IREDELL COUNTY PUBLIC LIBRARY
201 NORTH TRADD STREET
STATESVILLE, NC 28677
(704) 878-3145

P9-CFA-550

CRE▲TIVE
HOMEOWNER®

ULTIMATE GUIDE TO

Gazebos

and Other Outdoor Structures

CREATIVE HOMEOWNER,® Upper Saddle River, New Jersey

COPYRIGHT © 1995, 2007

CRE▲TIVE
HOMEOWNER®

A Division of Federal Marketing Corp.
Upper Saddle River, NJ

This book may not be reproduced, either in part or in its entirety, in any form, by any means, without written permission from the publisher, with the exception of brief excerpts for purposes of radio, television, or published review. All rights, including the right of translation, are reserved. Note: Be sure to familiarize yourself with manufacturers' instructions for tools, equipment, and materials before beginning a project. Although all possible measures have been taken to ensure the accuracy of the material presented, neither the author nor the publisher is liable in case of misinterpretation of directions, misapplication, or typographical error.

Creative Homeowner® is a registered trademark of Federal Marketing Corp.

ULTIMATE GUIDE TO GAZEBOS

MANAGING EDITOR Fran J. Donegan
EDITORIAL ASSISTANTS Nora Grace, Jennifer Calvert
COVER DESIGN Maureen Mulligan
ILLUSTRATIONS James Randolph, Paul M. Schumm,
FRONT COVER PHOTOGRAPHY Jessie Walker
BACK COVER PHOTOGRAPHY *top* courtesy of Lancaster County Barns–Walter Kuhn *bottom left to right* Rodale Stock Images–Mitch Mandel; Bob Crimi; udigthis photography

SECOND EDITION PRODUCED BY THE HEARTWOOD GROUP
EDITOR Jeff Day
LINE EDITOR Cheryl Winters Tetreau
PAGE LAYOUTS Sandy Freeman
PHOTO RESEARCHER Donna H. Chiarelli
DIGITAL TECHNICIAN Thomas Wolf
ILLUSTRATIONS Bob Crimi
COPY EDITOR Barbara McIntosh Webb
INDEXER Nan Badgett

CREATIVE HOMEOWNER

VICE PRESIDENT AND PUBLISHER Timothy O. Bakke
PRODUCTION DIRECTOR Kimberly H. Vivas
ART DIRECTOR David Geer
MANAGING EDITOR Fran J. Donegan

Current Printing (last digit)
10 9 8 7 6 5 4 3 2 1

Ultimate Guide to Gazebos and Other Outdoor Structures, Second Edition
First Published as *Gazebos & Other Outdoor Structures*
Library of Congress Control Number: 2007922558
ISBN-10: 1–58011–370–2
ISBN-13: 978–1–58011–370–0

CREATIVE HOMEOWNER®
A Division of Federal Marketing Corp.
24 Park Way
Upper Saddle River, NJ 07458
www.creativehomeowner.com

safety

Although the methods in this book have been reviewed for safety, it is not possible to overstate the importance of using the safest methods you can. What follows are reminders—some do's and don'ts of work safety—to use along with your common sense.

- Always use caution, care, and good judgment when following the procedures described in this book.
- Always be sure that the electrical setup is safe, that no circuit is overloaded, and that all power tools and outlets are properly grounded. Do not use power tools in wet locations.
- Always read container labels on paints, solvents, and other products; provide ventilation; and observe all other warnings.
- Always read the manufacturer's instructions for using a tool, especially the warnings.
- Use hold-downs and push sticks whenever possible when working on a table saw. Avoid working short pieces if you can.
- Always remove the key from any drill chuck (portable or press) before starting the drill.
- Always pay deliberate attention to how a tool works so that you can avoid being injured.
- Always know the limitations of your tools. Do not try to force them to do what they were not designed to do.
- Always make sure that any adjustment is locked before proceeding. For example, always check the rip fence on a table saw or the bevel adjustment on a portable saw before starting to work.
- Always clamp small pieces to a bench or other work surface when using a power tool.
- Always wear the appropriate rubber gloves or work gloves when handling chemicals, moving or stacking lumber, working with concrete, or doing heavy construction.
- Always wear a disposable face mask when you create dust by sawing or sanding. Use a special filtering respirator when working with toxic substances and solvents.
- Always wear eye protection, especially when using power tools or striking metal on metal or concrete; a chip can fly off, for example, when chiseling concrete.
- Never work while wearing loose clothing, open cuffs, or jewelry; tie back long hair.
- Always be aware that there is seldom enough time for your body's reflexes to save you from injury from a power tool in a dangerous situation; everything happens too fast. Be alert!
- Always keep your hands away from the business ends of blades, cutters, and bits.
- Always hold a circular saw firmly, usually with both hands.
- Always use a drill with an auxiliary handle to control the torque when using large-sized bits.
- Always check your local building codes when planning new construction. The codes are intended to protect public safety and should be observed to the letter.
- Never work with power tools when you are tired or when under the influence of alcohol or drugs.
- Never cut tiny pieces of wood or pipe using a power saw. When you need a small piece, saw it from a securely clamped longer piece.
- Never change a saw blade or a drill or router bit unless the power cord is unplugged. Do not depend on the switch being off—you might accidentally hit it.
- Never work in insufficient lighting.
- Never work with dull tools. Have them sharpened, or learn how to sharpen them yourself.
- Never use a power tool on a workpiece—large or small—that is not firmly supported.
- Never saw a workpiece that spans a large distance between horses without close support on each side of the cut; the piece can bend, closing on and jamming the blade, causing saw kickback.
- When sawing, never support a workpiece from underneath with your leg or other part of your body.
- Never carry sharp or pointed tools, such as utility knives, awls, or chisels, in your pocket. If you want to carry any of these tools, use a special-purpose tool belt that has leather pockets and holders.

contents

dreams and schemes

You sit back, enjoying a gentle breeze wafting across your face. All is quiet except for the chirping of birds. You feel as if you are a million miles from the hustle of daily life, but in reality you didn't have to travel at all to get there. You are enjoying a gazebo, pavilion, or arbor right in your own backyard. Your satisfaction with your outdoor retreat is enhanced because you crafted the structure with your own two hands.

This book is designed to help you create an outdoor structure that perfectly fits your family's needs and desires. The book is divided into two parts. The first part is filled with chapters that will show you how to customize your project into exactly the structure you want. The second part contains step-by-step plans for several gazebos, pavilions, and arbors. If one of these plans matches your needs, then by all means, build it just as described. But if you have something different in mind, the first part will help you transform your vision into reality. You'll learn how to lay out your project, build a foundation, construct the frame, install the deck, design the rafters, and build the roof. You'll learn the pros and cons of various outdoor finishes, and you'll even find a chapter that will help you choose a paint scheme. A chapter on maintenance will help you keep your project beautiful for many years to come.

Building a garden structure is one of the most enjoyable projects that a do-it-yourselfer can undertake. Unlike most home projects, these won't make a disrupting mess inside your house. You'll be out in the sunshine, exercising your creative carpentry skills.

When you embark on your outdoor building project, you'll be joining a legion of artisans dating back nearly to the beginning of gardening itself. Some of the first to appreciate the luxury of a small structure in their gardens' midst were the Egyptian pharaohs. In fact, the pharaohs ordered murals of their gardens painted on the walls of their tombs so that they might take the beauty with them into the afterlife. In China, the Taoist religion revered natural beauty, and garden structures were an essential component of many compositions. The Chinese embraced these simple structures because they provided an escape from the pressures of an advanced civilization (and that was in 4,000 B.C.). Many centuries later, outdoor buildings caught on in the rest of Europe. By the start of the Renaissance, no proper garden was complete without its own outdoor structure.

Gazebos and other outdoor buildings had their most profound impact on the Victorians. With the advent of the Industrial Age, more people were living closer together, and the pressures associated with this new urban lifestyle necessitated more garden retreats. Gazebos were a delightful complement to these garden hideaways.

By the mid-1900s, these types of buildings had lost favor to front porches and open-air decks. But today, homeowners are rediscovering the pleasures of a special outdoor structure. Nothing can match the look of roses trained to envelop an arbor, or the snug feeling inside a gazebo during a summer shower. No wonder these structures are enjoying a new surge in popularity.

A bit of advice: you'll save untold amounts of time, work, money, and frustration if you take the time to plan your project carefully before you begin building. If you do not plan, you might just end up "managing crises" and will probably be disappointed in your final project.

Whether you look out over a wide expanse or a simple lawn, a gazebo, arbor, or pavilion can be your private retreat.

GUIDE TO SKILL LEVEL

 Easy.
Even for beginners.

Challenging.
Can be done by beginners who have the patience and willingness to learn.

Difficult.
Can be handled by most experienced do-it-yourselfers who have mastered basic construction skills. Consider consulting a specialist.

GAZEBOS

By definition, a gazebo is meant to be a "gazing room," an isolated structure intended to offer a panoramic view of the surrounding landscape. It is meant to serve as a haven, a quiet place in which to take a moment to catch one's breath and relax or contemplate as the busy world continues outside the garden.

During the late 1800s, gazebos became a focal point in proper Victorian and Edwardian English gardens. By the mid-1900s, their popularity began to wane as more people opted for more modern-looking front porches and, still later, open-air decks. Today, gazebos are being added to homes where front porches and decks already exist.

Gazebos are the most complex, but also the most adaptable, projects described in this book. Your gazebo can be very open, or it can be entirely screened in, essentially giving you a room separated from the rest of the house.

PAVILIONS, OR PERGOLAS

The pavilion, or pergola, originated alongside the gardens and pools of India. Along with the desire for water in their gardens, the people of India sought shade from the grueling sun and a place to sit, contemplate, and enjoy their surroundings.

The pavilion remains a great place to relax or to entertain during the summer months. Classically, it is a simple rectangular structure with either a slat roof or a lattice roof. Often, it is set above a concrete or paved deck. The pavilion may be freestanding or attached to your house, sometimes acting as a transition between the home and a pool.

The simplicity of this structure should encourage you to try your hand at a little custom design. Depending on your preference, you can roof your pavilion with lattice, or you may decide to build a conventional rain-shedding roof like the one on the "Pavilion with Gable Roof" project on page 166. Similarly, the side walls may be completely open, or you could install lattice panels and plant some climbing vines to provide additional

ARBORS

Ancient Egyptian wall paintings depict vine-covered structures that resemble the arbors of today. But it was the Romans who took the idea of the arbor and ran with it, creating an abundance of designs most similar to the arbors we now know. During ancient times, these structures provided shade from the scorching sun. Arbors still do that, but today they often serve as decorative entrances to many gardens.

Arbors are a perfect example of the beauty that can result when people work in harmony with nature. We build the arbor, plant vines at the base, and then let nature weave a fragrant flowering cover. Because the plants serve as roof and walls, the basic framework for an arbor is quite simple. Posts set directly into the ground act as vertical support members; cross beams and joists form the open framework of the roof. Grid facing constructed of wood slats or sturdy lattice also can be fastened to the framework to provide additional support for the climbing vines.

One way, besides its overhead structure, that an arbor differs from its lighter cousin, the trellis, is that it is designed to support the heaviest of vines. Of course, you can use your arbor to support the lighter varieties, too. Check with your local nursery to see which vines will flourish in your area.

1 planning and design

Function, more than anything else, should determine the size and shape of your outdoor structure. For example, let's say that you know you want a gazebo with a hot tub, and you like to entertain. After thinking it over, you realize that you usually have about 10 guests. Now you have enough information to establish some basic design parameters. If you want an additional seating area, the space would get larger. If you add a gas grill, the space would get larger still. As you add equipment and activities, you take on more people-circulation problems, requiring still more space. You might start out thinking that you want an 8-foot octagonal gazebo, but after analyzing what you want to do in the gazebo—its function—you may realize that the four-sided pavilion serves you better.

GO WINDOW-SHOPPING

Unless you are very comfortable working in two dimensions and envisioning how something will look in real life based on a set of plans, you are going to have a number of questions concerning general qualities of your project. It is impossible for this book to determine whether or not a specific project can accommodate this year's Memorial Day picnic, or if a roofline will look too steep next to the neighbor's shed, or if one project would look better than another if it were placed next to your rose garden.

The most effective preliminary research is simply to study existing outdoor structures. When you see a structure that you really like, think about what it is about the structure that excites you. You can learn just as much by a close look at structures that you immediately dislike. Look for the design mistakes you want to be sure to avoid. Town parks, botanical gardens, and new housing developments can all offer invaluable research material. You might even try introducing yourself to those individuals who have a project in their yard; explain your interest, and ask whether you might get a closer look at how it was constructed. There's a good chance that they will be flattered by your interest and will be happy to answer a few questions for you.

Look at all the different applications for these projects. Some may be used primarily for entertaining guests, others as quiet nooks to sit in and enjoy the sun. Electric lights, barbecue grills, even hot tubs can be incorporated into the design to accommodate the desires of the owner.

ABOVE Study existing outdoor structures to analyze your likes and dislikes.

Take the time to sketch out your project before construction begins. Include in your drawing any furniture or accessories that you may want. Careful planning will help you choose the right project for your needs.

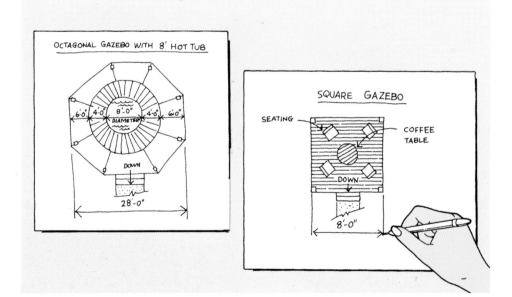

OCTAGONAL GAZEBO WITH 8' HOT TUB

6'-0" 4'-0" 8'-0" DIAMETER 4'-0" 6'-0"

DOWN

28'-0"

SQUARE GAZEBO

SEATING

COFFEE TABLE

DOWN

8'-0"

Take time to inspect the details of how the structure was constructed. Was the project set in a concrete foundation, or is it resting on concrete pilings? Notice how some techniques and materials influence the overall appearance of the design. For example, metal fasteners can help create a strong structure, but they may look mechanical compared with hand-cut joinery. Pressure-treated wood creates a different effect from redwood or cedar. Seeing these woods in real life, perhaps after they've weathered for a few years, will help you decide which wood you like best. Some of the designs discussed in "Customizing Options" on page 22 are more time-consuming than others, but seeing just how much a little trim can enliven a project might inspire you to try cutting your own custom slat balusters.

This is also a great opportunity to compare different solutions to problems. For example, when trying to build in a little privacy, did they use lattice, shrubbery, or a more creative option? What problems did they discover? What do you see as problems in their particular design?

Finally, take note of how the projects are placed in relation to the rest of the yard. Does a particular structure seem to fit better snuggled into a corner, or should it be set off as the center of attention? Has a brick or gravel path been laid directly to the gazebo, or does this structure blend more naturally into the rest of the landscape? This is also an excellent time to start noticing which flowers or plants you may want to use around your project.

SITE CONSIDERATIONS

Of course, you want to build a structure that will withstand the extremes of your climate. For example, depending on the severity of your winters, a project may require 36-inch-deep footings to get beneath the frost line. That same project in Florida may require only a 6-inch foundation, or it might even rest on concrete pilings. Although building concerns are addressed throughout this book, specific questions can be answered best by your local building inspector.

Other design decisions are motivated by personal preference rather than by structural concerns and, therefore, depend much more on how you intend to use your project. Your choice of roofing material may not significantly affect the longevity of your project, but choosing a composite (asphalt) roof instead of a lattice roof will make a big difference to you when it starts to rain.

The site you choose for your outdoor structure is one of the most important design decisions you'll make. You can show off the gazebo or pavilion, making it a focal point in the overall plan of your home and grounds. Perhaps you'll want to plan your garden around the gazebo, planting shrubs and flowers to enhance and highlight the beauty of the site. Or you can treat your gazebo as a secluded retreat. Achieving either goal takes careful planning of the site and surrounding plantings.

Planning also includes the surrounding landscape. A brick path leads to this quiet retreat within the trees.

Do you plan to eat and/or cook frequently in your pavilion or gazebo? If so, you'll want to consider placing the structure near the kitchen. And you'll want to make the structure big enough to accommodate the tables, chairs, and supplies that accompany eating and drinking.

Regardless of the distance from the house, consider building a walkway to your project. Concrete, brick, and treated wood are all good materials for walks. Gravel makes an effective informal walk, but it will need to be bordered with concrete, brick, or treated wood to hold it in place.

Sometimes it's tricky to predict traffic patterns in your lawn. How often have you seen a concrete walkway with a dirt path beaten into the lawn nearby? That's a sure sign that somebody made a wrong traffic-pattern prediction. If you are unsure what path your walkway should take, don't build one for a month or two after you complete the outdoor structure. The most popular route will be recorded by the beaten path.

Rain and Moisture

Few things are as enjoyable or refreshing as a gentle summer shower. Unfortunately, it's easy to have too much of a good thing. If you live in an area that's prone to more than a few downpours, you should consider ways of maximizing the time you can spend outdoors and lengthening the life span of your project.

The most obvious accommodation you can make to Mother Nature is in your choice of a roof. As much as you may enjoy the look of lattice, if you live in an area that gets frequent showers, a cedar or asphalt shingle roof will save you from scrambling for the house at the first hint of rain.

Frequent rainfall can contribute to other water-related problems. One of the most serious concerns is drainage. Even pressure-treated wood will suffer if water is allowed to puddle around the posts. To avoid this problem, provide proper drainage away from your project by positioning it on higher ground, by elevating the posts on concrete piers, or by crowning the top of the concrete where it contacts the posts. These basic precautions are covered more thoroughly in the basic construction steps outlined in "Laying the Groundwork" on page 88.

Sunlight

If you want climbing plants or vines to eventually envelop your project, you must position the structure on a site that provides at least 4 hours of direct sunlight daily. Otherwise, it will be difficult to grow much of anything. Southern and eastern exposures are the most desirable.

Lattice and climbing vines provide ample shade from the summer sun.

On the other hand, it is possible to have too much of a good thing. Lattice and slat-style roofing are two effective ways of diffusing excess heat while still letting you enjoy the summer sun. Installing lattice on the sides of your project and encouraging plants to climb up it is another excellent way to create a shady spot.

MAKING A SITE PLAN

Building a gazebo, pavilion, or arbor is a great chance to express your own style. Because the project scale is small, you needn't be daunted by fancy details. If you want to install fancy frieze boards, you aren't committing yourself to making endless runs of them. On the other hand, you may wish to express your craftsmanship through a simple design.

Before beginning the project, be sure to read Chapters One through Eight. Then you can design the structure knowing specifically what kind of trim, lattice, railings, steps, decking, and roof treatment will be used. Don't feel bound by what you see in the projects here. As long as you do not alter the structural framework of the design, feel free to mix and match ideas.

Building an outdoor project usually involves two sets of plans—the design of the project, and the site plan detailing the yard. These two plans are essential for explaining what your project will be and where it will be built.

Even if you have already selected a site for your project and plan to leave the rest of the yard pretty much as it is, you'll still need some sort of a site plan to show to the building department. If this project is but one step of a bigger landscaping project that will eventually include adding, removing, or relocating other plants and structures, then it's important to develop a site plan to help you (and the others involved in your project) visualize how the building fits into the overall scheme.

To make a site plan, you'll need to buy some graph paper for a base map (a scale of $1/4$ inch equal to 1 foot is standard) and some tracing paper for overlays. If you have the original map or site plan for your property, this could also serve as your base map. If you don't have the original map, use a 50-foot tape measure to help measure the size of the lot and to locate various features within it (house, trees, paths, etc.). Here is how to proceed:

1 MARK PROPERTY LINES. **On the graph paper, mark the property lines as shown. If only a portion of the property will be affected (for example, the backyard), you needn't include the entire lot. Indicate north and, if you can, the directions of the prevailing summer winds.**

At this point, it's a good idea to check with the zoning department to determine setbacks (how close a structure may be to property lines); mark setbacks as dotted lines on your plan.

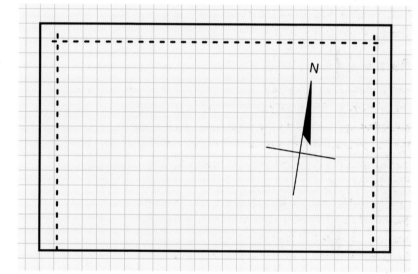

2 LOCATE EXISTING STRUCTURES. **Starting from a front corner of the house (marked X on the drawing), measure the dimensions of the house and transfer them to the plan. Again, if only one yard (front, back, or side) will be affected, you need only show the part of the house that faces it. Include the locations of windows and exterior doors that will be facing your project. Measure and mark the locations of other buildings and permanent structures, including patios and decks, fences, and paved walks. Also show any underground or overhead fixtures, such as utility lines and septic systems. Most public service companies will locate your utility line for you for free. Their phone numbers should be in your phone book. The site map of your property might also have the utility locations drawn in, especially if you live in a newer home.**

(continued on the next page)

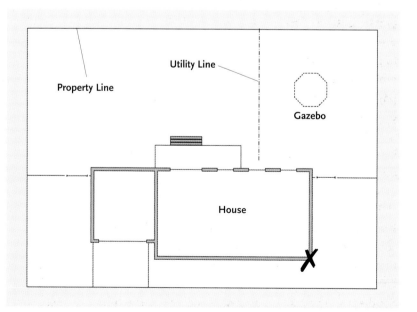

(continued from the previous page)

3 LOCATE PLANTINGS. **Mark the locations of trees, shrubs, and other major plantings; then specify which ones are to be kept and which ones are to be removed or relocated. If applicable, make notations on the shade cast by trees, tall shrubs, fences, or other structures near the project site.**

Give each member of your family a copy of the plan, and encourage everyone to sketch anything that may come to mind. There are no bad ideas at this point—brainstorming is the best way of finding new solutions to old problems.

This is also a good time to formulate a "master plan," or at least a "wish list" for the rest of the yard. Even if you are not planning to tackle the entire yard at once, it will save time later if you consider what kinds of improvements you'd like to do over the next few years. For example, if you would eventually like to include a pond on the north side of your gazebo, it would not be smart to invest a lot of money in flowers and shrubs for that spot. Sketch in smaller additional projects such as walkways, fences, or outdoor lighting.

4 LOCATE PROJECT ON OVERLAYS. **On a tracing paper overlay, draw in the exact size and location of the proposed project. Draw the final overlay neatly, and then attach it to the base map. Make copies to show to building officials or anyone else involved in the project.**

At this point, you should start checking your materials list to see just how much your project will cost. Take your materials list to your local supplier and price it out.

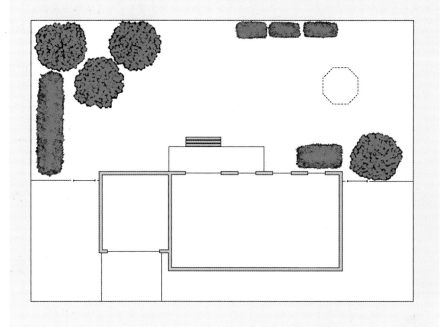

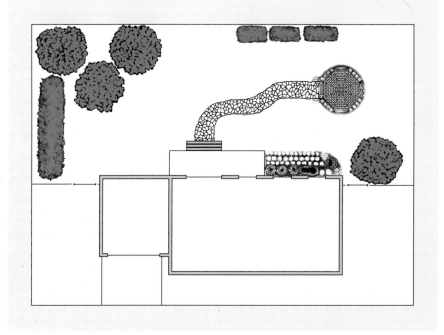

smart tip

DRAFTING AIDS How-to kits, which are available in most home centers, can take a lot of the pencil work out of drafting your yard. Computer programs are also available that will not only help you lay out your project but also show you how your changes will look, at the click of a mouse.

THE STAKE-OUT

When deciding on the final layout of your project, it will help if you can see exactly how it will fit into the real space of your yard. Use some scrap wood for stakes and some string to lay out the perimeter of the project. This will let you get a feel for how much room you will have in the structure and to check the views from the selected site. Staking out the project is also a good way to ensure that you didn't overlook something when you drew up the site plan.

COMPLYING WITH CODE

Building codes and zoning ordinances apply to permanent structures. In this context, permanent means any structure that is anchored to the ground and/or your house. In other words, if you sink posts in concrete or support your project on a ledger bolted to your house, the structure is considered permanent. It also means that you'll probably need a building permit. So check with your municipal building inspector before you break ground.

Obtaining a building permit can seem like a real hassle. It's a bunch of paperwork that you'd rather not deal with, and it can sometimes delay your work while the paper winds its way through the bureaucracy. Plus

you have to pay a fee. As a result, you might be tempted to skip the permit process. Don't skip it. Permits are accompanied by visits from the building inspector. If you do any electrical or plumbing work, that will be inspected, too. The purpose of the permit and inspections is to make sure the structure is safe and does not infringe on the rights of other property owners.

Building codes regulate building practices and materials. Footing depths, joist sizes, and post spacing are some of the things that must adhere to certain minimum requirements. Zoning codes regulate the amount of setback that must be maintained from the property line. A typical setback would be 10 feet to the sides and 25 feet in the front and back.

Look at your building inspector as an asset. If he or she spots a design problem in your plans, it could save you a lot more money than the cost of a permit.

And think of this: there will probably come a day when you want to sell your home. If you've got a permit and have passed inspections, these will be on record at the town hall. It will be the buyer's guarantee that the gazebo in the backyard was built to code. If there is no record of your structure, its safety is in question. And no bank will approve a mortgage if there is any possible violation of setback requirements.

Neighborhood Regulations

You may also want to check with your neighbors or any local neighborhood committees. Very often, some communities set their own architectural standards, either to preserve local traditions or to beautify the area. Not only will compliance with these standards help maintain good neighborly relations, but some communities actually codify these standards; in this case, they carry the full weight of the law.

Tax Effects

Like it or not, there's a good chance that your project will affect your real-estate tax bill. As soon as you apply for a building permit, your tax assessor will know that your house's value is about to increase. Once the project is completed, there's a good chance that he or she will stop by to reassess your property. (Small projects, such as a trellis, may not warrant a permit or new assessment.) This is an annual cost, so it would be a good idea to visit the assessor's office to see what effects your project might have on your taxes.

2 customizing options

Whether it is a railing of your own design or custom brackets, a few simple changes can make the difference between a "nice" gazebo and a project that perfectly complements your property.

Some of the options discussed in this chapter can be purchased pre-made at your lumberyard or home center. (Take your plans along so that you'll have the dimensions handy and will know whether or not an accessory will fit your project.) Other options will let you spend a little time in the workshop. Making these accessories from scratch will not only save you money but also allow you a chance to showcase your style and woodworking skills. And whether you make it in the shop or buy it at the lumberyard, the results are sure to be worth the extra effort.

POSTS

With the introduction of steam-powered woodworking machinery in the 1850s, elaborately-turned posts were produced by hundreds of small mills. Because most of these mills were closed down in the last century, some people think they have no alternative but to use ordinary square-cut posts. This is not the case. Today, you can still purchase turned posts through a variety of specialty mill-work catalogs and even in some lumberyards that carry special materials for restoration work.

Using turned posts instead of typical square-cut 4x4s can dramatically enhance the appearance of your project. Although they may look small when compared with square-cut posts, they have about the same compression strength as the thicker members and can be worked into any project in this book without structural changes. Pressure-treated pine, redwood, and cedar spindles are available to match any project, although you may need to special-order some materials. If you are planning to seal and paint them anyway, you can save money by using poplar turned posts. Just be sure that your posts are de-

signed to be load-bearing and are built for outside use.

Another nice thing about turned posts is that most manufacturers also make matching turned balusters. Using turned posts and balusters is a quick way to transform your project into a very elegant addition to your property. These turned elements do cost more than the typical square-cut variety, but considering the relatively small size of your project and all the years that you will enjoy your outdoor haven, it is money well spent.

Embellishing Square Posts

Even if you decide not to use turned posts, you don't have to settle for plain square-cut 4x4s. It's easy to build up your posts to resemble formal columns that would have cost hundreds of dollars if you had ordered them.

Both baseboard and crown moldings can be used to jazz up nondescript square posts. Build up the bottom with a combination of molding treatments to create a solid-looking pedestal.

Carefully miter the small sections of molding, using either a miter box or a power saw. Fasten the pieces onto the posts using finishing nails. Fill the nailholes with

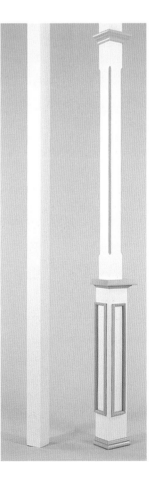

LEFT Small details, such as custom-cut slat railings and corner brackets, can transform a plain gazebo into something special.

RIGHT A few simple moldings and router cuts transform a plain 4x4 post into an architectural column.

Ready-made finials dress up a simple square post. A large screw coming out of the base makes it easy to drill a hole and then screw the finial in place.

A little extra sawing and sanding finishes a rail with a handcrafted look.

putty, creating an even surface, and paint the entire post for a more elegant effect.

Another option to use alone or in conjunction with molding, is to rout decorative edges. By equipping your router with a few decorative bits, it's possible to do your own custom millwork. You can rout the posts themselves, or you can rout pieces of 1-by and apply them to the posts.

RAILINGS AND BALUSTERS

Of all the decorative accessories mentioned in this chapter, the railing deserves special attention because of its structural significance. People depend on the rail for support and protection; invariably they will be leaning against it or even sitting on it. It will have to withstand a great deal of use and abuse.

For these reasons, building codes have placed special requirements on the construction of railings. Whether or not your project is required to adhere to code (if you received a building permit, it will), it makes sense to follow the code's specifications to ensure a safely built project. Most building codes specify that railings must be 36 to 42 inches high. Whenever a deck is above a certain height (typically 18 inches), balusters should be placed no more than 4 inches apart. And, above all, make sure that your railing is securely fastened to the posts.

The simplest railing option is to use a 2x4 horizontally

Attach rails to posts using metal connectors or angle irons for strong construction. Horizontal rails may be supported on a wood cleat and toenailed to the post and cleat.

between each set of 4x4 posts. Cut the lengths to fit snugly. The rails can be secured either by toenailing them to the post or by using metal connectors, angle irons, or simple wood cleats. Additional 2x4 railings or 2x2 balusters can be installed to provide even more support.

But if you are reading this chapter, you're interested not just in function, but also in form. There are several ways of beautifully integrating the railing into the rest of your project.

Balusters

There's no reason why you have to settle for square-cut 2x2 baluster when turned spindles cost only a fraction more. These spindles are also available in pressure-treated wood as well as redwood and cedar. Spindles, like turned posts, are an attractive option because they offer just as much strength and security as square-cut stock but look lighter and less confining.

Most suppliers offer matching posts and spindles, which create a very elegant effect.

Premade Rails and Channels

Premade rail and channel-molding pieces can speed up assembly while giving you professional-looking results. Essentially, these are 2x4s or 2x2s that have a double groove routed on one face to receive either 2x2 balusters or lattice panels. The grooves ensure that the balusters or panels are properly seated and reduce the amount of toenailing required.

The top 2x4 rail pieces are milled to look and feel like a traditional curved rail. To fasten the balusters to the rail, nail through the top directly into the ends of each baluster. Lattice may require using additional strips of lath on the edges to provide a larger nailing surface and to help wedge the lattice into the groove.

Premade mortised rails are one of the easiest ways to add an elegant detail to any rail unit. These rails are also designed to work with standard 2x2 rails, so you can "mix and match" various stock pieces to create your own unique railing.

LEFT Turned balusters are a beautiful alternative, costing only a bit more than square-cut balusters.

BELOW Premade rails and channels make assembly easy and solid.

Railing slats can be made in an endless variety of styles.

CUSTOM-BUILDING A SLAT RAILING

Factory-cut slats are available through many custom mill-work companies, but the cost of these pieces might be a little intimidating. Following are instructions for cutting 1-by slats that can be used instead of typical 2x2 balusters. Use these instructions as a guide; you may decide to use one of the patterns presented here, or you can create your own. The patterns shown have been drawn on a grid in which 1 box equals 1 inch.

Using a design element from your house is a great way to integrate your project with the rest of your property. Just remember that you will have to do a lot of cutting, so try to keep the design simple. When cutting custom slats, try to make sure that your slat width will fit evenly between the posts. The best way to prevent having to cut a strip off one or more slats is to set all of the slats in place before you fasten them to the rail. That way, any large gap on one side can be evenly worked into the spaces between each pair of slats.

When cutting balusters, or any of the other custom accessories in this chapter, it helps to first use a drill or drill press equipped with a circle cutter to cut out the circles. A Forstner bit, a hole saw, or even a sharp spade bit will cut the curves quickly and more uniformly than a saw blade. A drilled hole also allows a blade more room to negotiate sharp turns.

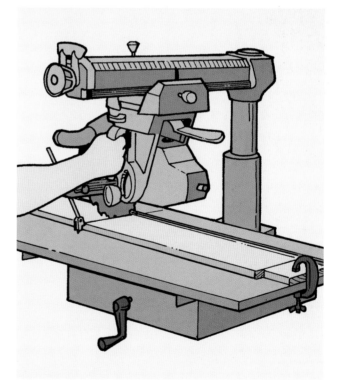

1 CUT SLATS TO SIZE. Using 5/4 x 6-in. decking boards, 1x6 stock, or a good-quality plywood (at least ⅝ in. thick), rip and cut the desired number of slats. All of the slats in the patterns are 29 in. long, which will create a rail that is 36 in. tall. You can adjust the length if you want a lower rail.

(continued on the next page)

(continued from the previous page)

2 CREATE THE TEMPLATE.
Enlarge one of our designs or draw your own slat pattern on a scrap of hardboard. Cut the hardboard using a band saw or a saber saw to make a template. Use this template to mark the pattern on all the slats. (Note: If you can stack and cut the slats, you'll only have to mark every other or every third board.)

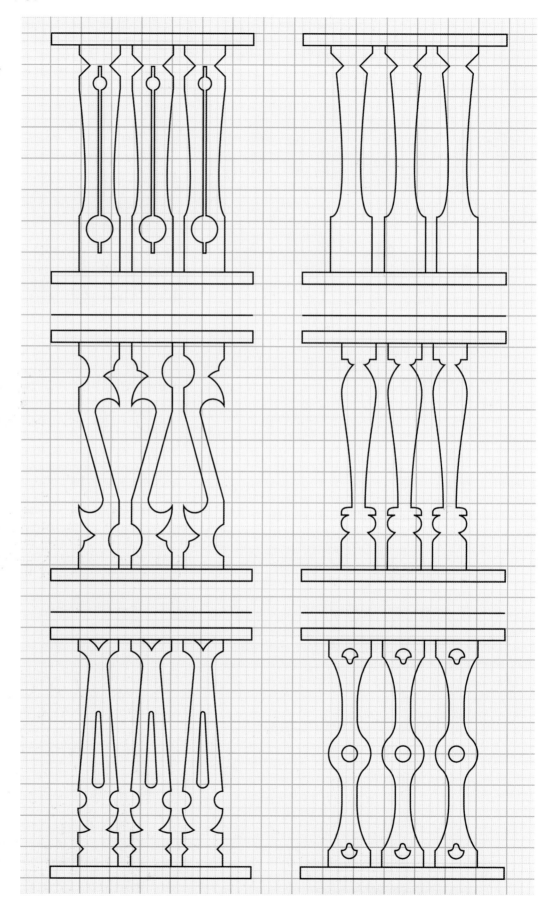

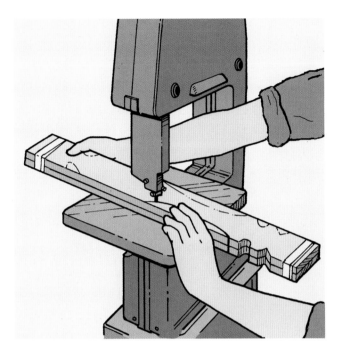

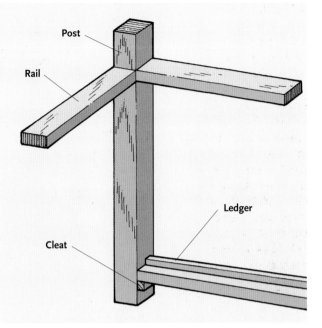

3 CUT THE SLATS. If you have a band saw, stack and tape two or three slats together, with the marked slat on top. Cut the pattern. If you are using a saber saw, you might still be able to stack and tape two slats at a time. Cut slowly to prevent the blade from drifting off the pattern line.

4 INSTALL RAILS AND LEDGERS. Rip ¾ x 1-in. ledgers from 1x4 stock. Cut the two outside ledgers to fit between the posts, one underneath the top rail and one above the bottom rail. Nail the outside ledgers in with 6d common nails or use 1½-in. bugle-head screws.

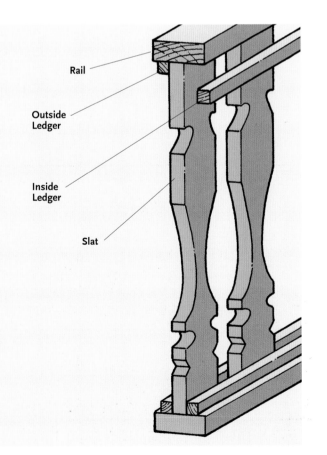

5 INSTALL SLATS AND INSIDE LEDGER. Place the slats between the top and bottom rails and against the outside ledgers, spaced ½ to ¾ in. apart. Adjust the positions of the slats until they appear to be spaced evenly. Use 6d common nails to toenail the slats in place into the top and bottom rails. Cut the inside ledgers to fit between the posts. Nail these ledgers in with 6d common nails.

smart tip

WATER HAS A BAD HABIT OF COLLECTING IN THE ROUTED GROOVES OF BOTTOM RAIL SECTIONS AND CHANNEL MOLDINGS. EVENTUALLY, THIS WILL LEAD TO SOME SORT OF WATER DAMAGE UNLESS YOU TAKE THE PROPER PRECAUTIONS. WHEN USING THESE PIECES, DRILL ⅜-INCH-DIAMETER WEEP HOLES. SPACE THESE HOLES ABOUT EVERY 8 INCHES.

CORNER BRACKETS

The corner bracket is commonly referred to as "Victorian gingerbread" because it resembles the sugar-frosting trim common on a gingerbread houses. These trimmings, also called carpenter's lace, bric-a-brac, and carpenter Gothic, have been integral to American architecture since the middle of the nineteenth century. A striking result of the advent of steam-powered woodworking machinery, these brackets add a sense of weight and solidity to the homes

of that period. Corner bracket treatments are an excellent way to integrate the roof with the posts and the rest of the structure.

These elements are available in just about any home center or millwork catalog; but because they are particularly labor-intensive, they can be costly. There's no reason why you can't make these brackets on your own. All you need is a saber saw (or band saw) and a little patience. Make sure that you use a water-resistant glue.

Note: Because of the short span between the posts on most of the projects in this book, corner brackets may not work well with other pieces of top trim, such as a frieze board. For this reason, you should decide which element you would most prefer to incorporate into your project before you start building.

Mahogany, cedar, redwood, and oak all make fine corner brackets. Fir, pine, and poplar are also good choices, especially if the brackets will be painted. It is important to use tight-grained, knot-free wood on larger, more elaborate pieces; but you'll discover that No. 2 pine can be used effectively on smaller jobs. When laying out your pattern, run the longest dimension parallel with the grain of the wood.

Brackets can be secured with finishing nails, but because you have spent extra time building your brackets, you may want to screw them on through predrilled holes, minimizing the chance of splitting or dinging the bracket with a poorly aimed hammer stroke. For the templates shown, 1 square equals 1 inch.

CORNER BRACKET TEMPLATES

FRIEZES

A frieze is a band, or line, near the roofline that can add a classic element to your project. The frieze is built like a railing, but the stock dimensions are smaller.

You may choose to copy one of the patterns below, which are shown against a grid in which 1 box equals 1 inch. Most older houses, and some newer ones, have a particular pattern right under the roofline. Copying this frieze pattern would be one way to integrate your project with the rest of your property.

BUILDING A FRIEZE

1 CREATE AND CUT OUT THE PATTERN.
Trace your frieze pattern on a scrap of hardboard. Cut the hardboard using a band saw or saber saw to make a template. You will use this template to mark the pattern on all the slats. If you have decided on a repeating pattern, it is not necessary to create a pattern that will reach the full length of the frieze. Instead, make a template of one or two repeating units that you can move down the board.

Using 1-by stock that is wide enough to fit your entire pattern, cut each board to length to fit exactly between each pair of posts. Remember that on some projects, the edges will have to be mitered to fit flush. Label each board to ensure that they are installed between the posts that they were cut to fit.

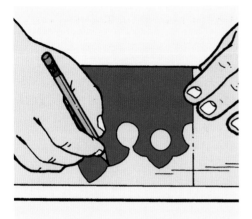

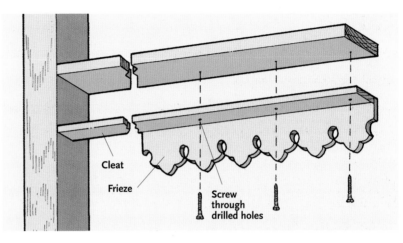

Cleat

Frieze

Screw through drilled holes

2 LAY OUT AND CUT THE FRIEZE. Mark the center of each frieze board. Starting from the center, transfer the template pattern onto each of the boards. Starting at the center and working out is the best way to ensure that the pattern ends evenly on both sides of each board.

3 ATTACH FINISHED FRIEZE. Rip 1½-in. strips from a piece of 1-by stock and cut them to the same lengths as the prepared frieze boards. You will have to miter the ends of the cleats to fit against the posts, or you can simply cut the cleats 1 in. shorter on each end so that they can clear the posts. Attach the frieze board to the cleats using either 6d finishing nails or 1½-in. screws. Use 1½-in. screws to fasten the cleats to the 2x4 cap plates. Drill these screw holes to prevent splitting.

LATTICE

Lattice can be incorporated into your project in a variety of different ways. It can provide shade, privacy, or simply a place for climbing flowers to grow. It's easy to use lattice as a railing treatment, in a frieze panel, or even as a wall-size panel.

Lattice panels are available in pressure-treated wood, redwood, and even plastic. A panel is composed of two layers of strips oriented to overlap each other at a 90-degree angle, forming a grid that is stapled or nailed together. Vinyl lattice panels are fused together with a solvent during production. Several different grid densities are available. Stiffer, heavier lattice panels are made from ³⁄₈-inch-thick lattice strips and would be a good investment if you expect the panels to receive a lot of abuse.

Building with Lattice

Because the panels are relatively delicate, lattice must be handled and installed carefully. Store lattice panels flat until you're ready to use them. Left standing on their edge, these panels will bow or even come apart. Lattice panels should be installed in a frame to hide and protect their edges. Channel molding is very helpful when using lattice; that way, the panel's entire edge can rest in the groove.

The following instructions describe how to use lattice panels to build an enclosed railing. Because the installation steps for including lattice in any of these applications is nearly identical, simply substitute your specific measurements and use these steps as a general outline.

Lattice can provide shade, privacy, or in the case of this gazebo, visual appeal.

LATTICE PANEL INSTALLATION

1 **INSTALL CHANNEL MOLDING OR BACKING CLEATS.** For a post-and-rail framework, first fasten the backing cleats to the posts and rails, using either galvanized finishing nails or screws. If you use screws, drill holes to avoid splitting the wood.

If you opt to use channel molding, install bottom and side pieces with galvanized 4d finishing nails, but leave the top molding off until the lattice panel can be slid into the side and bottom channels. Drill ³⁄₈-in.-dia. drainage holes (weep holes) through the bottom channel molding about every 8 in.

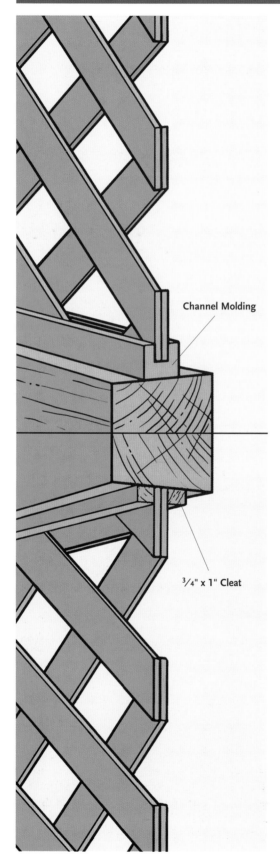

Channel Molding

³⁄₄" x 1" Cleat

2 **CUT AND INSTALL LATTICE.** Place the panel on a flat surface, such as a sheet of plywood. Mark the cutting lines by snapping a chalk line or using a pencil and straightedge. Use a straightedge jig as described on page 123. Adjust your saw's depth of cut to match the thickness of the panel before making the cut. Most lattice panels are stapled together at each intersection. Don't worry—it's okay to cut through these staples, but it's all the more reason to invest the extra money in a carbide-tipped blade. As always, make sure that you are wearing safety glasses or goggles.

Find someone to help hold the panel against the backing cleats until the front cleats are installed. You can also try tacking the panel to the backing cleats with several brads.

Install the front cleats, holding each one firmly against the panel. If you're using molding, fasten the top piece to the underside of the top rail, and then install the top rail.

TONGUE-AND-GROOVE FLOORING

Gazebos are usually built with tongue-and-groove flooring, not unlike the floors once installed in many homes.

Tongue-and-groove floors are not only neater-looking, they're locked together as a single unit, and they distribute loads better than regular decking. Don't use tongue-and-groove in gazebos with slat roofs, however. With no spaces between the boards, water is likely to puddle.

INSTALLING TONGUE-AND-GROOVE FLOORING

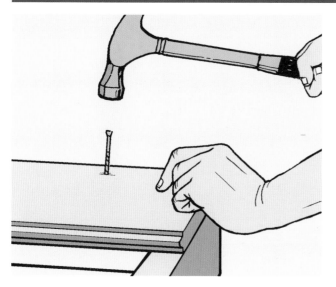

1 LAY STARTER BOARD. Snap a line that is $1/2$ in. less than the width of the board. Position the board so the groove is on the outside edge, and put the line you drew right at the edge of the framing, allowing the board to overhang. Pre-drill holes for galvanized casing nails, and drive them into the framing.

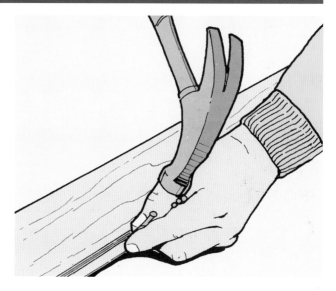

2 NAIL THROUGH THE TONGUE. Drill holes through the tongue of the first course of boards and into the joists. Nail the boards in place. To keep from marring the board with the hammer, leave the nailhead exposed, and hammer it home with a nail set.

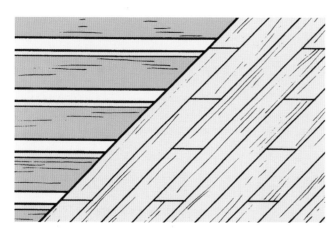

3 LAYING THE FIELD. Lay out several courses of boards in the way that they are to be installed. Cut to length as needed so that each joint is centered over a joist. Stagger the joints so that no two joints are next to each other. Cut the boards so each row runs over the edge of the deck by at least $1/2$ in. (The excess will be cut off later.)

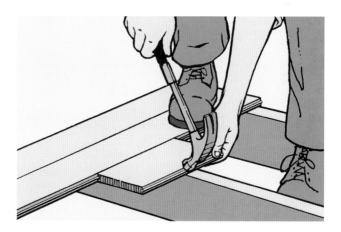

4 FITTING AND NAILING. As you lay each row, use a scrap tongue-and-groove board to tap the floor boards together. Nail through the tongue and into the joists. Once you've installed all the flooring, trim the edges using a circular saw so that they're uniform.

3 the use of color

Don't let your gazebo design end with the wood, and don't necessarily let your color palette stop at white. Victorians—who invented gazebos—loved both ornateness and color. You don't need to be an artist to incorporate some of the time-proven color combinations explained in this chapter. Once you've made your selections, you have two ways to achieve the look you want. Paint is the traditional choice, and the only option the Victorians had. But modern stains let you create a color scheme that protects the wood while leaving the grain visible.

You may eventually settle on white—after all, it's a color, too, and it may be perfect for your yard. But look here first, and at least dream in color before you pick up your brush.

the use of color

EFFECT OF COLOR

Used properly, color can make your project feel larger or smaller, act as a link to your house and the rest of your property, draw attention to your gazebo, or let it hide in a shady corner of the yard. However, your overall goal should be to unify the architectural elements so that no single one is dominant and the features of the structure appear balanced.

In general, the same rules that apply to interior design also work outside. Light colors will make your project feel larger; darker colors will make it feel more intimate. Depending on the surroundings, both light and dark colors can be used to make your building stand out, as long as the color contrasts with the background. Traditionally, when painting Victorian homes, architects would choose a darker paint for houses that were exposed and a very light shade for houses that were concealed by trees or shrubs.

It's possible to enhance the effect of shadows by using light colors on projecting elements and dark colors on the insets. But don't go overboard when applying accents. Subtle changes in color and small details will do more for your project than you might imagine, so whatever you think you like, try cutting it in half.

A high-contrast scheme focuses the eye on each detail and will make your project appear smaller. To make your project seem larger, opt for a low-contrast scheme. Pale colors reflect more light, heat, and UV rays, so they tend to last a little longer; however, they also show more flaws in the prep work.

Blue makes this gazebo stand out from the background, and as with all pastels, its colors work well together.

Color Considerations

Your color choices also depend on how your project will complement your house and yard.

First, consider the elements that you cannot or will not change. These may include the colors of the roofing material, the nearby landscape, your house, or your neighbor's house. For example, matching the color of your gazebo to your house is a great way to tie your project in with the rest of your property; using a contrasting color will give the gazebo its own identity. Likewise, you will want to avoid clashing with the colors you can't change. Realize, too, that if other elements are close enough, their reflected light can actually affect the way you perceive your chosen color.

Of course, it's possible to overdo your concern with these details. During the Victorian period, some people tried to "blend" their homes with the surroundings by copying the harmonious colors of nature, such as soil, rocks, and wood. The result, some said, was too often a dirty yellow house that seemed to spring up out of the mud!

USING A COLOR WHEEL

A color wheel not only demonstrates the relationships between colors, but also identifies particular associations between colors. Whether one color complements or contrasts with another is more than a matter of taste—it depends on where the colors fall on the wheel. For example, colors that lie next to one another share a common base color and are considered harmonious. Contrasting colors lie on opposite sides of the wheel. Here are some other examples, which are illustrated on pages 41 and 42:

- *Similar colors* are neighbors on the color wheel. Using colors that are too similar can create an awkward look. If the colors come from adjacent wedges of the wheel, or even the same wedge, vary them by pairing pastel, muted, or shaded versions. This is a great way to add visual interest to your scheme.
- *Complementary colors* are any two colors opposite each other on the wheel. They create a familiar contrast and are generally considered harmonious. When complementary colors are placed close together, they intensify each other, and the result can be particularly vibrant. But contrasting colors used in equal amounts tend to compete with each

White is a simple, elegant color choice that has withstood the test of time.

other and can create an uneasy effect. Make sure one color dominates by using it on at least two-thirds of the project. Use the second color to accent specific architectural elements.
- *Triad harmony* uses three colors that are equidistant on the wheel to create an exciting trio. Choose a dominant color so the scheme does not feel too busy.
- *Split complementaries* consist of one color combined with the hues on either side of its contrasting color.

White, Black, and Gray

White, black, and gray are unique because they can be used to enhance the appearance of any color placed next to them. White will make colors appear deeper, black will make colors look lighter, and gray will make colors look richer.

● UNDERSTANDING THE COLOR WHEEL

It is said that the human eye can distinguish more than 10 million different colors. Yet every one of them is based on red, blue, and yellow, plus black and white.

The color wheel shows how these basic colors relate to one another and how they combine to make all the other colors.

Primary Colors

The three key colors are pure red, pure yellow, and pure blue. These colors are considered primaries because they cannot be mixed from other colors. All other colors are mixed from the primaries, white, and black.

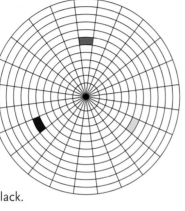

Secondary Colors

Orange, green, and violet are mixed from equal amounts of two primaries.

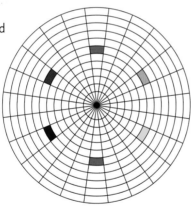

All Other Colors

In between the secondary colors comes an infinite array of intermediate colors. This chart slices the color continuum into 24 segments.

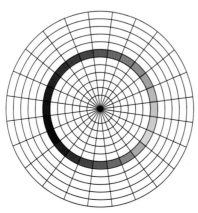

Pastel Colors

A pastel is simply a color mixed with white. Any pastel color will coordinate with any other pastel, even those opposite on the color wheel, because they all contain a lot of white. Pastels blend effortlessly with the lighter range of muted colors and with modern and traditional styles. Pastels can be used to create a light, airy feel.

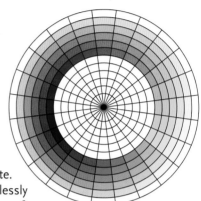

Shaded Colors

Pure colors that are darkened with black are known as shaded colors.

Muted Colors

Muted colors are pure colors mixed with varying amounts of black and white. The most neutral color of all is gray, which is simply a mixture of black and white. The gray scale on the drawing shows various mixtures of black and white. The boxes running along the top and right side of the drawing represent a wedge from the color wheel. All the other boxes show muted colors of a single hue.

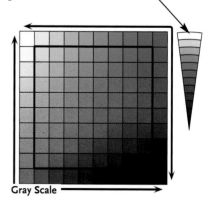

Gray Scale ➞

SIMILAR COLORS

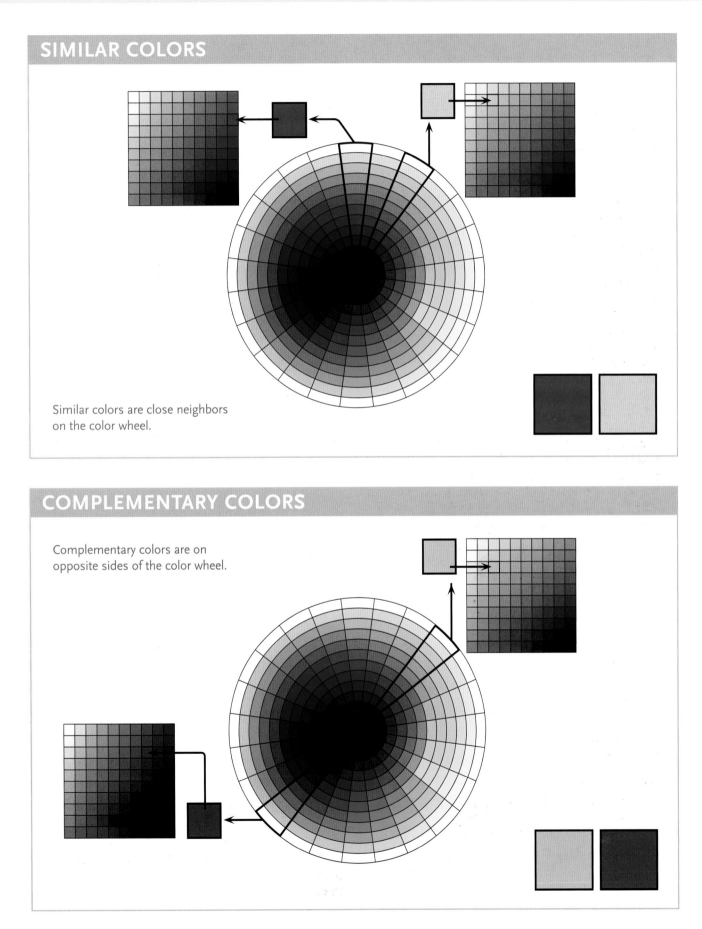

Similar colors are close neighbors on the color wheel.

COMPLEMENTARY COLORS

Complementary colors are on opposite sides of the color wheel.

TRIAD HARMONY

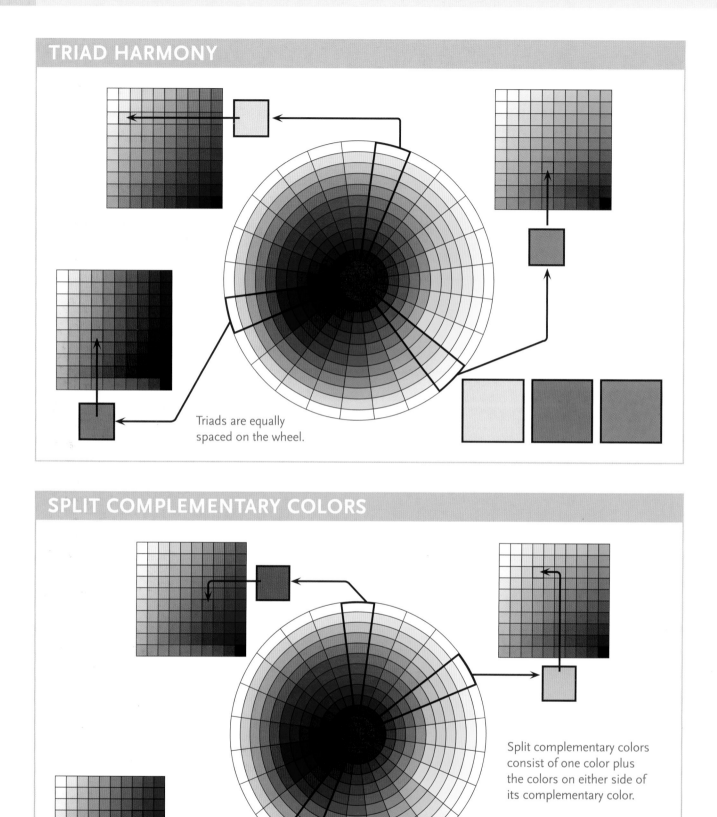

Triads are equally spaced on the wheel.

SPLIT COMPLEMENTARY COLORS

Split complementary colors consist of one color plus the colors on either side of its complementary color.

SELECTING A COLOR SCHEME

Even when you understand the effects of color and how colors interact, selecting a scheme for your particular project can still be daunting. Here are some procedures you can follow to help you zero in on the perfect color combination for your garden structure.

Determine the Color Values

You can start deciding on color placement without actually using color. Trace or sketch a line drawing of your project and then make several photocopies so you can try different schemes. Using a pencil, try shading different features to experiment with highlighting possibilities. Decide which features you would like to emphasize and which ones you would like to hide. The different degrees of shading will later correspond to appropriate values of color. (*Value* refers to the lightness or darkness of a color.) The goal here is to create a well-balanced whole in which no element seems to dominate.

Color In the Sketch

You can experiment with various color possibilities by coloring a sketch of your project. By "prepainting" in this manner, you will not only avoid disappointment but you will also be encouraged to try some distinctive schemes before you pick up the paintbrush.

Some paint stores and Web sites feature programs that will "paint" your house for you right on the screen; these systems can also give you a sense of how to paint your gazebo. The better in-store programs are even equipped to scan a high-contrast photo of your project. Even if you are unable to get an exact reproduction of your gazebo, these programs will give you an idea of what combinations are pleasing and demonstrate some ideas for how you might distribute color on your project.

Testing Color

Everyone knows what white looks like. But should you decide to use something a little different, you should invest some time in testing your choice to make sure that it's the color you think it is. Remember, perceived color is affected by several factors:

- Colors look different in different types of light. What you thought was a wonderful pink under the fluorescent lights of the paint store may appear too pale or even garish in sunlight. The best place to compare colors is outside, preferably on an overcast day or in the shade. That way, you'll be able to study the color under the full spectrum of light, but without worrying about glare.
- Color is affected by the colors nearby. Pink might make a wonderful contrast to a blue trim, but it could also clash horribly with the pine trees in the yard.
- The amount of color affects how you see it. It's possible to have too much of a good thing. What looks fine on the can lid may not look as becoming when it covers your entire project. Colors seem to intensify with size.

Before you select a color from a chip, isolate it from the other colors on that card. Cut out a small frame of white paper to expose just one color value at a time. When you begin selecting color combinations, try framing them against a white background, and then against a black background, which will help bring out the undertones in the colors.

Most professional color designers will not pick colors from chips, which are too small to adequately show the impact the color will have on a large project. And because chips are printed from printer's inks and not pigment, you cannot be sure that the chip color will match the actual paint.

You can avoid later disappointment by purchasing quart-sized cans of paint and testing the colors on a scrap board or piece of plywood (this is called *swatching*). Paint large swatches, and be sure that the colors that will be used together are located next to each other on your test. Try to swatch roughly the same percentage of area that each paint will cover on the project.

Position the test board next to your project, and note the colors at different times of the day, because different levels of sunlight will also affect how a color "reads." Remember also that the colors will seem to darken as the paint dries. Also look at your test board from a distance so that you can get some idea of how the color scheme will work in with the rest of the yard.

PAINTING: WHAT GOES WHERE

Now that you have selected a color palette for your gazebo, it's time to decide which colors should be assigned to its specific architectural elements. Of course, you can just go ahead and paint your project however you like, but chances are you won't be 100 percent delighted. Whether you realize it or not, you have already chosen the "look" of your gazebo. And just as you've chosen the colors through a set formula, how you treat each piece of your project must also follow certain guidelines in order to look "right." While these guidelines do have a certain design basis, they are also the result of a long evolution in the use of color. People have been experimenting with color for centuries. When something looked good, others would be more likely to repeat it; when it didn't, it was probably buried under another coat of paint.

We'll discuss each major architectural element of your structure, along with appropriate color suggestions. Because you will be adapting these ideas to suit your own project, these approaches are meant to be used as a general outline.

Use the drawing on page 45 to help you identify various elements of a gazebo.

Roof

"A roof should not be painted in a light color, but some dark color that will strongly contrast with the main paint on the building." This advice from a Sherwin-Williams promotional book is as true today as it was in 1884, the year it was published.

In the Victorian scheme, a dark roof helps define the structure's boundaries and creates a feeling that the gazebo is firmly rooted to the ground. Victorians typically stained or painted roof shingles dark red, dark reddish brown, or dark olive green. Even if you are using composite (asphalt) shingles, a large variety of organic colors is available to assist your color scheme. These colors will also help the structure blend in with its natural surroundings.

Frieze

An historically appropriate treatment for the frieze is to use both the trim and body colors. Be careful not to introduce too many colors, though, or the effect will be too busy.

Corner Brackets

These are probably the most popular elements on Victorian structures and the ones that are most often incorrectly painted. Brackets should be considered part of the overall structure and should be painted so they do not appear to be "floating free" of the structure. Use the principal trim color. Avoid using too much color. Some painters add a leading edge of scarlet to their cornices. This may look nice, but it's a misunderstanding of Victorian exterior decoration.

Posts

If you have simple rectangular wood posts, you probably don't want to emphasize them with their own color. Paint them to match either the overall trim or the body paint. However, if your posts have special millwork, such as a chamfer on a square post or a ring on a turned post, it is perfectly acceptable to highlight these decorations with a flourish.

Rails

The rails are essentially extensions of the posts, so they are usually painted in the same color as the posts.

PREFAB COLOR SCHEMES

Deciding on the specific colors in a multicolor scheme can be a little tricky. For that reason, almost every major paint company has created "combo cards" to help you pick base and trim colors in one step. These colors are available in historic shades designed to match the most prevalent color schemes of a particular period. One nice feature of these cards is that the trim and accent color chips often appear next to the body color, which more realistically shows how the colors will look together.

Balusters

Try painting the balusters a lighter color than the rails. If the posts and rails have been treated in the main body color, try using the trim colors to make them stand out. Even if you have elaborately-worked balusters, don't use too many colors to demonstrate your handiwork. Besides the amount of time that would be involved in detailing each baluster, the effect will be too busy.

Floors and Ceiling

Because a Victorian-style gazebo is a sort of detached porch, your gazebo will look most traditional if you base your floor and ceiling color scheme on traditional porch colors. Back then, porches needed to be painted in light colors to keep them from being too dark. Painting porch ceilings blue is a technique that has been used for cen-turies to suggest the sky overhead. The gray floor is even more practical; it is less likely to show dirt and footprints. The trim or body color can also be used if it is neither too light nor too dark.

If the underside of your gazebo ceiling rafters is exposed, you might paint them by using a combination of the body and trim colors.

Steps and Risers

The risers of wood steps are normally painted the trim color, while the treads carry the deck to the ground and should be painted in the same color as the deck.

The handrails and balusters on the steps follow the same rules applied to the gazebo itself: top and bottom rails should be in the trim color, and the balusters should be painted in the body color.

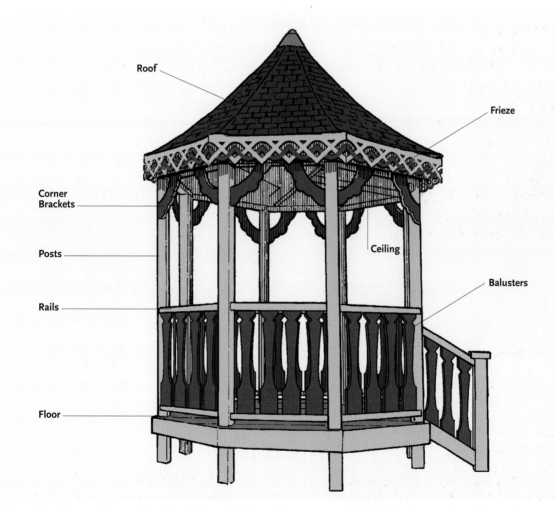

Roof

Frieze

Corner Brackets

Posts

Ceiling

Balusters

Rails

Floor

Assigning colors to specific architectural elements is an important part of designing a color scheme for your gazebo or other outdoor project.

STAINS

Stain has excellent hiding power and good color retention. Overall, it provides a more mellow look than paint, because it allows the natural texture of the wood to show through. A stain penetrates into the surface of the wood, while paint creates a waterproof shell on the surface. In stained wood, moisture moves freely in and out, so stain does not blister or peel off. There is no surface buildup with stain, thus no cracking or any of the other problems you find with multiple coats of paint. One possible disadvantage to stain is that once you have chosen a color, you might be able to darken it with another stain, but you can't use another stain to lighten it. However, you can cover over a dark stain with a light paint.

Stains come in a variety of colors, from the lighter shades of gray to the darker wood tones. How well a particular stain performs depends not only on the product itself but also on the type of wood it is covering and the climate of your area. Because they are not as durable as

paint, stains require more frequent periodic refinishing.

Stains are available in both water- and solvent-based formulas. Water-based stains have less odor and are easier to clean up, but they tend to sit on the surface of the wood and may not last as long. Solvent-based stains sink deeper into the wood's pores to provide a longer-lasting finish.

Semitransparent Stains

Semitransparent stains are classified as pigmented penetrating finishes. The resin or oil in semitransparent stains soaks into the pores of the wood, acting as a sealer. Enough pigment remains on the wood's surface to affect the color without covering the grain pattern or creating a surface film. The pigment particles in a semitransparent stain act as UV blockers, with the oils acting as the penetrating sealers. If you want the stain to resist both water and rot, choose one that contains a preservative and is water repellent.

Because they are relatively thick and contain pigment, semitransparent stains should be mixed frequently to ensure color consistency. Be sure to order more than enough stain to finish the job. Manufacturers sometimes discontinue or alter their selection of tints, so that one may not exactly match others made in a different batch.

Solid-Color Stains

Solid-color stains are a hybrid between paints and stains. Although they are highly pigmented, they still allow some wood texture to show through. Because they contain more pigment, solid-color stains will provide better UV protection than semitransparent stains. However, they do not penetrate the surface of the wood as deeply as the lighter-bodied stains and are generally less durable than semitransparents.

Solid-color stains are designed primarily for use on exterior siding and aren't recommended for horizontal surfaces, such as decks, where they would be worn down quickly by foot traffic. Latex solid-color stains do not penetrate as deeply as the oil-based variety and are even less weather-resistant. When applying solid-color stains, make sure to pretreat the lumber with a paintable wood preservative to ensure a more even coat. Also choose a product that can accept a topcoat of stain.

"CEDAR"   "DRIFTWOOD"   "REDWOOD"

Natural-looking toners can transform pressure-treated southern pine into a host of attractive alternatives.

A natural finish will look right at home in a natural setting.

Deck Stains

Deck stains are specially formulated to withstand not only the weather but also the abrasion a deck receives from everyday foot traffic. They are typically made with alkyd oil and contain water repellents to provide protection from moisture. Because they are available in shades that resemble cedar and redwood (see the photo on page 46), deck stains are a way to change the look of your pressure-treated deck. Check with the manufacturer to be sure that the stain is an appropriate finish.

Deck stains are formulated for immediate application to new pressure-treated wood as well as periodic application to older decks. You can apply them in a variety of methods—spray or roll them on; apply with a pad; you can even dip smaller pieces. Your deck should be dry enough to use 24 hours after application.

SELECTING THE PROPER PAINT

Paint not only looks traditional, but is the best way to protect wood from the elements. Paint forms a protective film that seals your project against moisture, insects, and everyday wear. Because paint contains the highest proportion of pigment, it is the most effective way to protect your project from the effects of UV radiation and to cover knots or other imperfections in the wood.

These days, latex paints are preferred over oil-based paints. Latex paint dries more quickly, retains its color better, and adheres longer than oil-based paint. Latex paints dry to a rubbery film, which can withstand the flexing caused by changes in temperature and humidity. It is also more porous than oil-based paints, so moisture can pass through it (this is called "breathing"), to help prevent peeling.

By using latex paint, you avoid the entire problem of volatile organic compounds (VOCs)—the gases formed by the solvents in oil-based paints. Several VOCs are known health and environmental threats; others are strongly suspected. Some states and municipalities have made it virtually impossible to obtain and apply oil-based paint.

Finally, latex paint costs less than oil-based paint. And with latex, you do not have to buy expensive solvents for cleanup—soap and water is sufficient. There are not many applications that still require the use of oil-based paints. When painting redwood or cedar, you may decide to use oil paints to block resins that bleed from the wood and stain the paint job. However, there are latex paints available that are specially designed to prevent bleeding.

Watching the Weather

Proper painting requires a dry and clean surface. Unfortunately, the weather doesn't always cooperate with your plans. Heat and cold can affect paint, and rain can wash latex paint away if it's not fully dry.

Painting in Hot Weather

The hotter the weather, the quicker latex paint dries. But when paint dries too fast, brushes and rollers can gum up, the paint fails to bond properly with the surface underneath it, and uneven drying times cause a patchy appearance.

The ideal painting temperature is around 70 degrees F. If the temperature is between 55 degrees F and 70 degrees F, plan your work so that you are in the sun. If the weather is warmer, stay out of direct sunlight. Try not to paint on hot, windy days because wind speeds up drying.

Painting in Cold Weather

Latex paint does not cure at temperatures below about 45 degrees F, which is why manufacturers' specifications always call for latex paint to be applied at temperatures no lower than 50 degrees F. Try to avoid painting in the winter, or anytime that the temperature falls below 50 degrees F. There are few things more discouraging than watching paint slide off the walls in sheets.

smart tip

CHECKING FOR MOISTURE
IT IS OKAY TO APPLY LATEX PAINT TO A SURFACE THAT IS SLIGHTLY DAMP (COOL TO THE TOUCH) BUT NOT WET. LET WET SURFACES DRY OUT BEFORE PAINTING. IF RAIN OR DEW GETS ON LATEX PAINT BEFORE IT IS DRY, THERE MAY BE NO EFFECT, BUT THE PAINT MAY ALSO MOTTLE AND BLISTER OR WASH OFF ENTIRELY. IF THE PAINT BUBBLES, IT HAS TO BE SCRAPED OR SANDED OFF BEFORE THE SURFACE CAN BE REPAINTED.

Porch and Floor Paint

If you choose to paint the decking of your project, use porch and floor paint. This is a heavy-duty paint that is formulated to resist peeling and withstand the abuse of foot traffic and furniture scraping. Porch and floor paint usually comes in dark colors (black, battleship gray, dark green) to hide scrapes and markings. Prime new lumber with oil-based primer. When the primer is dry, sweep the deck clean and then roll the porch and floor paint on. This paint is extremely thick and does not need to be brushed in. You'll probably want to throw away the roller cover, as porch and floor paint is very difficult to clean off. This paint dries to a hard, glossy finish and should last for several years.

PRIMERS

Priming is not so much the first coat of paint as it is the last step of preparation. Primer seals the surface of the wood, insuring a smooth base and more even absorption of the finish paint. It allows the finish paint to stick, and stay stuck, to the surface. Primer provides resistance to moisture, fills in cracks in the wood, and keeps stains, such as turpentine that weeps out of knots in the wood, from bleeding through the finish coats. The two major types of primer are oil-based and latex. It is important to understand the proper applications for each, as well as their advantages and disadvantages.

Oil-Based Primer

An oil-based primer is considered best for general exterior use. These primers dry more slowly than latex primers and are absorbed deeper into the wood's pores. Latex primers depend on a good surface bond, so they may not adhere as well. Oil also has a moderate advantage in its ability to inhibit stains, like those from knots. Once it has dried, you can use either latex or oil-based paint as a topcoat. Be sure the surface is very dry, or the oil primer will not adhere. If water gets between the wood and the primer, the primer can lose its bond, causing the paint to peel down to the bare wood.

Latex Primer

There are two disadvantages to using latex primers: Latex-primed surfaces sometimes require an extra topcoat, and they can allow rust stains from nailheads to show through the finish paint. (Even if you use hot-dipped galvanized nails, the rust-resistant coating takes a beating from hammers and nail guns.) If rust stains show through, your only alternative is to spot-prime the nailheads with an oil- or shellac-based primer.

Working with Primer

When applying a primer, cover everything that you intend to paint. With fascia and other trim pieces, it's a good idea to "backprime," which means covering all the surfaces, including the sawn edges that don't show. Backpriming will help restrict moisture movement and will extend the life of these decorative elements. Although it seems like an extra

CHEMICAL COMPATIBILITY

It's important to look for chemical compatibility when choosing a water-repellent primer and topcoat. Buying materials from the same manufacturer helps ensure compatibility; however, check all the labels just to be sure.

step, try priming the wood before installation. This will save you time and money later on.

If you cannot adequately seal the more resinous knots, try a shellac-based primer. These primers dry very quickly; most are ready for a topcoat in less than 1 hour. The downside to these primers is that they are more expensive than latex- or oil-based primers, and because they dry so fast, they are not intended for large surfaces. For that reason, you might want to purchase just a small can to spot-prime the most difficult spots. When the patch has dried, you can finish up with the regular primer.

As a general rule, the faster the primer dries, the sooner you should start painting. If the primer is allowed to weather beyond a critical point, it will fail or will cure so hard that the topcoat cannot stick to it. Read the manufacturer's specifications for the optimum time between priming and applying the topcoat. With some primers, you should recoat in a matter of hours. With others, you can wait a few weeks. Whatever you do, do not prime in the spring and plan to finish painting in the fall—you will end up redoing the entire job.

WHEN AND HOW TO PAINT

In an ideal world, you would paint or stain your project before it's even brought outside. Painting protects the boards from UV radiation, which breaks down the lignin in the wood. This breakdown affects the adhesion strength of any topcoat. In fact, painting tests have shown that bonding strengths are affected by as little as four weeks of exposure.

Realistically, you should aim to finish your project as soon as possible to avoid any damage to the wood. If your lumber is visibly wet, you will have to let it "weather," but for no more than a few weeks at most. The old rule of "waiting a year" is no longer considered the right way to do the job—by then, the wood will be damaged enough to prevent you from applying a finish that will adhere well.

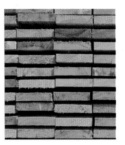

4 tools and materials

Your project begins as a pile of lumber, hardware, and tools. It pays to have a good understanding of each. Part of your concern is budget, but what do you sacrifice by setting the budget too low? What do you gain by spending a few extra dollars? Faced with stacks of lumber, which pile do you head for? Are galvanized connectors better than nails?

The best advice: read this chapter, and then seek quality. With proper care, your gazebo and your tools are going to last a lifetime. Invest wisely.

TOOLS

This chapter should not be read as a wish list. For generations, carpenters—skilled craftsmen—have managed quite well with little more than a hammer, a saw, some chisels, and a few planes. Except for the additions of the electric drill and circular saw, your toolbox does not need to include more than that same basic cache. Remember that power tools have been created for convenience—no one purchase will ever be able to replace skill, experience, and a little creativity.

Too many carpenters confuse *want* with *need,* and end up buying tools that they really have no use for—tools that wind up collecting dust and rust at the bottom of the box. In most cases, one tool can do another's job just as conveniently; which one you use often depends simply on which one you already own. At other times, you will find that, given a little extra time, it's possible to "make do" with what you have. Carpentry is an exercise in improvisation.

This section outlines the basic tools used in the construction of outdoor projects. The tools fall into three major categories: tools for layout and excavation, tools for cutting and joining, and tools for everything else.

Purchase the least expensive tool that will meet or exceed all of your criteria. This usually means purchasing the best tool you can afford. (Best does *not* always mean most expensive, so be sure of what you're buying.) A "bargain" tool, on the other hand, will not seem to be such a great bargain if its limitations remind you of that fact every time you pick it up.

One-time jobs can be done very professionally and economically with rented tools. Rental shops deal with professional-caliber tools that will perform better than their less-expensive counterparts. Renting is a great opportunity to use a more exotic tool at a fraction of its purchase price. And should you eventually decide to purchase that particular type of tool, your on-site experience will better enable you to pick out the model that's right for you.

Excavation and Layout Tools

Laying out is both vitally important and very simple. You'll do most of it with shovels, sticks, and strings—not that different from the way the Egyptians laid out the pyramids.

Marking Out the Site. A tape measure is essential for just about any building project. For this type of work, you'll find that a 25- or 30-foot tape will be the most useful for both long and short measurements. Good tape measures will have the first foot divided into $1/32$-inch lengths for really precise work. Tapes with a 1-inch-wide blade are a little more bulky than $3/4$-inch blades, but the blades are much more rigid and can be extended farther without folding. This can really come in handy for one-person measuring jobs.

A chalk line is simply a roll of string held inside a chalk-filled container. It only takes a couple of seconds to "snap a line." Stretch the string against a flat surface and pluck it to produce a straight, chalked layout line. Although red chalk may be a little easier to see, stick with blue: the red pigment is permanent and can stain anything it gets in contact with (hands, wood, etc.).

A plumb bob relies on gravity to enable you to drop a perfectly vertical line from a given spot. The heavy pointed bob is suspended on a string and is useful for aligning posts, with pinpoint accuracy. Some chalk lines can also be used as plumb bobs.

smart tip

> *BUYING OR RENTING TOOLS*
> *INVARIABLY, THERE WILL BE SOME TOOL THAT YOU WILL SIMPLY HAVE TO HAVE. NO MATTER WHAT THE PURCHASE, YOU FIRST HAVE TO UNDERSTAND WHAT YOU EXPECT THE TOOL TO DO. FOR EXAMPLE, IF YOU NEED A MEASURING TOOL, YOU MUST FIRST ASK YOURSELF: "HOW LARGE A SPAN WILL I BE WORKING WITH?" "WHAT KINDS OF TOLERANCES WILL I REQUIRE?" "HOW MUCH USE (ABUSE) WILL I EXPECT MY TOOL TO TAKE?"*
> *A POWER TOOL WILL WARRANT ITS OWN SPECIAL SET OF QUESTIONS: "WHAT KINDS OF OPERATIONS WILL I BE EXPECTING FROM THIS TOOL?" "WHAT WILL I BE CUTTING (OR DRILLING)?" "HOW MUCH SPACE AM I WILLING TO DEDICATE TO THIS MACHINE?" OF COURSE, YOUR BUDGET WILL ALSO BE A PRIME CONSIDERATION.*

TOOLS FOR EXCAVATION AND LAYOUT

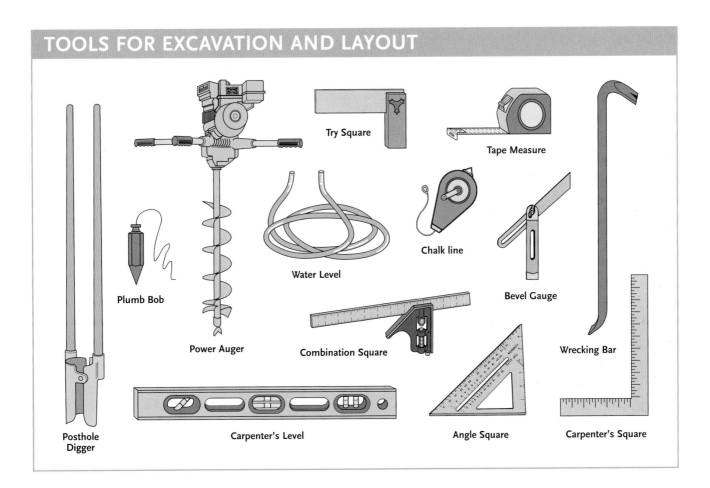

Try Square

Tape Measure

Chalk line

Water Level

Plumb Bob

Bevel Gauge

Power Auger

Combination Square

Wrecking Bar

Posthole
Digger

Carpenter's Level

Angle Square

Carpenter's Square

Digging Holes. If you have to sink only a few posts or if you have a really strong back, you can dig holes by hand using a posthole digger. This double-handled tool is designed to cut deep, narrow holes and scoop out the dirt with its clamshell-like blades.

For larger projects, you'll thank yourself for renting a power auger to speed up the job. Power augers are powered by a gasoline engine and work just like a giant drill. Some models can be handled by one person; others require two. You will still need a posthole digger to clean out the holes when you're finished with the auger.

Whether you are using the auger or a posthole digger, if you run into rock, you'll need a wrecking bar (also referred to as a breaking bar) to break up the stone or to wedge it loose. Roots can also slow down your progress; cut them out using either a hand ax or branch pruners.

Levels. There are two levels that can assist you in making sure that the longest spans are "on the level": a water level and a line level.

A water level consists of a pair of clear graduated vials fitted onto a long tube (your garden hose will do nicely).

Water naturally seeks its own level; when the water levels in the two tubes are even, the points are level with each other. This is the most accurate method for measuring over long distances. A line level consists of only a single vial. It's designed to be hooked to a string for leveling long spans. Make sure that the string is taut to ensure an accurate measurement.

The carpenter's level is a workhorse on any construction site. Available in 2-foot and 4-foot lengths, you will use one for leveling beams and ledgers, and making sure posts are plumb. Take special care of your level—all it takes is one good drop to make it inaccurate. One way to test your level is by setting it on top of a level surface. Now flip it over. The bubbles should still be in the center; if they've moved, then your level is off.

A torpedo level is a good tool for plumbing up concrete forms and J-bolts as you set them in wet concrete. Its compact size makes it a handy addition to your toolbox.

Squares. A carpenter's square is made from a single piece of steel or aluminum and is useful for laying out stair stringers and rafters. Its large size makes it good for

53

squaring up large boards and calibrating your other squares; but when you're setting individual tools, such as your circular saw, you will probably find that it's more convenient to use a smaller square.

A combination square is adjustable. The body has both 90- and 45-degree sides and can slide up and down the blade if you unlock the thumbscrew. This is the ideal tool for measuring depth or running a line along a board.

Angle squares are thick, strong, triangular castings of either aluminum or plastic that are tough enough to withstand the rigors of general construction without losing their accuracy. The angle square's triangular shape enables you to lay out a 45-degree angle as quickly as a 90-degree angle. Using markings on the body, it is also possible to lay out other angles, as when laying out rafters. The edges of this square can also be used as an accurate cutting guide.

Probably the best tool for gauging and transferring angles other than 45 and 90 degrees is a sliding bevel gauge (also known as a T-bevel). A bevel gauge has a flat metal blade that can be locked into a wooden or plastic handle at any angle. A bevel gauge is great for transferring an existing angle on the actual project; it can also be used in conjunction with a protractor to record a specific angle (for example, if you wanted to draw a 25-degree angle).

Cutting and Joining

Most people consider cutting and joining to be the most enjoyable part of carpentry—the result of working with the wood, cutting and shaping it to fit your design. The feeling will be enhanced if you work with the correct tools. More important, having the right tool for a specific job and knowing how to use it are the best ways to avoid wasting material and to prevent injuries.

TOOLS FOR CUTTING AND JOINING

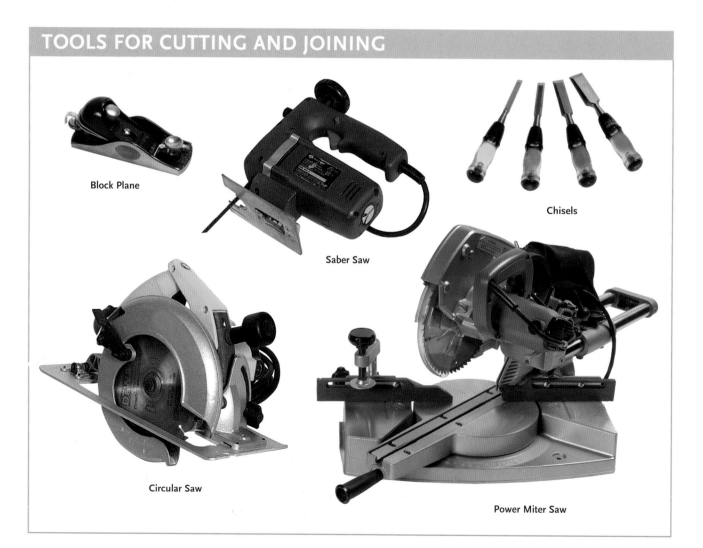

Block Plane

Chisels

Saber Saw

Circular Saw

Power Miter Saw

● SAFETY EQUIPMENT

Common sense should tell you not to do carpentry without first having some basic safety equipment, such as eye and ear protection.

Wear safety goggles or plastic glasses whenever you are working with power tools or chemicals—period. Make sure your eye protection conforms to American National Standards Institute (ANSI) Z87.1 or Canadian Standards Association (CSA) requirements (products that do will be marked with a stamp). Considering the cost of a visit to the emergency room, it doesn't hurt to purchase an extra pair for the times when a neighbor volunteers to lend a hand or when you misplace the first pair.

The U.S. Occupational Safety and Health Administration (OSHA) recommends that hearing protection be worn when the noise level exceeds 90 decibels (db) for an 8-hour workday. However, considering that a circular saw emits 110 db, even shorter exposure times can contribute to hearing impairment or loss. Both insert and muff-type protectors are available; whichever you choose, be sure that it has a noise reduction rating (NRR) of at least 20 db.

Your construction project will create a lot of saw-dust. Wear a dust mask if you are sensitive to dust, or if you are working with pressure-treated wood. Two types of respiratory protection are available: disposable dust masks and cartridge-type respirators. A dust mask is good for keeping dust and fine particles from being inhaled during a single procedure. Respirators have a replaceable filter. Both are available for protection against nontoxic and toxic dusts and mists. Whichever you purchase, be sure that it has been stamped by the National Institute for Occupational Safety and Health/Mine Safety and Health Administration (NIOSH/MSHA) and is approved for your specific operation. When you can taste or smell the contaminate or when the mask starts to interfere with normal breathing, it's time for a replacement.

Work gloves are also nice for avoiding injury to the hands—catching a splinter off a board or developing a blister when digging postholes is not a good way to start a workday. Similarly, heavy-duty work boots will protect your feet. Steel toes will prevent injuries from dropped boards or tools; flexible-steel soles will protect you from puncture by a rogue nail.

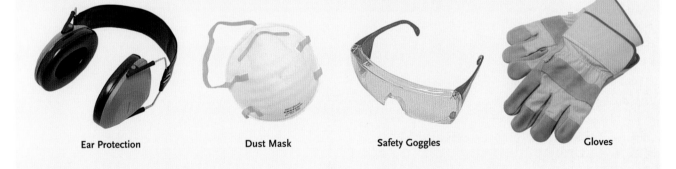

Ear Protection   Dust Mask   Safety Goggles   Gloves

Cutting. The circular saw has replaced the handsaw in almost every situation. That's because a circular saw is capable of crosscutting, ripping, and beveling boards or sheets of plywood quickly and cleanly. It can be used to create a variety of common joints, such as miters, laps, and dadoes.

The most popular saws with carpenters and do-it-yourselfers alike are the models that take a 7¼-inch blade. This blade size will enable you to cut to a maximum depth of about 2½ inches at 90 degrees. (Larger saws are available for cutting thicker material, but they're generally too bulky for this type of use.)

Choosing a Circular Saw. There are many options that distinguish one saw from another, the most important of which is its power. Don't judge a saw's performance by its horsepower rating, but by the amount of amperage that the motor draws. Low-cost saws may have only 9- or 10-amp motors with drive shafts and arbors running on rollers or sleeve bearings. A contractor-grade saw is rated at 12 or 13 amps and is made with ball bearings. This extra power will enable it to better withstand the wear it will receive while cutting through a lot of tough pressure-treated lumber.

It is no longer a plastic housing that signals an inferior tool; it's a thin, stamped-metal foot. A thin, stamped-steel base won't stay as flat as a thicker base that is either extruded or cast.

For safety's sake, be sure that your saw is double-insulated to minimize any chance of electric shock. Some saws have an additional safety switch that must be depressed before the trigger will work. Another feature to look for on a saw is an arbor lock. The lock secures the arbor nut and prevents the blade from turning while you are changing blades.

Choosing a Blade. For general all-purpose use, carbide blades are the best for achieving smooth, precise cuts. Carbide blades may cost a few dollars more than a comparable blade made from high-speed steel, but you can expect it to cut 5 times longer before it needs to be resharpened.

A 24-tooth blade is usually adequate for deck construction and general use. (There is a trade-off between the number of teeth and the cut rates and cut quality. For example, a blade with fewer teeth will cut faster, but the cuts will tend to be ragged. More teeth will produce a finer cut, but your saw will also have to work harder to move more teeth through the wood, and it will cut slower.) It's a good idea to have an extra blade or two on hand: wet wood and dense pressure-treated wood will dull your saw's blade relatively quickly.

For angle cuts, you'll want to use a motorized miter box. These tools—also called chop saws or cutoff saws—are simply circular saws mounted on a pivot assembly and are designed to make precise crosscuts in boards, planks, and pieces of trim. Chop saws are more expensive than circular saws, but they make it possible to cut difficult angles precisely and quickly. You'll be cutting through some big stock, so consider a saw with a 12-inch blade.

A saber saw is a good choice for cutting decorative curves on the ends of rafters and for making elaborate pieces of trim. A saber saw can cut curves, make cutouts, and finish cuts started by a circular saw.

For certain types of cuts, nothing will completely replace a good handsaw. A handsaw is just the thing when you have just a few cuts to do, for those spots where a circular saw can't reach, or when you want to finish off a circular saw cut. A 15-inch saw with 10 to 12 teeth per inch (tpi) will cut well and still fit into your toolbox.

Joinery Tools. No matter how adept you become with your power tools, sooner or later you will end up falling back on certain old reliables to achieve close-fitting joints. A block plane is great to carry along with you on the site. A properly set plane will trim a shaving off at a time, until the joint matches up perfectly. A plane is also handy for softening hard edges that might otherwise splinter or catch someone's clothing.

A set of three chisels, ¾ inch, 1 inch, and 1½ inches, will also be useful for close paring. The blades must be kept as sharp as possible for these tools to work safely and smoothly. Pressure-treated wood will dull steel edges more quickly than other types of wood.

Other Construction Tools

There are a few tools that don't really fit into one specific category or that seem to apply to more than one category. For that reason, they warrant their own special mention.

For every project in this book, it is assumed that you have an electric drill. If you don't, you should pick up one with a ⅜-inch chuck, variable speed control, and a reverse switch. Make sure that your drill is sufficiently powered (at least 3 amps) to handle the kind of abuse that it will receive on the job. You will discover that if you insert the proper bit in the chuck, your drill will be able to drive screws faster than you could ever do by hand.

If you're in the market for a second drill, a cordless drill will provide you with all of the attributes of an ordinary drill, but without the hassle of having to drag around a cord. An adjustable clutch is a desirable option, because it will allow you to drive screws to a set depth without overloading the motor or stripping the screwhead.

And how can you build anything without a hammer? You can manage quite well with a standard 16-ounce hammer; a lighter hammer is ideal for fastening railings, trim, and other light members when you are concerned primarily with control. When driving 12d or 16d nails into the beams, or joists, you will quickly learn to appreciate the way a 20-ounce framing hammer can sink a nail in just a few blows. If you are considering roofing your project with wood shingles or shakes, you may find that, with practice, a roofer's hatchet is handy.

One problem in driving nails with a hammer is the "rosettes" that seem to spring up when you are trying to drive the nail flush with the wood. A nail set picks up

ADDITIONAL TOOLS

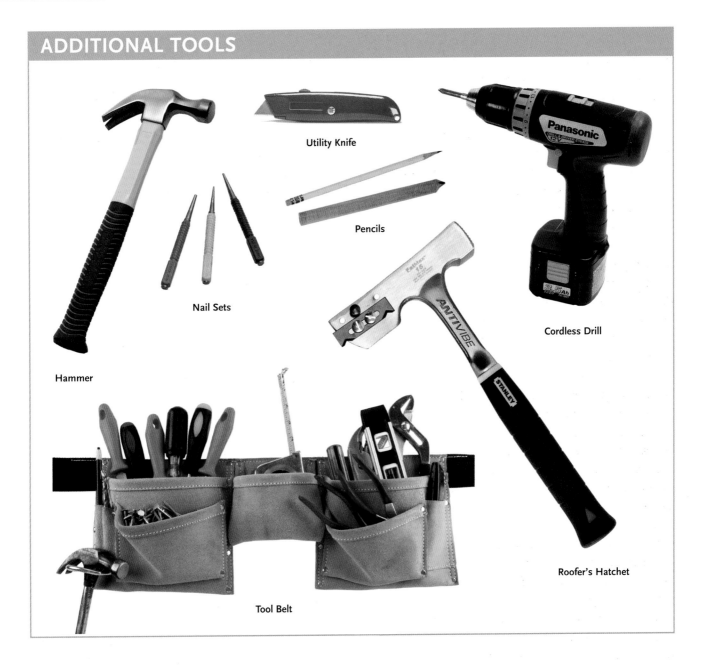

Utility Knife

Pencils

Nail Sets

Cordless Drill

Hammer

Roofer's Hatchet

Tool Belt

where most hammers leave off. A nail set is a small shaft of metal with one square end and the other tapered to a point. The tapered point is sometimes cupped to hold the nailheads. With a nail set, not only can you drive a finishing nail flush with the surrounding wood, but you can also countersink nails so that they can be filled with putty, to produce a nail-free finish. Nail sets come in various sizes to match different types of nails; use the nail set sized to the nail being driven to avoid enlarging the hole.

Unless you want to spend most of the day trying to remember where you left everything, a tool belt or work apron is a must. A good tool belt will have a spot for your hammer, tape measure, chalk line, and block plane, and

still have a pocket left over for nails and screws. A utility knife will probably be the most reached-for tool in either your toolbox or pouch. You will use your utility knife for everything from sharpening your pencil, marking cut lines, and cutting shingles, to shaving off wood so you can ease in a close-fitting joint. For general use, you should invest in a fairly heavy-duty knife that has a large angular blade held in place within a hollow metal handle. As with all cutting tools, sharp blades are safest because they provide the most control with the least amount of effort. Discard blades as soon as they're dull.

And there's one thing that a carpenter can never have enough of—pencils, pencils, pencils.

HARDWARE

There's a wide variety of hardware involved in building a gazebo—screws, nails, lag bolts, and framing hardware, to name a few. Spend as much time choosing them as you do your wood. Make sure everything you get is hot-dipped galvanized to resist rust. Buy a few extra from a store that will let you return what you don't use. If given a choice between a good piece of hardware and a better piece of hardware—get the best. Rusty or weak hardware is the beginning of the end for a gazebo.

Fasteners

Regardless of the type of outdoor structure you're planning to construct, you'll need a variety of nails, bolts, or screws, and some framing hardware to join materials and strengthen joints. Metal fasteners will free you from having to cut and fit complex joints. And considering that cuts made on site are sometimes less than perfect, metal fasteners offer some leeway while still ensuring that the joint will be strong and secure. Some metal fasteners are essential for joining different materials together—no amount of nails can replace a post tie for joining a wooden post onto a concrete footing.

But metal fasteners do have some disadvantages. Large fasteners, such as rafter ties and decking cleats, can save time, but the job will cost you more than if you simply use nails. This price difference can be significant if your project incorporates many metal fasteners into its design. Sometimes metal connectors, even nails, can be visually obtrusive and take away from the overall appearance of a carefully built project.

Remember, some local building codes may require structural fasteners in addition to nails. Be sure to check before building.

Nails

The most basic of metal fasteners is the nail. As commonly used, the term *penny* (abbreviated as *d*) indicates a nail's length. The number did not originally refer to the length of the nail but to the cost of 100 nails of that size. The length of the various penny sizes of common and finishing nails are listed at the bottom of page 207.

The best overall choice for outdoor use is hot-dipped galvanized nails. These nails should be used where rust

NAILS

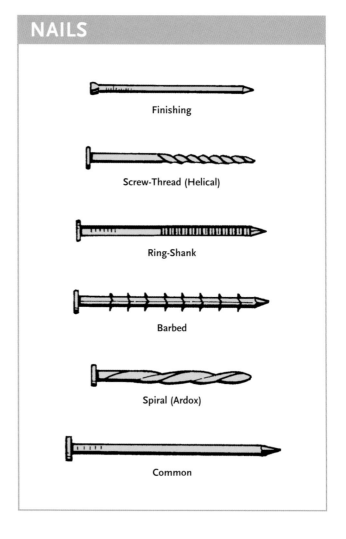

Finishing

Screw-Thread (Helical)

Ring-Shank

Barbed

Spiral (Ardox)

Common

staining could become a problem. But even though they are coated with a layer of zinc, galvanized nails will rust over time, especially at the exposed nailhead, where the coating has been damaged by hammering. You must also be wary of "galvanic corrosion," which can happen anytime galvanized nails are used to join a dissimilar metal, particularly in a humid environment. Galvanic corrosion is a reaction between the two metals that creates accelerated weathering at the point of contact. Always select nails that are compatible with any metal being attached to the wood (i.e., use aluminum nails to attach aluminum gutters, copper or brass nails for copper flashing, etc.).

Because they will not rust, stainless-steel and aluminum nails are also suitable for exterior use. Aluminum nails are softer and tend to bend easier than steel nails. Both types of nails are usually more expensive than galvanized nails (stainless-steel nails can be twice as expensive as hot-dipped galvanized), but where excessive corrosion

NAILING SCHEDULE FOR LIGHT OUTDOOR STRUCTURES

Area	Application	Method	Quantity/Spacing	Size	Nail Type
Frame	Header to joist	End-nail	3	16d	Common
	Header to sill	Toenail	16" o.c.	10d	Common
	Joist to sill	Toenail	2	10d	Common
	Ledger to beam	Face-nail	$3/16$" o.c.	16d	Common
	Double top plate	Face-nail	16" o.c.	10d	Common
	Ceiling joist to top plate	Toenail	3	8d	Common
	Rafter to top plate	Toenail	2	8d	Common
	Rafter to ceiling joist	Face-nail	5	10d	Common
	Rafter to hip or valley	Toenail	3	10d	Common
	Ridge board to rafter	End-nail	3	10d	Common
	Rafter to rafter	Toenail	4	8d	Common
	Collar tie (2") to rafter	Face-nail	2	12d	Common
	Collar tie (1") to rafter	Face-nail	3	8d	Common
Roof	Asphalt, new	Face-nail	4	$7/8$"	Roofing
	Asphalt, reroof	Face-nail	4	$1^3/4$"	Roofing
	Wood shingle, new	Face-nail	2	4d	Shingle
	Wood single, reroof	Face-nail	2	6d	Shingle
Sheathing	$3/8$" plywood	Face-nail	6" o.c.	6d	Common
	$1/2$" and thicker plywood	Face-nail	6" o.c.	8d	Common
	$1/2$" fiberboard	Face-nail	3" o.c.	$1^1/2$"	Roofing
	$3/4$" fiberboard	Face-nail	3" o.c.	$1^3/4$"	Roofing
	$3/4$" boards	Face-nail	6" o.c.	8d	Common

could be a problem, like for a deck near the ocean, it might be the best investment.

Common nails are preferred for general construction because they have an extra-thick shank and a broad head. You can also purchase common nails that have been cement-coated (actually nylon-coated) to increase their holding strength. Their coating is melted by the friction of being driven through the wood, and it quickly resets. Try to drive cement-coated nails home in a few quick blows.

"Deformed" nails, such as helical, barbed, or ring-shank nails, also exhibit greater withdrawal resistance. These nails' shanks have been adapted to increase friction (helical nails are actually threaded like a screw) and have a 40 percent greater withdrawal resistance than common nails. These nails are harder to drive.

If you don't want the nail's head to show, choose finishing or casing nails. Casing nails are similar to finishing nails but have a duller point and thicker shank; they have more holding power than a finishing nail of the same size. After you drive the nails nearly flush, sink them with a nail set. You can fill the hole with wood putty.

Holding Power. Several characteristics determine the holding power of a nail—its shape, diameter, point (pointed, chisel, or blunt), and the coating of the shank. Think of a nail as a small wedge being driven against the fibers of the wood; anything that would enable this wedge to contact more wood fibers without damaging them or that can attach the wedge more securely to the existing fibers will increase the nail's hold. And holding power is a key part of keeping framing square, plumb, and level.

A thicker nail, for instance, will be more difficult to remove than a thinner nail. The resistance of nails to withdrawal increases almost directly with their diameter; a nail's holding power is doubled with a proportional increase in diameter, because more wood fibers are acting against the wider wedge. A pointed nail will have a greater resistance because it is driven between wood fibers that a dull nail would tend to sever. And a deformed or textured nail, such as a ring-shank or a coated nail, will have greater withdrawal resistance than a smooth shank because the wood fibers have a textured surface to grip.

The characteristics of the wood also contribute to overall resistance. Hard, tight-grained woods, such as oak, will grip a nail tighter than a softer wood, such as pine. Oak and other hardwoods offer so much resistance that to drive the nail without bending it, you'll usually have to drill before nailing. Dry wood will hold a nail better than wet wood. Withdrawal resistance is also determined by how a nail is driven in relation to the wood's grain.

Using more nails will also increase overall holding strength; just make sure that the nails do not end up splitting the wood. Staggering a row of nails will help. Even slight splitting will greatly affect holding power.

Screws

Bugle-head screws are commonly known as drywall screws because they were originally developed for installing wallboard. These handy screws have become popular for all kinds of woodworking and carpentry projects. Drywall screws have an aggressive thread and do not require a pilot hole. "Bugle-head" refers to the taper beneath the flat head of the screw that allows you to drive them flush in softwood and drywall without drilling a countersink hole.

Screws have greater holding power than nails and can actually pull two boards tightly together. They also create a clean finished appearance by eliminating the possibility of hammer dents and scuffs; and unlike nails, screws will not "pop" (work themselves loose) after a couple of seasons. And because screws can be removed cleanly, they

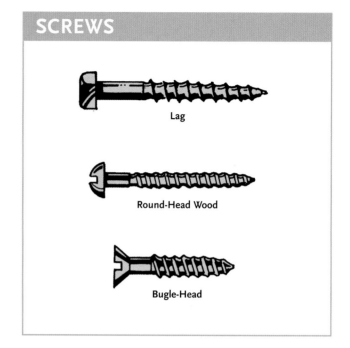

SCREWS

Lag

Round-Head Wood

Bugle-Head

facilitate disassembly or the removal of a damaged board. But, while screws can be used anywhere nails are used in outdoor construction, they cost considerably more than nails. As a result, screws are usually limited to two applications—installing deck boards, and finish trim work.

In the United States, drywall screws are most readily available with Phillips heads. Some woodworking supply catalogs offer them with a square recess for driving the screws. Square-drive screws are more readily available in Canada. You'll need a power drill or driver to install drywall screws. The square drives are superior because you can't easily strip the drive hole or the bit.

Drywall screws are available in a black oxide finish, suitable for interior work, and in a hot-dipped galvanized finish, for exterior projects. You'll usually find the exterior version sold as "deck screws." The most common lengths are 1, $1\frac{1}{2}$, 2, $2\frac{1}{2}$, and 3 inches.

If you need to toe-fasten pieces in an area of your project that will be highly visible, you can avoid ugly hammer dents by toe-screwing instead of toenailing. Put the boards in place, and drill a starter hole with a bit approximately equal in diameter to the shank of the screw.

Sizing. When determining nail or screw length, the general rule for softwoods is that the nail penetration into the bottom piece should be equal to or greater than the thickness of the top piece. For example, if you are nailing 1-inch-thick (5/4) decking boards to joists, 8d nails would do the job. You'll get even better holding power with 10d nails.

smart tip

PLANNING AHEAD

KEEPING A FEW SPARE POUNDS OF SCREWS AROUND CAN COME IN HANDY FOR A DIFFICULT JOB. PURCHASE A POUND EACH OF $1\frac{1}{2}$-, $2\frac{1}{2}$-, AND 3-INCH SCREWS FOR THOSE SITUATIONS WHERE YOU NEED ADDITIONAL STRENGTH OR FOR THOSE SPOTS THAT ARE TOO TIGHT TO SWING A HAMMER.

BOLT AND LAG SCREW SCHEDULES

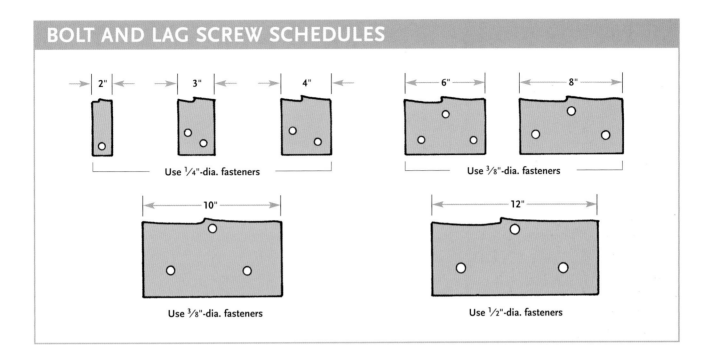

Use ¼"-dia. fasteners

Use ⅜"-dia. fasteners

Use ⅜"-dia. fasteners

Use ½"-dia. fasteners

When fastening plywood, the choice of the nail depends on the thickness of the panels. For ¾- and ⅝-inch plywood, use 8d common nails. For ½- and ⅜-inch panels, use 6d common nails. Space nails every 6 inches along the edges and 12 inches in the field. Ring-shank or screw-thread nails are recommended for this application, to prevent the nails from working their way loose when the wood expands and contracts with moisture changes.

The chart "Nailing Schedule for Light Outdoor Structures" on page 59 tells you what kind of and how many nails to use in the various connections you'll make.

Although not recommended for framing, screws can be used effectively for installing sheathing. For ¾- to ⅝-inch plywood, use a 1½-inch screw. For ½- to ⅜-inch plywood, use a 1¼-inch screw. Space screws 12 inches along the edges and 24 inches in the field.

Bolts, Rods, and Lag Screws

The most rigid joint fasteners are bolts and lag screws. These heavy-duty fasteners are recommended for connections that must be extremely strong, such as post-to-beam connections or where a ledger joins to the house. For strength and appearance, a single lag screw or bolt can replace three or four bugle-head screws.

Bolts pass all the way through the pieces they join (or are "through-bolted") and are secured with washers and nuts. The bolt-hole diameter should equal the stated diameter of the bolt. Two types of bolts are commonly used in outdoor construction: machine bolts and carriage bolts. Machine bolts resemble lag screws, in that they have a hexagonal head that remains above the surface of the lumber.

Carriage bolts work just like machine bolts, but they have a round head instead of a hex head. Just beneath the head, the shank is square. When tapped into a tight-fitting hole, the square shank seats the bolt into the wood, so that the nut can be tightened. A carriage bolt does not always require a washer beneath the head, but a washer is needed beneath the nut. Because the head is pulled almost flush with the surface of the lumber, carriage bolts are typically used on railing posts or in other places where a lag bolt might be visually obtrusive or snag clothing.

Bolt lengths range from 3 to 12 inches, and diameters range from ¼ to ¾ inch, in 1/16-inch increments. For longer lengths, you can purchase threaded rod. Bolts should be approximately 1 inch longer than the thickness of the combined pieces to accommodate washers and nuts. Threaded rod uses washers and nuts on both ends, so size it 2 inches longer than the combined thickness. Plan to drill bolt holes using a bit that's the same diameter as the bolt. When setting or removing lag bolts or carriage bolts, try not to damage the threads by striking them with a hammer or against a metal surface: damaged threads will make it impossible to thread on the nut. If you must tap the threaded end, protect it with a scrap of wood or hit it with a plastic mallet.

BOLTS

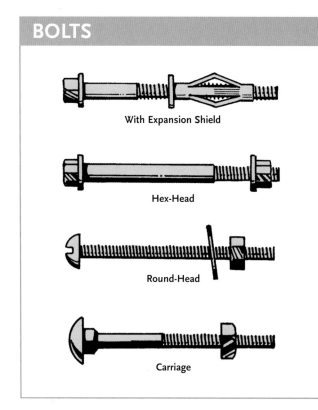

With Expansion Shield

Hex-Head

Round-Head

Carriage

Lag screws are available in the same size and length as machine or carriage bolts. Because they have a bolt-shaped head, lag screws are sometimes confused with lag bolts; but unlike bolts, they do not protrude through the objects being joined. They're particularly useful in tight spots where you can reach only one side of the connection with a wrench (a socket wrench is easiest). Drill a lead hole about two-thirds the length of the lag screw, using a bit 1/8 inch smaller than the lag screw's shank. Place a washer under each lag screw's head.

It is a better idea to make connections with several small-diameter bolts or lag screws instead of fewer large-diameter bolts. See "Bolt and Lag Screw Schedules" on page 61 to help you estimate the sizing and spacing for joining boards with lag bolts or screws.

Framing Hardware

You'll find many types of framing connectors in sizes to fit most standard-dimension rough and surfaced lumber. There are several major manufacturers of structural wood fasteners. Their basic product lines cover nearly all applications, but you may need to ask about special fasteners such as the gazebo roof peak fastener, hip rafter ties, or truss plates. Explain your needs to the

FRAMING HARDWARE

A Post Anchors. These connectors secure the base of a load-bearing post to a concrete foundation, slab, or deck. In areas where there is a lot of standing water or rain, choose an elevated post base that raises a post 1 to 3 inches above the surface.

B Joist Hangers. Joist hangers are used for butt joints between deck joists and beams. Single- and double-sized hangers are available. Rafter hangers are similar but are used to hang roof rafters from a ledger board.

C Saddle Hangers or Purlin Clips. Available in single and double designs, these clips are ideal for installing crosspieces between joists or rafters.

D Rafter Ties. These ties are used to provide wind and seismic ties for trusses and rafters.

E Ridge Rafter Connector. These connectors resemble joist hangers with an open bottom. Use them to fasten 2x6 rafters to ridge boards or ledgers. The open bottom can accommodate slopes of up to 30 degrees.

F Truss Plates. These plates are used in the construction of roof trusses. They can be designed with or without a lip. Various sizes are available.
Caution: Not all plate-type fasteners are designed for truss applications. Be sure the plates you buy are specified for roof truss construction. Special truss nails may also be required.

G Twist Tie. These straps are ideal for tying pieces that cross at 90-degree angles, such as joists, rafters, and beams.

H Hip Corner Plate. A hip corner plate connects a rafter or joist to double top plates at a 45-degree angle.

I Gazebo Roof Peak Tie. Two of these connectors are used at the peak of a six-sided gazebo roof to tie together all rafters. A key block is not needed.

J Hip Rafter Gazebo Tie. Similar to a hip corner plate, this connector is angled to tie roof rafters to the top plate of a six-sided gazebo.

K Hurricane Ties. Use these ties to secure rafters and trusses to top plates.

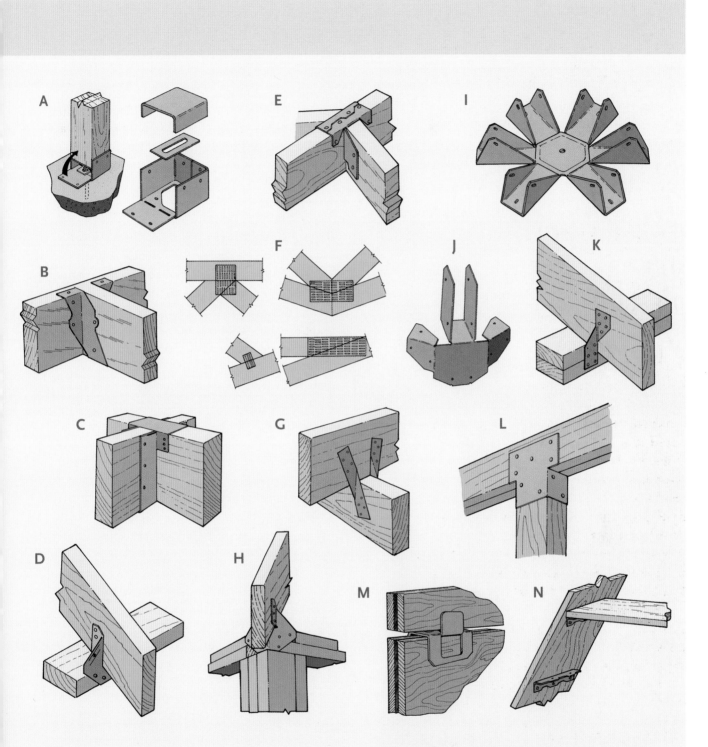

L Post Caps. These fasteners can be used at the top of a post to join it to a beam or to strengthen a splice connection between two beams.

M Panel Clips. These clips are slipped between the edges of plywood panels to lock them together where they span between rafters. Panel clips will also help maintain a sufficient gap between panels to allow for thermal expansion.

N Stair Angles. These clips support stair treads.

salesperson. While an effort has been made to select the generic name for the fasteners described in this book, one manufacturer's hurricane clip may be another's storm tie. The fasteners you do buy may also look a little different from those illustrated here. Just make sure they are designed to do the same job.

Remember that most of these fasteners are simply metal accessories designed to assist with, or replace, other traditional joinery techniques. If you cannot find a particular fastener or you wish to maintain a metal-free appearance, consider other options.

WOOD

Once you've decided on a design for your gazebo, arbor, or pavilion, the next important decision is selecting the wood for your project. The wood you choose must fulfill many requirements. Your project must weather years of exposure without losing its strength or stability. It must resist the combined effects of sun, rain, mold, and wood-boring insects. In addition, the wood you use should be easy to work with, attractive, and reasonably priced.

Trying to find wood at your local lumberyard that will best meet all of these requirements should not be intimidating. This section (pages 64–71) is designed to introduce you to the types and grades of woods typically used in exterior construction. After reading this section, you will be able to select the wood that is best suited for your particular project. This section will also guide you through the purchase of your lumber.

Choosing Wood

Lumber is divided into softwoods and hardwoods. Softwood comes from coniferous trees (evergreens), while hardwood comes from deciduous trees (those that lose their leaves in the fall). While most hardwoods are harder than most softwoods, this is not always the case. Southern yellow pine, which is a softwood, is harder than poplar, which is a hardwood.

Nearly all outdoor construction today is done with softwood lumber because it is more readily available, easier to work, and generally less expensive than hardwood. Although more costly, hardwoods are typically used in smaller decorative elements because they can be cut or milled more sharply and because they have attractive grain patterns. (Premade cornice pieces and frieze boards are typically made of poplar, because this hardwood cuts cleaner and weathers better than pine.)

Of the softwoods, redwood, cedar, and cypress are considered the most highly desirable outdoor building materials because of their beauty and natural resistance to decay. These woods are used for decks, gazebos, lath- or lattice-style roofing, shingles, siding, and shakes. Unfortunately, due to their popularity, they are also the most expensive of all softwoods and may not be available in all regions.

But don't think that you have to use higher-priced redwood or cedar for a great-looking outdoor project. Other softwoods are available in various regions of the country—for example, pine, fir, spruce, and larch. Granted, these woods will require additional weather protection, but the extra care will enable you to build the same beautiful project for a lot less money.

Redwood. The redwood trees of the Pacific Northwest are legendary for their size and for the quality of the lumber they provide. Redwood's beautiful, straight grain, natural glowing color, and weather resistance have traditionally marked it as the Cadillac of all outdoor building materials. Unfortunately, past overlumbering has affected the availability (and price) of redwood today.

There are two "types" of redwood in each log. The younger, outer portion of the wood is called sapwood; the older, denser center is referred to as heartwood. The sapwood is lighter in color and less weather-resistant than the heartwood. Redwood heartwood is extremely stable and can be milled to produce very smooth surfaces. When it is sawn, the reddish heartwood produces a wonderful fragrance, releasing the same chemicals that discourage wood-boring insects. If you like, you can let redwood age naturally to a light gray patina; however, it will also accept paint or stain readily.

There are several grades of redwood. The two grades preferred for outdoor construction—because they consist entirely of heartwood—are Clear All Heart and Construction Heart. Of the two, Clear All Heart is more expensive because it is knot-free. Its price will probably limit its use to railing and other important trim pieces that must be smooth and clear. In comparison, Construction Heart, or Con-Heart, does contain some minor imperfections, but should be ideal for almost every other element of your outdoor project. Because they contain some sapwood, Clear, B-Grade, Construction Common, and Merchantable are not recommended for deck framing or decking. They can be effectively used for accessories around your project, such as fences, planters, or trellises.

Although it is weather- and rot-resistant, redwood does not last as long as pressure-treated lumber under ground-contact conditions.

It's a good idea to raise the deck of your project several inches above the ground by setting your posts on concrete pillars. Another popular and attractive (and cost-effective) option is to build the understructure from pressure-treated wood and use redwood only for the parts that will be visible.

Western Red Cedar. Western red cedar is more decay-resistant than eastern cedar varieties. Western red cedar trees are also significantly larger and yield a reasonable selection of dimension lumber. Like redwood, cedar is a fragrant, dark-colored wood that is extremely stable and rot-resistant. It can be left to develop a gray patina, or it can be painted or stained.

Cedar does have some drawbacks. Because it is softer and weaker than other species, cedar is not the best choice for framing members. The popularity of cedar shingles, clapboards, and shakes limits the use of cedar for other applications by driving up the price.

Cypress. Bald cypress is the South's answer to redwood. Native to the swamps and lowland areas throughout the southeast, bald cypress is extremely resistant to decay and insect attack. Cypress is similar to redwood in hardness and strength, although it's not as stable. In the southern United States, local sawmills can be a very economical source for your building materials. Cypress isn't usually stocked outside of its native region, but it can be custom-ordered by northern consumers.

Other Decay-Resistant Woods. Depending on where you live, you may have some local woods that are quite resistant to rot. Osage orange, black locust, and white oak are all excellent for outdoor projects. However, most of these species will not be readily obtainable through a home center. Availability is limited—you'll have to get them from a local sawmill.

REDWOOD GRADING

Grades of Redwood

Grades Containing Only Heartwood
Clear All Heart
Select Heart
Construction Heart
Merchantable Heart

Grades Containing Some Sapwood
Clear
B-Grade
Construction Common
Merchantable

FROM LEFT TO RIGHT Clear All Heart, Select Heart, Construction Heart, Merchantable Heart, B-Grade, Select, and Construction. Use heartwood for outdoor construction.

PRESSURE-TREATED LUMBER STAMP

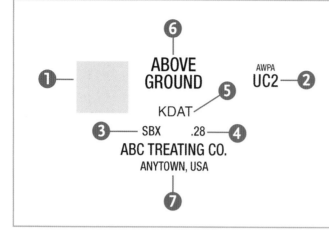

1. Trademark of inspection agency accredited by American Lumber Standard Committee (ALSC)
2. American Wood-Preservers' Association (AWPA) use category
3. Preservative used for treatment
4. Preservative retention
5. Dry or KDAT, if applicable
6. Exposure category
7. Treating company and location

Pressure-Treated Lumber. Pressure-treated lumber (typically southern yellow pine, Douglas fir, ponderosa pine, or Engleman spruce) is wood that, in addition to being graded, has been factory-treated with preservatives to repel rot, insects, and other causes of decay. Pressure treatment is the most effective method of applying preservative, because it forces the chemical deeply into the wood's fibers. The chemical injection process is what gives pressure-treated wood its characteristic green tint. Like redwood and cedar, pressure-treated wood will fade to a pleasing mellow gray if left to weather naturally.

Working with Pressure-Treated Wood. In 2004, the most widely used pressure-treated wood, chromated copper arsenate (CCA), was restricted to industrial use. In its place, wood treated with one of two new arsenic-free preservatives entered the market. From the builder's standpoint, both alkaline copper quat (ACQ) and copper azole (CBA-A, with boron, and CA-B, without) work equally well.

The amount of preservative needed varies, depending on the intended use of the board and on the preservative used. Labels printed on the end of the board help you sort things out. "Pressure Treated Lumber Stamp," above, shows you how to read the label. The chart "Pressure-Treated Wood Types & Uses" tells you what to look for on the label based on the end use of the board. In general, unpainted wood requires one type of wood, and painted wood requires another.

Both ACQ and CBA are more corrosive than CCA. Make sure you get hot-dipped galvanized nails, screws, and connectors. Other types are not as durable.

When you are working with pressure-treated lumber,

you should take precautions against the preservatives. Wear a long-sleeved shirt and long pants, a dust mask, and eye protection (always!) to protect yourself from direct exposure. Do all of your sawing outside; whenever possible, try to avoid sanding. Be sure to wash thoroughly before eating or drinking. And should you happen to get a

PRESSURE-TREATED WOOD TYPES & USES

Use	Exposure Category	Use Category
Decking, painted or unpainted	Above Ground, Exterior	3B
Joists, beams	Above Ground, Exterior	3B
Railing components	Above Ground, Exterior	3B
Support posts, sawn	Ground Contact or Fresh Water	4C
Trim, brackets, lattice, other, painted	Above Ground, Exterior	3A
Trim, brackets, lattice, other, unpainted	Above Ground, Exterior	3B

splinter, remove it immediately—splinters from pressure-treated wood can be especially irritating.

After you complete your project, make sure that you clean up all scraps and sawdust. You should either bury these scraps or discard them in the trash. Do not burn pressure-treated wood: burning will cause the wood to release poisonous gases.

It's not a bad idea to hose down your completed project or to let it sit through a few rainstorms before allowing small children or pets to use it.

Buying Lumber

Dimension softwood is sold by the lineal foot, in lengths of even 2-foot increments from 6 to 24 feet. Many of the projects in this book call for standard lengths, such as 8, 10, or 12 feet, to minimize the amount of cutting (and waste) involved.

You cannot always count on the lumberyard to provide square ends, particularly on lower grades of lumber. Examine the ends of any critical-length lumber to make sure that it is not slanted or damaged. Take a measuring tape with you to make sure that the boards measure up to (or preferably, a little over) their specified lengths. If you have to square-cut the ends yourself, plan on losing $\frac{1}{2}$ to 1 inch of length.

You can also move up to the next available length and trim to exact plan dimensions. But, unless there's some use for all the generated scrap, you'll save a lot of money by adapting the plan to the material.

Not all suppliers stock every lumber grade in every possible length, so you might have to make adjustments. Make sure that the critical support members (posts, beams, joists, and rafters) are lengths that match or exceed those required. For lumber that will be cut into smaller pieces, it is more economical to buy several smaller lengths than a single long length. For example, it's cheaper to buy two 6-foot 2x4s than a single 12-foot length.

Nominal vs. Actual Dimensions. When a 2x4 is sawn from the log, it really does measure 2 by 4 inches. But then the piece of lumber is surfaced to make it flat and smooth and is left to dry, so its dimensions begin to change. As a result, the 2x4 actually measures $1\frac{1}{2} \times 3\frac{1}{2}$ inches by the time it gets to you. A 1x4 actually measures $\frac{3}{4} \times 3\frac{1}{2}$ inches, while a 2x8 is only $1\frac{1}{2} \times 7\frac{1}{4}$ inches. See the chart "Nominal and Actual Sizes," at right.

smart tip

RETREATING PRESSURE-TREATED WOOD EVEN AFTER PRESSURE TREATMENT, THE CHEMICAL PRESERVATIVES DO NOT PENETRATE THROUGHOUT THE ENTIRE DEPTH OF A BOARD. THE WESTERN WOOD PRODUCTS ASSOCIATION (WWPA) DOES NOT RECOMMEND RIPPING FOR WIDTH OR RESAWING FOR THICKNESS, BECAUSE THESE OPERATIONS CAN EXPOSE LARGE UNTREATED SECTIONS OF WOOD ON THE TREATED BOARD. OF COURSE, SOME CUTTING IS INEVITABLE. THE WWPA SUGGESTS BRUSHING OR DIPPING SOME ADDITIONAL PRESERVATIVE ON ALL FRESHLY CUT SURFACES UNTIL THE WOOD IS SATURATED.

NOMINAL AND ACTUAL SIZES

Lumber	Nominal Size (inches)	Common Actual Size (inches)
Boards	1 x 3	$\frac{3}{4} \times 2\frac{1}{2}$
	1 x 4	$\frac{3}{4} \times 3\frac{1}{2}$
	1 x 6	$\frac{3}{4} \times 5\frac{1}{2}$
	1 x 8	$\frac{3}{4} \times 7\frac{1}{4}$
	1 x 10	$\frac{3}{4} \times 9\frac{1}{4}$
	1 x 12	$\frac{3}{4} \times 11\frac{1}{4}$
Dimension Lumber	2 x 2	$1\frac{1}{2} \times 1\frac{1}{2}$
	2 x 3	$1\frac{1}{2} \times 2\frac{1}{2}$
	2 x 4	$1\frac{1}{2} \times 3\frac{1}{2}$
	2 x 6	$1\frac{1}{2} \times 5\frac{1}{2}$
	2 x 8	$1\frac{1}{2} \times 7\frac{1}{4}$
	2 x 10	$1\frac{1}{2} \times 9\frac{1}{4}$
	2 x 12	$1\frac{1}{2} \times 11\frac{1}{4}$
Posts	4 x 4	$3\frac{1}{2} \times 3\frac{1}{2}$
	4 x 6	$3\frac{1}{2} \times 5\frac{1}{2}$
	6 x 6	$5\frac{1}{2} \times 5\frac{1}{2}$

smart tip

WET VS. KILN-DRIED PRESSURE-TREATED WOOD IS AVAILABLE AS "WET" OR "KILN-DRIED AFTER TREATMENT" (KDAT). THE SPECIFIC TREATMENT SHOULD BE INDICATED ON THE WOOD'S STAMP. IF PAINTABILITY AND PRODUCT STABILITY ARE YOUR PRIMARY CONCERNS, YOU MIGHT WANT TO INVEST A LITTLE MORE AND USE KDAT. FOR EXAMPLE, KDAT WOOD WOULD BE A GOOD CHOICE WHEN BUILDING THE RAILS, BECAUSE THEY WOULD NOT TEND TO BOW OR CUP AND WOULD BE READY FOR PAINTING AS SOON AS YOU NAIL THEM IN. WET-TREATED WOOD ALSO WILL DRY OUT WITHIN A FEW WEEKS OF EXPOSURE, AND UNLESS IT IS USED IMMEDIATELY OR PROPERLY STICKERED, IT MAY BEGIN TO WARP OR CUP.

LUMBER GRADING STAMP

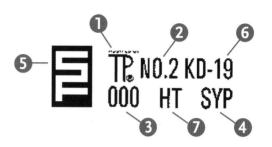

1. Inspection service: Timber Products Inspection, Inc. (TP)
2. Lumber grade
3. Mill identification number
4. Lumber species
5. (Optional) Logo denoting a member mill of Southern Forest Products Association (SFPA)
6. Moisture content (MC): Kiln-dried (KD) to a maximum of 19%
7. Heat-treated

Lumber Grades. Lumber is sorted and marked at the mill with a stamp that identifies the quality, moisture content, grade name, and in many cases, the species and the grading agency. Grade is determined by natural growth characteristics (such as knots), defects that result from milling errors, and manufacturing techniques used for drying and preserving the wood (they affect the strength, durability, and appearance of the wood).

Surfaced lumber is the standard material for most construction and is available in nearly all grades. Lumber that is surfaced on all four sides is termed S4S. If you want your project to have a rustic final appearance,

rough-sawn lumber may be just what you need. Because rough-sawn lumber is not reduced by surfacing operations, the actual dimensions will be quite close to nominal. And rough-sawn is cheaper than S4S because you don't have to pay for surfacing. Most lumberyards don't carry rough-sawn lumber, so you'll need to buy it directly from the sawmill.

The two major grades of softwood are select and common. Select softwood has two good faces. Select grades are further broken down into B and Better, C, and D. Select lumber, classified as "clear," is free from knots and other surface imperfections. You will usually

LUMBER GRADES

No. 1 Grade

No. 2 Grade

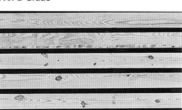

No. 3 Grade

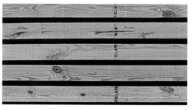

● LUMBER DEFECTS

BOW is a deviation from a flat plane of the wide face, end to end. It has no effect on strength and can be used as long as you can nail it back to a flat plane.

CUP is a deviation from a flat plane of the narrow face, edge to edge. Cupping tends to loosen fasteners.

CROOK is a deviation from a flat plane of the narrow face, end to end. It makes wood unsuitable for framing. Small crooks can be pried straight and nailed in place.

TWIST is the turning in opposite directions of the ends of the board. Twist makes lumber unsuitable for framing or decking.

CHECK is a rift in the surface caused when the surface of the timber dries more rapidly than the interior. Checks are generally cosmetic; they do not affect structural strength. Use kiln-dried wood to avoid checking.

SPLIT is a crack that passes completely through the wood. It constitutes a serious structural weakness. Lumber with splits should not be used for any structural members, such as joists or posts.

WANE is the presence of bark, or lack of wood at an edge. It is the result of the sawyer maximizing the amount of wood milled from a tree. Wane has very little effect on strength. Any remaining bark should be removed, because the bark will promote rot.

KNOTS are the high-density roots of limbs. The knots themselves are very strong, but they are not connected to the surrounding wood. The rules for knots in joists and rafters are (1) tight knots are allowed in the top third, (2) loose or missing knots are allowed in the middle third, and (3) no knots at all over 1 inch are allowed in the bottom third of the board width.

DECAY is the destruction of the wood structure by fungi or insects. Although it may enhance the decorative nature of the wood, it severely prohibits any structural applications.

PITCH POCKETS are accumulations of natural resins. They have little effect on strength, but because the pitch will bleed through, they should not be allowed in lumber that will be painted.

Defect	End View	Long View
BOW		
CUP		
CROOK		
TWIST		
CHECK		
SPLIT		
WANE		
KNOTS		
DECAY		
PITCH POCKETS		

have to hand-pick select clear lumber at a slight extra charge per piece.

Common-grade softwood is lower in quality than select grades. Common grades include 1, 2, 3, Const, Stand, Util, and Stud. You'll find that No. 2 is most readily available in lumberyards and home centers and is suitable for most general construction. You can save some money by planning where each board is to be used in relation to the project. Use lower-grade (No. 2) wood for the less visible areas, like the floor framing. You'll want to spring for No. 1 for the railing.

When purchasing lumber, you want to avoid as many defective boards as you can. A defective board is not only unsightly but can affect the structural integrity of your project. Some defects can be avoided by planning around the defect or by cutting it out of an otherwise good board.

However, if you encounter a significant percentage of defects, you should probably invest in a better grade of lumber. It is also a good idea to inspect several lumberyards because one may have better wood, even though it is advertised as the same grade.

Plywood

Standard softwood plywood is commonly used for roof and wall sheathing. Plywood panels measure 4x8 feet; their thicknesses range from $1/4$ to $3/4$ inch.

The appearance of the two sides of the panel determine its grade. Letters A through D designate the grades, with A being the highest and D the lowest. A/C (exterior) panels are an economical choice for projects where only one side will be visible. Face and back grades, glue type, and group number should be stamped on each panel, along with an association trademark that ensures quality.

When plywood is used as sheathing that will be covered on both sides, the most commonly used grade is CDX. As mentioned, the C and the D indicate the grade of the two sides. The X stands for "exposure"—not for "exterior" as many people assume. This means that the plywood is designed to weather a few rainstorms until you get around to applying siding over it. It doesn't mean that the plywood is intended to be used as permanently exposed siding. Siding-grade plywood will have a designation such as AC ext. The ext. marking on the panel is an abbreviation for "exterior."

When CDX plywood is used for house sheathing, the C side is set facing out because that grade makes

a fine nailing base for siding or shingles. However, in sheathing outdoor projects, the inside face is often left exposed. For example, you might sheathe and shingle the roof of a gazebo, leaving the rafters and inside face of the sheathing exposed. For this application, ACX would be a good choice. Face the C side out for a good nailing base, with the A face in for appearance. Exposure-grade is fine here, because the inside face is protected from the weather.

Delivery, Drying, and Storing Woods

Delivery. If you don't have access to a truck, you'll have to arrange for delivery to the site. Find out if there will be a delivery charge for your order. Make sure that the supplier will be able to deliver the wood when you need it.

It's also important to establish the dealer's policy regarding the return of unusable material. You should not have to pay for boards that are cracked, warped, or otherwise too defective to be used. For this reason, it's a good idea to be on hand when the delivery arrives so that you'll be able to give the wood a quick inspection before the truck leaves you with the defective wood.

Drying and Storing Wood. Some of the wood used in exterior projects, especially wet pressure-treated lumber, will still be fairly saturated with water when it is delivered to your construction site. Wet wood is not very enjoyable to work with: it will dull your saw's blade in record time, and some boards will even seem to "bleed" every time you sink a nail.

What's worse, wet wood will continue to shrink or otherwise distort until its moisture content matches that of its surroundings. The wood you are using can change shape as you are working with it; the parts that you carefully fitted one weekend may not fit by the next.

If you have to store your lumber for even a short time,

smart tip

WET WOOD FIELD TEST TO DETERMINE WHETHER YOUR LUMBER IS DRY ENOUGH TO USE, MAKE A TEST CUT AND RUB THE SAWDUST BETWEEN YOUR FINGERS. IF THE SAWDUST IS DRY, THEN THE BOARD IS READY TO USE.

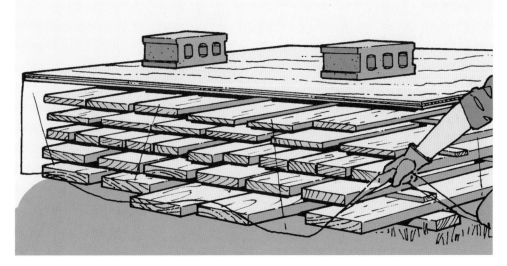

Protect your investment: carefully stack lumber to prevent moisture damage. Cull out the best pieces for special applications.

you must also consider the effects of moisture damage. It takes only a little water to promote mold and mildew, not to mention insects. The extra money you spent on kiln-dried wood will be wasted after the first rain unless the wood is protected and stacked in such a way as to dry uniformly. When wood is stacked incorrectly, moisture absorption will be uneven, causing the boards to cup or warp.

You can protect your investment by following a few simple steps. Store the wood in a protected and well-ventilated location. Stack wood a few inches off the ground so that your boards will not wick up extra moisture. Stack the boards in layers, separated by strips of ¾-inch furring, so that the air can circulate through the pile. Lay the furring, called "stickers," every couple of feet. Position them so that the stickers in each layer are directly above the ones below. Stones, bricks, or other weights placed on top of the pile will help to stabilize the uppermost pieces. Remember to cover your pile to protect it from a heavy rain.

Stacking lumber also offers you the opportunity to pick out the best pieces of wood to use in the most visible elements of your project. For instance, you may end up making the railing from the beautiful straight 2x4s that you found on the bottom of the delivery. The warped 2x4s that were originally piled on top can be cut to shorter lengths.

Storing Plywood and Siding. Plywood and siding should also be protected from direct exposure as much as possible. If you have the room, stack plywood flat; rest the bottom sheet on cinder blocks or some sort of frame to avoid ground contact. Plywood can also be stacked on edge. Rest the edges of the sheets on runners made from scrap dimension lumber so they don't touch the ground. Try to keep the sheets perpendicular to the ground to reduce the tendency of the wood to bow. In both cases, the sheets should be kept within a roofed enclosure, such as a shed or garage, or at least covered with a tarp, so they won't get saturated by every rainstorm.

5 techniques

Every carpenter has his or her own approach to a job. However, if you were to watch several people, you would start to notice similarities in the ways they get the job done. Many of these similarities evolve through trial and error. By working on your own, you, too, will eventually learn that certain systems work better than others. But you don't need to learn everything from the school of hard knocks. Starting off with a few basic techniques will provide you with a solid foundation to successfully (and enjoyably) build your project right on the first try, with a minimum of wasted time and materials. Some of these suggestions may seem to be common sense—the point is to learn to think like a carpenter. In time, you will come to use some of these suggestions reflexively.

PLANNING A WORK SPACE

The phrase "a place for everything and everything in its place" is not reserved solely for the Shakers. Good carpenters appreciate and abide by this well-worn saying.

Think back to your last project. Chances are that you probably wasted far too much time looking for a screwdriver, trying to find a free receptacle to plug another tool in, or carrying wood from one side of the yard to the other. And then there were the half-dozen trips to the hardware store. When you work this way, even the smallest project will devour the entire weekend. Planning out your project in relation to your tools and work space is an excellent way of making more efficient use of your time.

A well-planned work site is a lot safer, as well. For example, placing a few sawhorses or a chop saw right next to the stack of lumber will take the strain off of your back by minimizing the times you have to drag those 16-foot boards across the length of the site. Centralizing power tools in one corner also centralizes power cords, which could save you from tripping over the one that you "don't know how it got there in the first place."

Sometimes a quick sketch is all that it takes to visualize how everything will be able to work best on a given job. Plan how you want your site to work. Include all the major elements of construction: where you can park your car or truck, where the wood will be delivered, where the electrical cords are running from, and of course, the location of your project's foundation. Try to imagine how

In an efficient work site, the tools and materials are strategically placed to conserve steps while allowing you enough room to work.

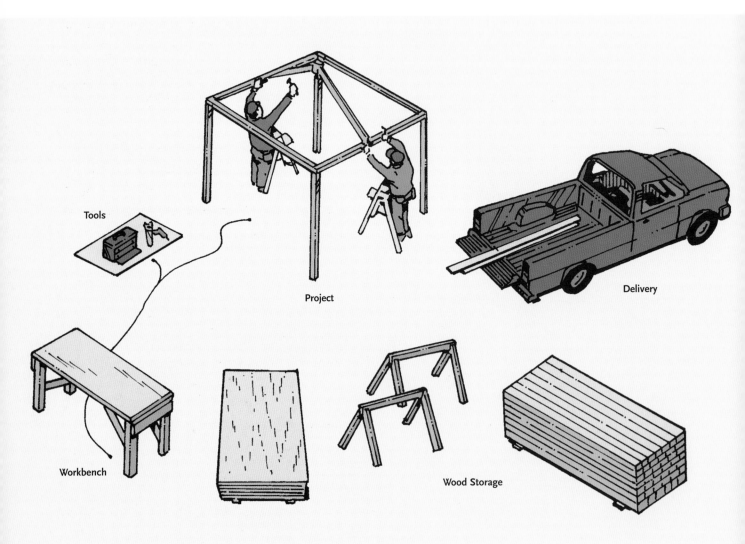

Tools

Project

Delivery

Workbench

Wood Storage

these elements will work with each other, and plan the work space accordingly. For example, if you are handling delivery of wood on your own, you will naturally want to keep wood-toting to a minimum. Make preliminary cuts near the side of the stack before carrying the boards to the foundation. Make sure that you'll be able to supply enough electricity at the cutting site. If you are working in an area that's inaccessible to extension cords, you might have to rent a generator for a few days. Planning out the site like this is an excellent way of identifying and solving problems before you begin.

Besides your time, your greatest investment in this project is wood. Be sure to stack your pile neatly to avoid unnecessary damage to the material as well as to your workers. The weight from a properly stacked pile will prevent boards from cupping and warping. Centralizing all of the material in one corner will prevent a lot of accidents throughout construction. Cutoffs and sawdust will also be centralized in one corner, which should make cleanup a little easier. Restacking your material gives you an opportunity to select pieces for special applications, such as railings and trim.

NAILING AND DRILLING

There's a little more to nailing than just a well-aimed blow. The structural strength of your project depends on using the right size and number of nails in the right locations.

Splitting

Splitting, in which the wood cracks (see page 64), is not a major problem with softwoods. But woods without a uniform texture, such as southern yellow pine and Douglas fir, do split more than the uniformly textured woods such as northern and Idaho white pine, sugar pine, and ponderosa pine. And all boards have a tendency to split near the end. Even a minor split will affect the holding power of the nail and the overall strength of the joint.

If you use several nails at a single joint, stagger their positions to prevent splitting. Another way to avoid splitting is to drill holes 75 percent of the nail diameter or to switch to a smaller-diameter nail. You can also reduce the chance of splitting by blunting the tip of the nail; but remember that a blunt point destroys wood fibers and will result in a reduced withdrawal resistance.

Skewing

Skewing creates a sounder connection by "hooking" the boards together, as well as by reducing the possibility of splitting. You can do this by simply driving the nails in at opposing angles.

Skewed nails are driven in at opposing angles to hook the boards together.

smart tip

CORRALING TOOLS TOOLS HAVE AN ANNOYING HABIT OF WALKING AWAY FROM A WORK SITE (EVEN WHEN YOU'RE WORKING BY YOURSELF). ONE WAY TO PREVENT YOUR TOOLS FROM SPROUTING LEGS IS TO MARK OFF A SPOT WHERE EACH ITEM SHOULD BE RETURNED WHENEVER IT IS NOT IN USE. (AN OLD BLANKET OR SCRAP SHEET OF PLYWOOD WORKS FINE.)

AT THE END OF THE DAY, MAKE IT A POINT TO PUT AWAY YOUR TOOLS ON YOUR OWN. THAT WAY, YOU'LL KNOW EXACTLY WHERE SOMETHING IS, BECAUSE YOU'RE THE PERSON WHO PUT IT THERE. THIS IS ALSO A PERFECT TIME TO GIVE EVERYTHING A QUICK INSPECTION TO CHECK FOR DULL BLADES, DEAD BATTERIES, OR OTHER DAMAGED OR MISSING PARTS.

Clinching

If nails go completely through both boards, you have three possible options. You could simply use shorter nails, or you could try driving the longer nail at an angle to make it travel through more wood. A third alternative is to "clinch" the nails, or to bend over the exposed tip. Although it's not the most attractive option, clinching increases holding strength as much as 170 percent over unclinched nails.

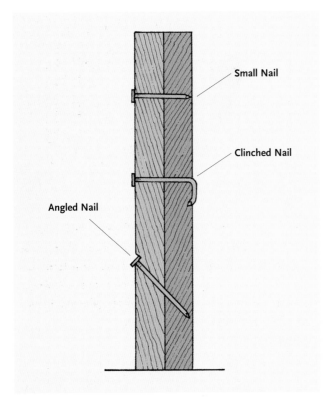

Small Nail

Clinched Nail

Angled Nail

Clinching ensures that a nail cannot work itself loose, and it more than doubles a nail's holding power.

Toenailing

Most of the time, when two boards need to be joined at a right angle, you can nail through the face of one board into the end of the other. But sometimes, the face that you'd prefer to nail into is inaccessible, or the piece you have to nail through is too thick. For example, you can't nail through a 4x4 post to attach a handrail. In cases like this, you need to toenail the pieces together. Toenailing means joining two boards by nailing at an angle through the end, or toe, of one board into the face of another. Position the nail on the first piece at least 1 1/2 inches from the second piece. Start the nail at a 60- to 75-degree

angle. When it is started, adjust it to a 30- to 40-degree angle. Move your hand and drive the nail home. If it is possible, drive another nail on the other side of the board as well, to increase holding power.

Screwing

Considering the popularity of cordless drills and drivers on today's construction sites, you probably will be using a few screws in addition to nails to put your project together. Screwing boards together does have its advantages. First, screws have a way of "pulling" two boards together to make a tighter-fitting joint if one board clears the threads. Using a driver also enables you to drive screws accurately in spots where you don't have the room to swing a hammer. Also, because of their threads, screws grip better than nails. At the same time, screws are easier to remove.

It does take a little practice before you can drive a Phillips-head screw at high speeds without stripping the screw head or the driver bit (buy a couple of #2 Phillips-

smart tip

NAILING RULE OF THUMB FOR A STRONG CONNECTION, ALWAYS TRY TO NAIL A THINNER MEMBER TO A THICKER MEMBER. THE NAIL SHOULD BE THREE TIMES THE THICKNESS OF THE THINNER MEMBER.

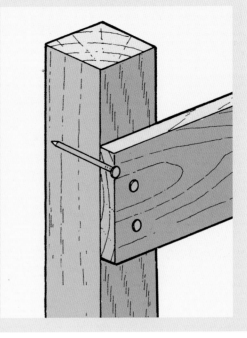

TOENAILING TECHNIQUE

To prevent a nail from slipping when toenailing, place the nail upside down on the spot where you want to start your toenail and give it a few light taps. Not only will this method give you a flat spot to start driving, it will also blunt the nail, reducing its chance of splitting the wood.

head bits just in case). When driving screws using a driver, start at a slow speed until the screw takes hold, and increase the speed until the screw is set. Maintain constant pressure parallel with the screw, and avoid stopping before it is in all the way. Friction exerted on these fasteners can sometimes catch the screw, and you may snap it if you

allow the wood fibers time to bind. When the head has countersunk itself into the wood, lift the driver as you take your finger off the trigger. If your driver has an automatic clutch, you don't have to worry as much about stripping or snapping the screw—the clutch will disengage the driver when the screw is at the correct depth.

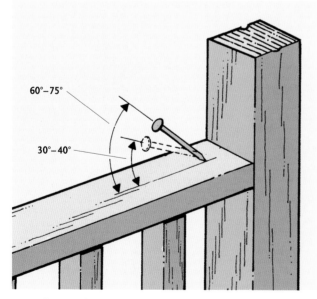

60°–75°

30°–40°

Start driving the nail at an angle of about 65 to 70 deg. to the work to keep it from slipping. Decrease the angle after you start.

Maintain constant pressure and start the drill at a low speed to prevent slippage. Increase the speed gradually as the screw goes into the wood.

CUTTING WITH A CIRCULAR SAW

You'll probably pick up the circular saw almost as frequently as your hammer. This tool is capable of performing very straight, precise cuts suitable for all types of joinery, as well as decorative ornamentation. The most elaborate effects are simply variations of a few basic cuts.

Choosing the Blade

It goes without saying that carbide-tipped blades are far better than steel blades. Although they cost a bit more, carbide stays sharp five times longer than steel—a definite advantage when cutting dense (and usually wet) wood such as pressure-treated southern pine. A sharp blade also puts less stress on your saw's motor and reduces the chance of binding or kickback.

But which type of carbide-tipped blade should you buy? For these projects, you should be able to do all of your cutting with an 18- to 24-tooth combination blade. Combination means that it cuts well perpendicular to *and* parallel with the grain. This blade also works fine when cutting posts and plywood. A coarser blade is designed for rough work, like demolition, and will produce a splintery cut. A blade with 36 or more teeth is too fine for this kind of construction and may tend to bind in wet wood.

Although a top-of-the-line blade may cut cleaner and stay sharper than a less-expensive blade, you might be better off with a middle-of-the-line model. A new, less-expensive carbide blade will outperform the best blade that has chewed through a whole stack of wet wood or has snagged a nail. Some very good 24-tooth blades can be purchased for less than half of the price of the premium blades. And once the middle-of-the-line blade is dull, just toss it. Why pay to have it sharpened when it's cheaper and easier just to buy a new blade?

Your saw will tell you when it's time to switch blades. Some indications of a dull blade include a slower cut speed, a "strained" motor sound, splintery cuts, and even smoking or burned cuts.

● KICKBACK

Kickback is the term describing that dreaded action when the saw suddenly kicks backward in the middle of a cut. What happens is that the teeth on the rear part of the blade catch the edge of the saw cut, causing the saw to jump out of the kerf. The threat is that the saw might buck up or perhaps even run backward toward you before you can release the switch. As soon as you feel the saw start to kick back, stop and correct the problem before continuing.

LEADING CAUSES OF KICKBACK:

▎**Binding Board.** Sometimes the stresses in the wood cause the kerf to close. Binding also will occur if the cut-off is not falling free and is pinching the blade.

▎**Twisting Blade.** A circular saw is not a jigsaw. If for whatever reason you started your cut off the line, do not try to correct your error in midcut. Stop the saw and start over.

▎**Backing Up the Blade.** Don't do it. Always stop the blade before backing up the saw.

▎**Dull Blade.** A dull blade will heat up and bind, which could cause it to kick back. It pays to have a spare blade handy.

Unfortunately, kickback is in the nature of the beast, and it happens even to experienced carpenters. For this reason, it's important always to keep your hands well away from the blade or cut path and position yourself to one side of the cut—never directly behind it.

ANATOMY OF KICKBACK

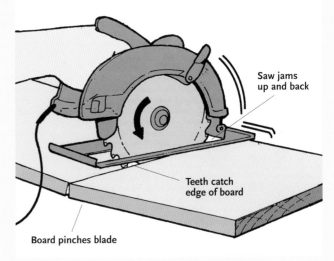

Saw jams up and back

Teeth catch edge of board

Board pinches blade

SQUARING THE BLADE

No matter what circular saw you have, you can't expect the angle markings stamped on the saw to be accurate. To ensure square cuts, use a square to set the blade.

1 SQUARE BLADE TO BASE. **Unplug the saw. Now turn the saw over and loosen the angle adjustment. Set an angle square or try to square against the blade and the base. Make sure you hold the square against the body of the blade without touching the teeth. The teeth are offset from the body and will throw off your adjustment. Tighten the angle adjustment when the blade and base bear evenly on the square.**

2 TEST FOR SQUARENESS. **Crosscut a small block off a scrap piece of 2x4. Flip the block and match the piece, cut-edge to cut-edge, with the 2x4. If your blade is not square to the base, you'll see a gap equal to twice the amount that your blade is out of square. If you do see a gap, repeat Step 1 and try again.**

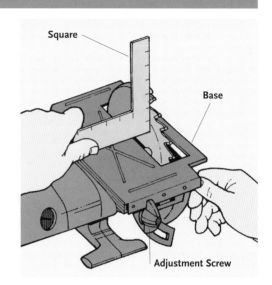

Square
Base
Adjustment Screw

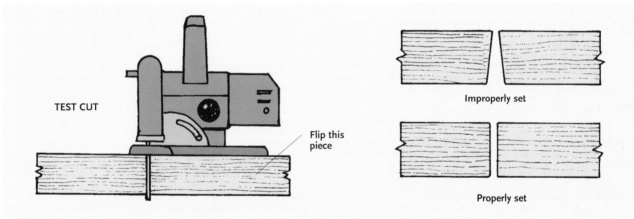

TEST CUT

Flip this piece

Improperly set

Properly set

MAKING SQUARE AND ACCURATE CUTS

1 POSITION WORKPIECE. **Before making the cut, your workpiece must be well supported on a stable surface that won't move during the cut. To avoid dangerous kickback, you must ensure that the piece you are cutting off can fall away without binding. If you are trimming a small piece off a board, position the board across two sawhorses and make the cut to the outside of one of the horses—never between the horses.**

When the piece being cut off is too long to let fall on the ground, you can do your cutting right on top of a stack of wood, as long as the stack is neat and stable.

(continued on the next page)

(continued from the previous page)

2 ALIGN BLADE TO LINE.

Use a square to strike a line where you want to cut the board. Make sure that the workpiece is well supported on a stable surface and that the waste piece will be able to fall away without binding the blade at the end of the cut.

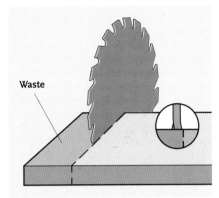

Waste

As mentioned, the teeth on a circular saw blade are offset. One tooth is offset to the left, the next to the right, and so on in an alternating pattern. Position the saw blade along the waste side of your cut line. Select a tooth that's offset toward the cut line, and align the saw so that this tooth just touches the line.

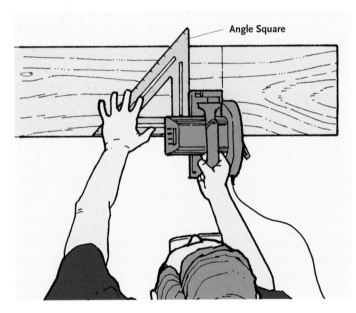

Angle Square

3 MAKE THE CUT.

With just a little bit of practice, you'll be able to cut squarely by following a pencil line. Get in the habit of keeping your eye on the leading edge of the blade, not the little notch or mark on the front of the saw base.

If you are new to using a circular saw, you might want to use your angle square as a guide until you get a feel for the saw. Even when you gain confidence, this is a useful technique for joinery cuts that will show in the final project. You can also use the angle square to make accurate 45-deg. miter cuts.

First, use the square to mark the cut line. Slide the square back onto the piece you mean to use, and hold it firmly with one hand against the edge of the stock. Set the base of your saw so that its edge bears against the square edge of the angle square. Adjust the saw and the square's position until the saw blade lines up with the cut line. Brace the square against the stock and make the cut, using the square's edge as a guide. Saw using light, steady pressure, allowing the blade to set the feed rate.

● RIPPING WOOD

Ripping Lumber. Cutting a board along its length is known as "ripping" it. When ripping lumber, you should use a rip guide. This is a steel guide that attaches to the base with a thumbscrew. The guide has a shoe that runs along the side of the board as you cut it along its length.

Ripping Plywood. One way to make a long, straight, accurate cut through plywood is to make a jig. Screw a thin strip of hardwood or plywood to the bottom of a straight length of 1-by stock. Guide the saw along the 1-by, trimming the plywood to width. Clamp or nail the jig to the trimmed edge along the line you want to cut, and guide the saw along the 1-by.

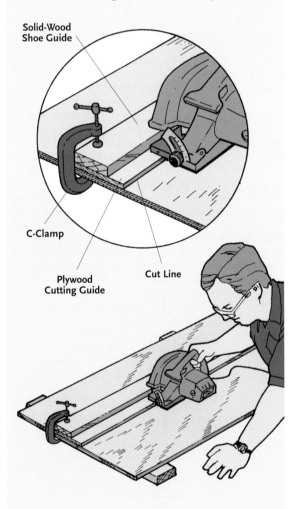

Solid-Wood Shoe Guide

C-Clamp

Plywood Cutting Guide

Cut Line

Setting the Depth of Cut

To use a circular saw safely and produce the cleanest possible cut, you want to set the blade so that it just penetrates the other side and clears itself of wood chips with the least amount of blade. The deeper the blade is set, the more heat it generates and the greater the risk of binding and kicking back, especially when cutting tricky materials such as plywood. Set the saw blade depth about 1/4 inch deeper than the thickness of the wood.

CIRCULAR SAW JOINERY

One way to gauge the level of craftsmanship used is to inspect the ways the builder joined one board to another. Skillful joinery has been used for many hundreds of years to join wood members—long before the invention of nails and screws. Besides being visually attractive, these techniques produce joints that are stronger than simply nail-ing one board to another. These joints will take some time to produce, but by working with a circular saw, you should have no problems cutting them quickly and consistently.

Miter joints can be cut in one pass. Notches, lap joints, and dadoes require three separate steps: kerfing, roughing out, and paring.

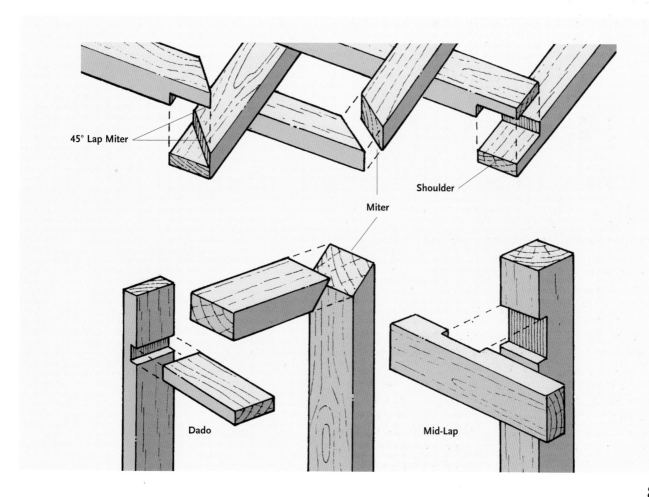

45° Lap Miter

Shoulder

Miter

Dado

Mid-Lap

1 KERF THE JOINT. Lay out the shoulders of the notch, lap joint, or dado that you wish to cut. Adjust the saw to the depth that you want the joint to be. (It's a good idea to make a test cut to make sure your setting is right.)

Make a series of closely spaced kerfs in the waste area of the joint. The first and last kerfs should be made using an angle square to ensure that the shoulder is square; because you are just cutting wood out of the notch, all the other kerfs need not be precise.

3 PARE OUT THE JOINT. With the chisel's bevel pointing up, pare away leftover ridges. Work from the outside edges in to the center. Use one hand to push the chisel into the waste, and use the other to keep the back of the chisel flat against the wood.

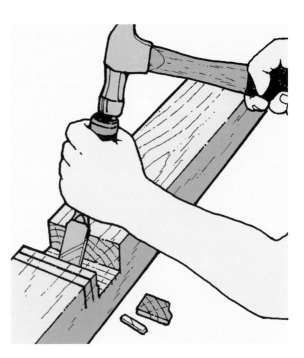

2 ROUGH OUT THE JOINT. Rough out the joint by chiseling out the waste. At this point, hit the chisel with a hammer to break the pieces free, but keep the chisel bevel pointing down to control the depth of cut. Chisel to the bottom of the joint in the center, leaving the edges high.

FIGHTING CROOKED STOCK

The challenge of carpentry is that you are trying to make something straight and square out of a natural material that resists our best efforts to make it regular. Almost every board you use will be at least slightly crooked, cupped, or twisted.

Carpentry is a constant battle to wedge and nail pieces of wood into the position and shape you want them to take. A smart carpenter uses the forces within the board to his or her advantage.

The most common example is "crowning" horizontal structural members such as beams and joists. This means sighting along the edges of a board to decide which way it bows and then installing the board with the convex edge facing up. This gives the board a head start in resisting sagging from the weight bearing on it.

If you are installing decking boards, there is no way to use crook to your advantage. If a board is badly crooked, use it to make short pieces. But if the crook is mild, there are a few ways to force it into place.

All of the methods start by fastening the straightest end of the board to at least two joists. Position the board so that the curve bends out away from the decking boards that have already been installed.

Once the board is in place, use a pipe clamp to pull the board straight. Concentrate on straightening the board on a joist-by-joist basis. As soon as one section of the board is properly positioned, nail it into place, and reposition the clamp as necessary to gain more leverage.

Another way of doing the same thing is to screw a temporary plank onto the joists in front of the crooked board. The brace should be positioned at an angle that approximates that of a wedge. Use a wooden wedge to force the plank into position. It is also possible to lever the board straight using a length of 2x4. Never use a pry bar to force a board into position: the metal can dig into the wood or dent the edge of the decking.

Good Side Up

Some carpenters believe that deck boards will shed water better if installed with the bark side down because boards will cup to shed water that way. Others prefer bark side up because boards installed bark side down will suffer more from grain raising and splitting along the annular rings.

The U.S. Department of Agriculture's Forest Products Laboratory has tested both of these theories. Their conclusion is, it doesn't matter which way the boards are laid. The laboratory's recommendation is simply to place the most attractive side of the board up.

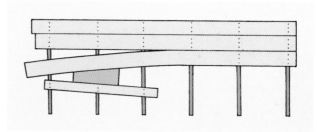

Pull the board straight with a pipe clamp if it is close to the edge of the deck.

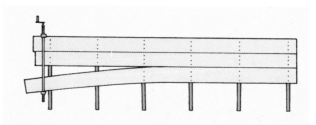

Wedge crooked boards in place with a temporary plank and a tapered piece of scrap.

SPACER JIG

When you use lumber decking boards, you need to leave a small space between each board for appearance and to let water through. One way to gauge the space is with the body of a 10d or 16d common nail. The problem with this method is that you wind up spending a lot of time fetching nails that fall through the spaces. Here is a handy spacer jig that will eliminate that problem.

All you have to do is rip a strip of wood at the desired gap thickness (about 1/8 inch). Tack the strip to a wider piece of scrap as shown.

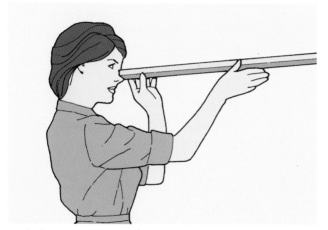

Look down one edge of the board to see whether it is straight, bowed, or crooked.

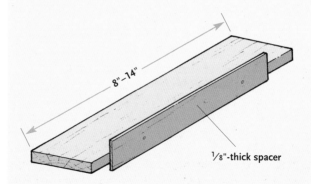

8"–14"

1/8"-thick spacer

LAYING OUT THE SITE

All of the projects in this book, including the six- and eight-sided gazebos, begin with a square or rectangular layout. You can easily check a project for square using the 3-4-5 layout method—if one side of a right triangle measures 3 feet and another measures 4 feet, the hypotenuse must measure 5 feet. If any of these measurements are off, the corner is not a true right angle. The same rule holds true for multiples of these dimensions: a right triangle with sides measuring 6 and 8 feet will have a hypotenuse of 10 feet.

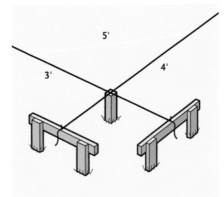

Use the 3-4-5 method to ensure a perfectly square layout.

BATTER BOARDS

1 ROUGH OUT DIMENSIONS. Use a tape measure to rough out the perimeter dimensions of the project. Drive in temporary stakes at each corner.

Erect batter boards at right angles to each other about 2 ft. outside the rough corner locations of the slab foundation or deck. These batter boards provide support for guide strings and a location to mark out key dimensions. The batter boards can be any scrap stock, as long as they are about 2 ft. long. Support each batter board with two short stakes. Use a line level to set the batter board crosspieces at the same height.

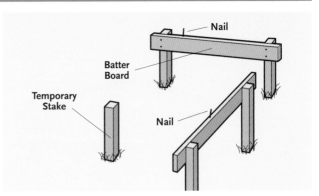

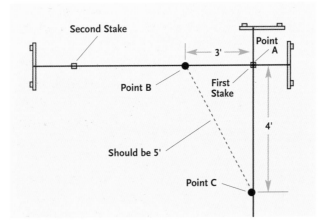

2 STRING THE LINES. Set up guidelines to outline the entire slab or deck. Make sure the lines are level. Make right angles at each corner by using the 3-4-5 triangle method. Measure from point A on the first stake along the line 3 ft. and mark point B. Run a second line perpendicular to the first across point A. Mark point C 4 ft. from point A. Move line AC so that the distance BC is exactly 5 ft. Angle BAC is now a 90-deg. angle. With all four string lines in place, double-check squareness by measuring the diagonals between opposing corners. Make any necessary adjustments.

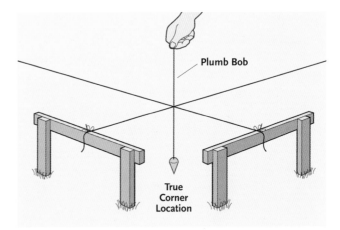

3 REPOSITION CORNER STAKES. Accurately reposition the temporary corner stakes, using a plumb bob to transfer the point of intersection to the ground.

SETTING POSTS

Projects that do not use a slab foundation require the setting of posts firmly in
the ground or on concrete footings. You
can use a clamshell-type posthole digger
to dig holes for the footings or posts.
If many holes are needed, renting a
gasoline-powered auger-type digger will
certainly speed up the work. You can rent
either one- or two-person models; the
size you choose depends on the number
of holes that you have to dig and the soil
conditions of the area. The manager of
your rental store will be able to suggest
which one will best meet your specific
needs. Be sure to read and follow safety
directions for all power machinery, and be
aware of hidden lines for utilities such as gas and water.

To prevent frost heave, your footing should extend below
the frost line. Follow local building codes concerning the
depth and diameter of the footing or post placement.

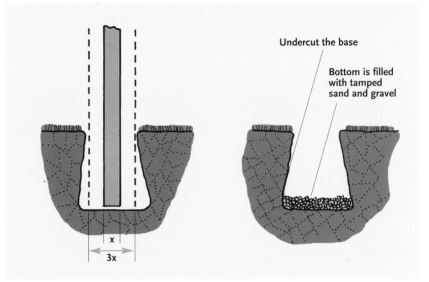

Set posts according to the "Rule of Three"—the hole should be 3 times the
width and one-third the length of the post.

Placing Posts Directly in the Ground

As a general rule, when setting posts directly in the
ground, the posthole should be about 3 times the width
of the post. It should also extend into the ground at least
one-third the overall post height. For example, if you need
8 feet of post above ground level, you should buy a 12-
foot post and dig the holes 4 feet deep. These are only
general guidelines; always check with your building inspector before deciding how deep to sink your posts.

Compact the base of the hole, and add 6 inches of
gravel to help drainage. Place the post in the hole. For
posts set in the ground, you should always use pressure-
treated wood.

Using premixed bag concrete is the most convenient
method of setting posts in the ground. Fast-setting mixes
are available that set up in minutes and reach final set in
several hours. With some brands, installation can be as
simple as positioning the post and adding layers of dry
mix and water until the hole is filled. Follow the concrete
manufacturer's directions.

Slope the top of the concrete away from the post to
drain water. Use a level to check for plumb and brace the
post firmly using lengths of scrap lumber, then recheck.

Post Footings

Another method of securing posts is to use metal post
anchors set in concrete footings. Metal post anchors
require the same amount of preparation as sinking posts
in concrete, and both require footings dug below the frost
line. However, because only the metal fastener is sunk
into the concrete, you can use shorter post lengths to
reach a given height, making it the most economical
choice for building a gazebo or pavilion.

A post anchor does not offer the same amount of lateral strength as sinking a post, so you wouldn't want to
use anchors for a fence or a project such as the "Arbor
with Picnic Table." But posts tied into a gazebo or other
structure with four or more sides don't have to handle a
significant lateral load.

The hole diameter for a 4x4 post should be approximately 12 inches. In firm soil, concrete can be placed
directly in the hole. Place a 6-inch layer of gravel in the
base of the hole, and fill it with concrete. When mixed to
the proper consistency, the concrete will find its own
level. Insert the post anchor before the concrete sets up.
Work quickly if you are using fast-setting concrete. Use a
torpedo level to make sure that the connector is plumb.
This is a critical point in the project, so check your work
several times and be sure anchors do not shift or sag.

In loose soil, you may have to dig a slightly larger hole
and set a wood form over it so that 5 or 6 inches of concrete are located above ground.

Another alternative is to use a ready-made form, available at most building supply stores. Simply cut the cylindrical cardboard form to length using a handsaw or saber saw and insert it into the hole. You can use the form to make the footing flush with the ground. Or if you are placing posts in a wet area, you can leave the forms longer to create concrete piers a few inches above ground level. Any cardboard that protrudes from the ground can be trimmed away after the concrete hardens.

If you are building a small structure in a region with little or no frost-heaving problem, you may not need a footing. Check with your building inspector. It may be permissible to place your project on precast concrete pier blocks. Pier blocks are available with post connectors already set in place. They create a wider, firmer base than a post set directly on the ground and prevent moisture problems by keeping the post out of the dirt.

Most water damage can be avoided simply by raising the posts off their anchors by less than ¼ inch. Cut a double-thick scrap of asphalt shingle to serve as a spacer.

smart tip

REMEMBER POST DIMENSIONS
KEEP IN MIND THAT FOR SOME PROJECTS, THE DISTANCE BETWEEN FOUNDATION POST LOCATIONS DOES NOT EQUAL THE OVERALL LENGTH OR WIDTH OF THE PROJECT. BUT IT'S EASIER AND MORE ACCURATE TO LAY OUT THE PERIMETER POST LOCATIONS AND ALLOW FOR SLIGHT OVERHANG THAN IT IS TO LAY OUT THE TRUE PERIMETER AND ADJUST INWARD. FOR ALL PROJECTS, CHECK YOUR PLANS CAREFULLY AND MEASURE ALONG GUIDELINES TO DETERMINE ALL KEY DIMENSIONS. FOR ATTACHED PROJECTS, THE SIDE OF YOUR HOME SERVES AS THE INITIAL GUIDELINE.

Lay out the posts carefully, and the angles and dimensions on an arbor like this will be uniform. Lay them out quickly, and every cut will be different.

POST-SETTING TECHNIQUES

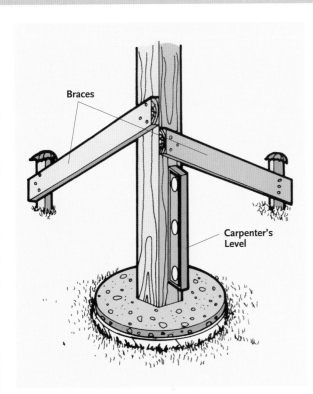

Use temporary braces to keep a post plumb until the concrete has a chance to set.

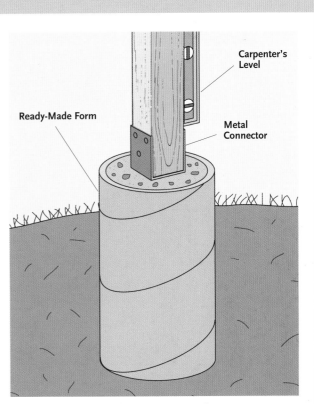

Install the metal anchor as soon as the concrete is stiff enough to support the extra weight.

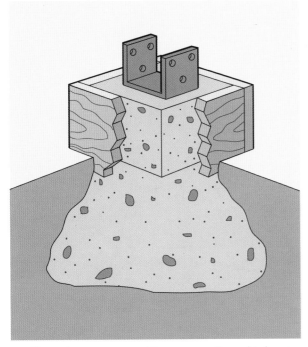

You'll need to use a wood form or cardboard tubes to retain the concrete in loose or sandy soil.

Place a double thickness of asphalt roofing under the post to protect the post bottom from water damage.

6 laying the groundwork

Begin your project with a foundation that is accurate and strong, and the rest of the construction process will be a pleasure. For the projects in this book, accurate foundation work means getting support posts firmly set in exactly the right positions. If you get the post support positions wrong, you'll spend the rest of the project compensating for it. Strong foundation work also means that the posts must be firmly anchored either in the ground or in concrete. If you decide instead to rest your project on a slab, the post anchor bolts must be accurately placed and the concrete surfaced to a smooth, hard finish.

PREPARING FOR A CONCRETE PAD

Projects in this book that are built on a concrete pad call for a pad 4 inches thick that is set $1\frac{1}{2}$ to 2 inches above ground level. In most parts of the country, the pad should sit on a 4- to 6-inch-thick subbase of 1-inch crushed stone. You can omit the stone if your soil is suitable, but check with your local building inspector before you do.

The pad should slope slightly to ensure proper drainage. On projects attached to the house, slope the concrete away from the house. If the pad is in the yard, slope it the same direction the ground slopes. A slope of $\frac{1}{8}$ to $\frac{1}{4}$ inch per foot is sufficient. To determine the proper pitch, multiply the length of the run in feet by the slope—$\frac{1}{8}$ or $\frac{1}{4}$, as the case may be. The product equals the number of inches your pad should drop from one end to the other. Move the layout lines down at one end, as shown in the illustration on the facing page, to lay out the slope of the pad and forms.

Most forms are constructed of 2x4s set on edge. Because a 2x4 is only $3\frac{1}{2}$ inches wide, stake the form $\frac{1}{2}$ inch off the ground so that you'll get a full 4-inch-thick pad. Some concrete will ooze out from underneath the forms when you pour, but it does no harm and it eventually gets covered by soil.

The wood used for forms needs to be strong, stable, and straight. You can use permanent forms, which remain in place after the pour, or temporary forms that you remove once the concrete dries. Use simple butt joints at all corners, and stake and nail the forms firmly in place so that they follow the path and slope of the layout lines. You can lay out the edges of the forms by running a string along the ground between corner posts. Establish the slope by measuring down a constant distance from the sloped lines.

Concrete pads have a reinforcing metal mesh running through them to keep them from cracking. Once you have the forms in place, set the mesh on wire supports (available at masonry supply stores) that position the mesh in the middle of the pad. Overlap individual pieces, tie them together with wire ties, and keep the mesh at least 6 inches from the edge of the pad.

When pouring a large pad, you can stake some 2x4 guides inside the form to help you level off the concrete. After the concrete has been poured, you can guide a 2x4 "screed" across the guides to flatten out the concrete in the forms. The guides can be either temporary or perma-nent. Permanent guides must be level with the tops of the forms and should be spaced evenly every 8 to 10 feet. For temporary guides, place one end of the 2x4 guide on top of the form, level it, and stake it into place.

If the guides are permanent, you can use a 2x4 as a screed. If they're temporary, nail a 1x2 block to the screed's top end, as shown in the top illustration on page 92.

Delivery Considerations

The standard unit of measure in the concrete industry is the cubic yard. To estimate the amount of concrete needed, divide the pad's thickness (in inches) by 12 and multiply that by the pad's width and length in feet to get cubic feet; then divide that by 27 to get cubic yards.

One of the quickest and most economical ways to obtain several yards of uniformly mixed concrete is to work with a concrete supplier. But you should take a little time to consider exactly what this step entails. Working alone, you won't be able to handle a large volume of truck-delivered ready-mix concrete. Assemble a crew of at least two helpers. Always have at least one helper with some experience in floating, final troweling, and edging. An experienced concrete finisher will keep the project moving and serve as an adviser to less-experienced crew members.

● ESTIMATING CONCRETE

Cubic Yards of Concrete Used in Pad Construction

Pad Size (sq. ft.)	Thickness of Slab		
	4"	5"	6"
25	0.31 yd^3	0.39 yd^3	0.46 yd^3
50	0.62 yd^3	0.77 yd^3	0.93 yd^3
75	0.93 yd^3	1.16 yd^3	1.39 yd^3
100	1.25 yd^3	1.55 yd^3	1.86 yd^3
200	2.50 yd^3	3.10 yd^3	3.72 yd^3
300	3.75 yd^3	4.65 yd^3	5.58 yd^3

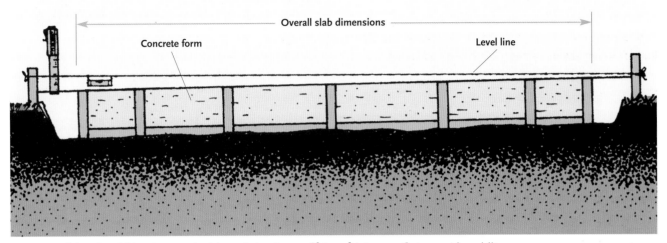

Concrete slabs should be designed with a slight slope of 1/8 to 1/4 in. per ft. to avoid puddling.

If you plan to do the work yourself, discuss the project with someone at the ready-mix plant. He or she should know the local codes and the concrete specifications used in your area. Also be sure to check with the building inspector. You'll probably need a permit, and the inspector can let you know in advance if your plans follow code.

Plan ahead for choice delivery times, such as Saturday mornings, and know the procedure for canceling delivery if the weather fails to cooperate. Be sure the truck will have access to your site, and keep in mind that a delivery truck can tear up lawn or sink into fresh fill.

Plan to work in good weather—late spring and early fall are ideal times for large concrete projects. At these times of the year there's usually no threat of freezing or drying out the concrete. Also, your workers won't have to contend with the hot summer sun.

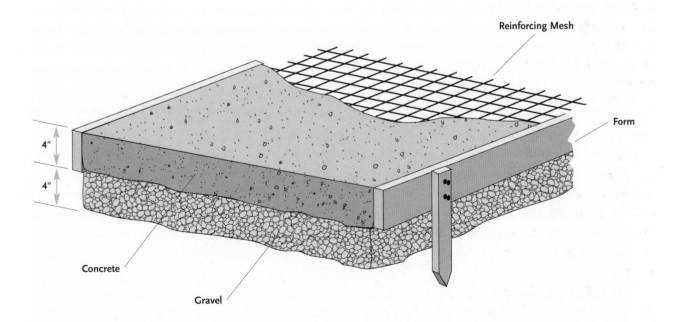

A concrete slab is only as good as its foundation. A gravel subbase helps to improve drainage and to ensure a level pour, and the reinforcing mesh helps to keep the slab from cracking.

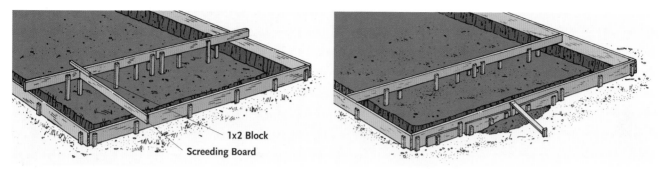

1x2 Block
Screeding Board

Remove temporary forms as soon as possible. Fill stake holes with concrete (left). Permanent forms serve as control joints for the finished slab (right).

MAKING THE POUR

Excavating and form building are jobs that you can take your time doing. But when the day of the pour arrives, have helpers ready. Things have to happen in order, but as the job progresses, you may need to do two or more things simultaneously. Have at least two helpers with wheelbarrows to fill hard-to-reach areas. Have two people ready to screed and someone ready with the float. Things happen fast, and the more help you have, the better.

POURING CONCRETE

1 EXCAVATE. Set up batter boards as directed on page 84. Drive two additional stakes at each corner, and tie level lines to them at the desired height of the slab— 2 in. above ground. Slide the lines up and down on the stakes to slope the patio $1/8$ to $1/4$ in. per ft. in the same general direction as the yard, but away from nearby structures. Mark where the lines are tied to the stakes. Dig up the sod within the lines and about 6 in. outside them. Dig down to a level 6 in. below the layout lines.

2 FILL AND TAMP. Lay a 2-in. layer of stone inside the excavation, and tamp it with a power tamper, available at rental stores. Lay a second 2-in. layer, and tamp it, too. Tamping in layers assures a firm base that will help prevent cracking

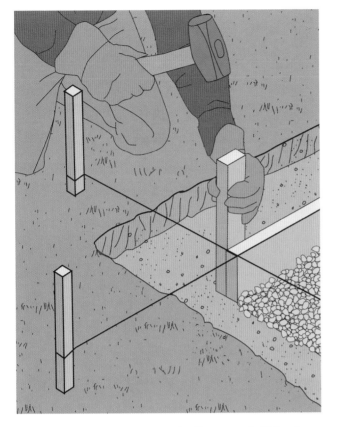

4 ATTACH THE FORMS. Nail the forms to the stakes, keeping the top of the form at the same height as the line running from the corner stakes. The stakes will be easier to remove later if you use duplex nails, which have a second head partway down the shank to keep you from driving the nail all the way in.

Cover the surface of the pad with wire reinforcing mesh. Rest the mesh on wire supports; overlap individual pieces; tie them together with wire ties; and keep the mesh at least 6 in. from the edge of the pad.

3 SET FORM SUPPORTS. The forms are held in place by 2x4 supports driven into the ground. Masons set the supports first, laying them out carefully and using them to position the forms. Start by tying the strings back on the corner stakes at the marks you made. Position a form support outside the layout lines by the thickness of the forms—use a short section of the form as a spacer. Drive the stake into the ground until the top is slightly below the level of the string line. Drive stakes every 4 ft.

5 FILL THE FORM. Plan the job before the truck arrives. Start pouring and spreading the concrete at the part of the form that is farthest from the truck.

Move the concrete with rakes and shovels. During the pour, fill all forms to their top edges. Use a shovel when necessary to lift material and move it back into low spots. Pay special attention to corners, along the edges of forms, or at any turns or curves in the forms. Work a spade into the concrete in these areas to release any trapped air. Spade the concrete in these areas.

Pour concrete in only one section at a time. When that is done, move to the next area while your helpers screed off the first section.

6 SCREED. Select a straight 2x4. Sight along the edge of the board to see whether there is any noticeable "crown." Place the concave side against the concrete. A slight crown will provide additional drainage.

Starting at one end of the pour, move the screed toward the front to strike off the excess concrete as you go. Move the screed back and forth sideways in a sawing motion as you progress to help slide it through the excess. This action not only removes the excess but also pushes the larger pieces of aggregate down just below the surface of the pour. If you find low spots behind the screed in some areas, use the shovel to move some of the excess concrete to fill these areas; then screed again.

FINISHING

The surface you see on concrete didn't just get there. It was the result of careful work that rounded over the edges, cut joints, and troweled the surface smooth.

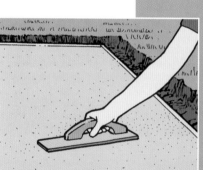

PREPARING THE SURFACE

1 FLOAT THE SURFACE. Floating removes excess water from the surface and knocks down the small ridges left by screeding. It leaves the pour smooth and level. Floating can be done with either a bull float or a large hand float, called a darby. The bull float is used on large surfaces, such as patios and floor slabs. The darby can be used for smaller surfaces or finishing off a slab after working the bull float.

Push and pull the bull float over the concrete. At the end of each stroke, lift the float and move it to make another parallel stroke. When pushing it forward, tilt it so the front edge is raised; when pulling backwards, tilt the back of the float so that it won't dig into the concrete.

After floating, cut the concrete away from the forms to a depth of 1 in., using a pointed mason's trowel.

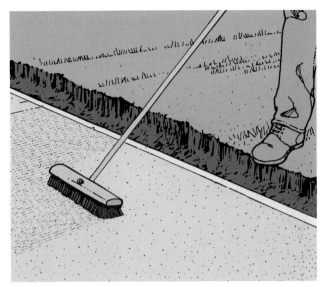

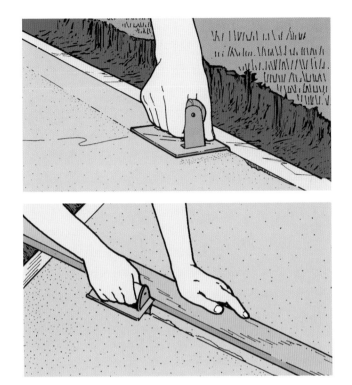

2 **CUT EDGES AND JOINTS.** Your concrete slab should be edged to create round, smoothed edges that chip less than a sharp edge would. Run a hand edger back and forth along the edge of the pour, holding the tool flat on the surface and against the inside of the wood form. Cut control joints unless you are using permanent forms, with interior dividers every 8 to 10 ft. Control joints provide a clean line along which the slab can crack if it settles. Without them the cracks will be random and jagged. Cut control joints with a grooving tool. To provide a straight line, place the tool against a 2x4 guide strip tacked across the forms or a plank laid on the concrete. Work the hand groover along just like the edger. The V-shaped bottom will cut through the wet concrete to form the joint.

3 **MAKE A TEXTURED "BROOMED" FINISH.** If you are pleased with the appearance at this point, you can choose to stop, or you may want to try a "broomed" finish. A broomed finish is a bit rougher than a floated surface. The roughness provides more traction so the slab will be less slippery to walk on when it becomes wet.

Brooming can be done with almost any stiff-bristle broom. Put the bristles down on the slab and pull the broom toward you. Lift the broom after each stroke. Don't push the brush, because this may cause it to dig into the surface. For best results, broom the surface at right angles to the traffic pattern rather than in the same direction. You may have to touch up the edges and control joints with an edger after brooming the surface of the concrete.

Curing

Concrete continues to harden, or cure, for five to seven days after it is poured. Once you've finished the surface of your pad, keep it wet. Concrete dries chemically instead of by evaporation, and the reaction requires water. A water-starved pad is likely to crack.

The best and simplest method of keeping the slab moist is to hose it down at regular intervals or to set up sprinkling equipment. In all but the hottest climates, a good dousing at nightfall will keep the slab moist until the next morning.

The slab can also be sealed with plastic sheeting to keep in the moisture. Lay it flat and seal it completely at joints and along edges. Patch discoloration of the concrete can occur if the sheeting becomes wrinkled.

Forms can be removed a day after placing the concrete, but curing should continue for five to seven days.

smart tip

TIMING THE FINISHING BECAUSE OF VARIATIONS IN CLIMATE AND CONCRETE MIXES, THE TIME YOU SHOULD WAIT BEFORE FINISHING VARIES. JUDGE BY THE CONCRETE—START FINISHING AS SOON AS THE SHEEN OF EXCESS WATER IS GONE AND THE CONCRETE CAN WITHSTAND FOOT PRESSURE. ANOTHER CLUE: THE CONCRETE FEELS GRITTY UNDER THE TROWEL.

7 roofs

A gazebo roof and a house roof may share a common structure, but the similarity ends there. Most house roofs rarely get a second glance. The roof of your gazebo or pavilion is closer to the eye. Details matter, and the steep pitch of most gazebo roofs makes them even more noticeable. Your choice of materials will influence the style of your project: standard asphalt shingles create a formal, practical structure; cedar shakes suggest a more natural setting.

And while the roof may be the most noticeable part of your gazebo, it is small and easily accessible. You can take all the time you need to carefully build details such as hips and peaks. A small project like this is a great opportunity to stretch your skills and build a roof that gets second, third, and fourth glances.

THE BASICS

Framing the roof on your gazebo is not as difficult as you might think. The layout is a bit more complex than other carpentry tasks, but the step-by-step instructions in this chapter will lead you through that. Once you understand the concepts, roof framing is just another bunch of straight cuts made with your circular saw.

There are some basic terms that you need to know before you can start laying out your roof.

The **span** is the horizontal distance covered by a roof. This length is usually the width of the building measured from the outer faces of the frame. The **ridge** is the uppermost horizontal line of the roof. The **total rise** is the total vertical distance that the roof rises above the cap plate, and the **total run** is the measure of the horizontal distance over which the rafter rises (usually half the span). The **line length** of a rafter is the hypotenuse of the right triangle formed, with its base as the total run and its altitude as the total rise.

Rafter **slope** is expressed in the number of inches a roof rises per 12 inches of run. For example, a roof with a very shallow angle might be a "4-in-12" roof; a steeper roof might be a "9-in-12" roof.

The most common type of roof, and the easiest to frame, is the gable roof. This is a roof with two slopes forming triangles on the gable ends. While gable roofs are very common on houses, they are not often used for gazebos. You will, however, often find gable roofs on pavilions, such as the "Pavilion with Gable Roof" on page 166. On a gable roof, the span runs perpendicular to the ridge. The total run is equal to one-half the length of the span. And the total rise is the difference in height between the ridge and the cap plate. The line length is equal to the length of a board connecting the ridge to the cap plate plus half the thickness of the ridge board.

There are three types of rafters you need to know about to build the projects in this book. These are the common rafter, the hip rafter, and the hip jack. In gable roofs, **common rafters** run from the top plate to the ridge at right angles to both. They are the only rafters you need for a gable roof. Although most gazebos don't have gable roofs, they do use common rafters. For example, the six- and eight-sided gazebo projects in this book use common rafters that run at right angles to the top plates to meet at a key block at the peak. The **key block** is cut to meet the rafters at a right angle. **Hip rafters** run on a 45-degree angle from the top plate to the ridge, forming the line of intersection for the two surfaces of a hip roof. **Hip jacks** run parallel to the common rafters, from the hip to the top plate. (See "Hip-Roof Framing System," opposite.)

No matter what kind of rafter you are making, all of the cuts will be either plumb or level. A plumb cut is any cut on a rafter that is vertical when the rafter is in position. A level cut is any cut on the rafter that is horizontal when the rafter is in position. With the help of a framing square, you can accurately lay out plumb and level cuts without lugging each board into position on the roof.

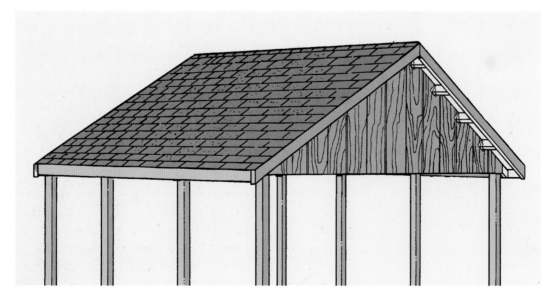

The simple gable roof is the most common roof form on houses in North America. It is also common on pavilions. Gable roofs use only common rafters. Although gazebos usually do not have gable roofs, they do use common rafters.

HIP-ROOF FRAMING SYSTEM

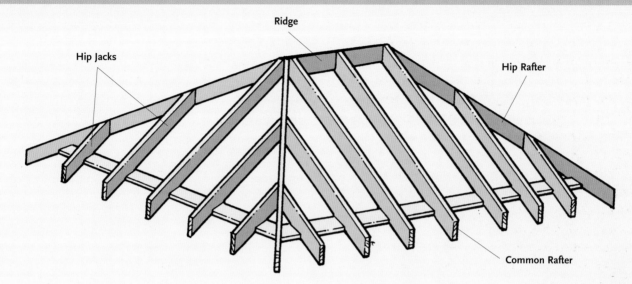

Ridge

Hip Jacks

Hip Rafter

Common Rafter

smart tip

USING THE FRAMING SQUARE
WHEN LAYING OUT RAFTERS,
IT'S EASY TO CONFUSE WHICH
WAY THE ANGLES ARE SUPPOSED
TO RUN AND WHICH PART OF
THE SQUARE TO MARK. YOU
CAN AVOID THIS CONFUSION
BY PRACTICING A CONSISTENT
TECHNIQUE WHEN USING THE
FRAMING SQUARE. ALWAYS USE
THE BLADE OF THE FRAMING
SQUARE (WIDE SIDE) FOR MARK-
ING LEVEL CUTS.

FRAMING SQUARE

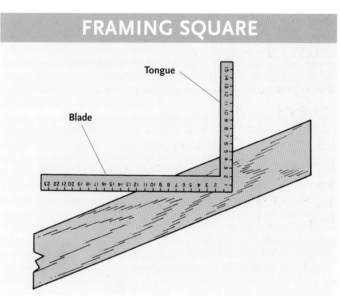

Tongue

Blade

The Framing Square

For many people, the framing square is little more than a handy measuring device or a quick way to check whether an angle is at 90 degrees.

But that same piece of metal is capable of doing much more. Besides estimating a rafter's length, the lowly framing square will precisely lay out the final cuts without the help of any complicated rafter charts or conversion books. That's because the design of the square already calculates roof slope in inches of rise per 12 inches of run.

LAYING OUT AND CUTTING THE COMMON RAFTER

As mentioned, the common rafter meets the top plate and the ridge at a 90-degree angle. The common rafter meets the ridge board or key block with a plumb cut called the "ridge cut." The bottom of the rafter fits over the top plate with a notch called a "bird's mouth." The bird's mouth consists of a level cut, called the seat cut, and a short plumb cut. The part of the rafter that overhangs the wall is called the rafter tail. In most designs, the rafter tail ends in a plumb cut. If there is no rafter tail, then there's no bird's mouth, either: the end of the rafter is flush with the wall.

99

Calculating Rough Rafter Lengths

You'll need to know approximate rafter lengths when you order lumber. You can use your framing square to estimate this length. Let the blade of the square represent the total run and the tongue represent the total rise. Using a scale of 1 inch = 1 foot, measure the distance from blade to tongue to find the length of the rafter. Don't forget to add any overhang into your final calculation if the rafter is supposed to hang past the plate. The overhang is traditionally measured in terms of a level measurement (how far it actually sticks out past the cap plate). Add that extra length to the blade before you do your calculations.

Essentially, what you are doing is making, and then measuring, a scale model of your roof. If you wanted to, you could draft a scale drawing and then measure the rafter on your plan. Not only is the framing square just as accurate, but it will save you all those steps!

RAFTER CUTS

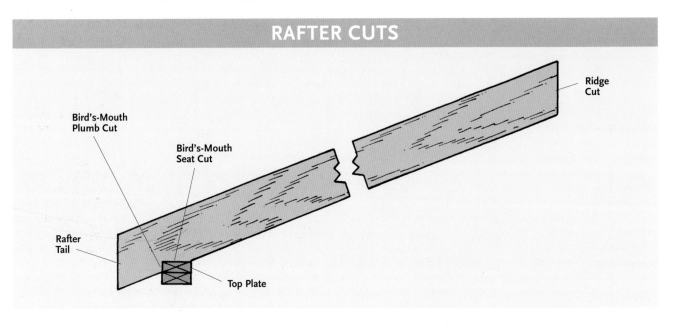

Bird's-Mouth Plumb Cut

Bird's-Mouth Seat Cut

Ridge Cut

Rafter Tail

Top Plate

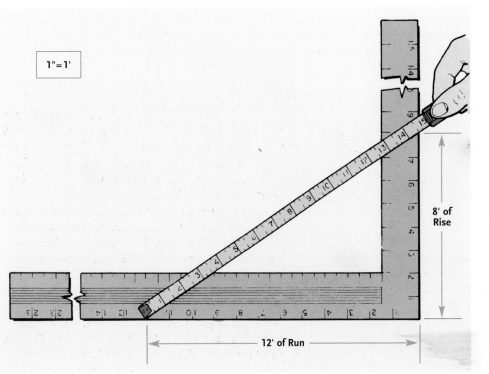

1" = 1'

8' of Rise

12' of Run

LEFT Using a framing square to estimate rafter lengths.

This estimate will be a little rough—it does not account for the vertical distance of the tail—but it should be adequate to determine which size stock you should be starting with. If your estimate is within less than a foot of a particular stock size, be sure to double-check your measurements. You might decide to purchase some longer boards, just to be on the safe side.

This method works for hip rafters as well as common rafters. Keep in mind though, that because a hip runs diagonally, it has a longer run than a common rafter on the same roof. If you know the common run, you can get the hip run by using the following formula:

Run of Hip Rafter = Run of Common Rafter x 1.41

CUT A COMMON RAFTER

Top of Rafter

12" 8"

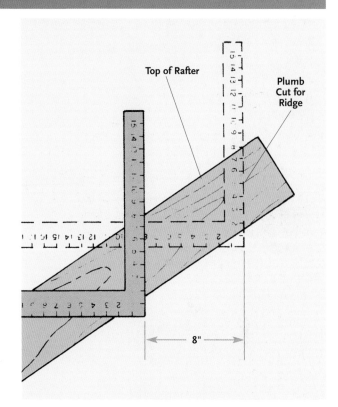

Top of Rafter

Plumb Cut for Ridge

8"

1 LAY OUT A RIDGE CUT. Lay out a straight piece of rafter stock across two sawhorses. Select the straightest piece possible, because this will be used as a pattern to mark the rest of the rafters. Position yourself so that you're on the crowned side of the rafter. It's easier to hold and work with the framing square from that position.

Let's say we are laying out an 8-in-12 roof. Lay the square down on the left end of the stock. Hold the tongue of the square with your left hand and the blade with your right. Move the square until the edge of the stock nearest you aligns with the unit rise mark (8 in. in this example) on the outside of the tongue and the 12-in. mark on the outside of the blade. Mark along the outside edge of the tongue for the plumb cut at the ridge.

2 STEP OFF A PARTIAL STEP. If your line length is not an even number of 12-in. units (for example, 6 ft. 8 in.), then you will have to include a "half-step" to accommodate this extra length. Mark off the partial step first, and then proceed from that mark to step off full 12-in. units as described in Step 1.

Starting at the top of the rafter, hold the square in position and draw a ridge line along the edge of the tongue. Continue to hold the square in the same position as you measure and mark the length of the odd unit on the blade. Now shift the square to your right along the edge of the stock until the tongue is even with the 8-in. mark. Mark off a plumb line on the tongue of your square.

When you begin stepping off full units, remember to start not from the ridge cut but from the plumb line that you just marked to determine the odd unit.

(continued on the next page)

(continued from the previous page)

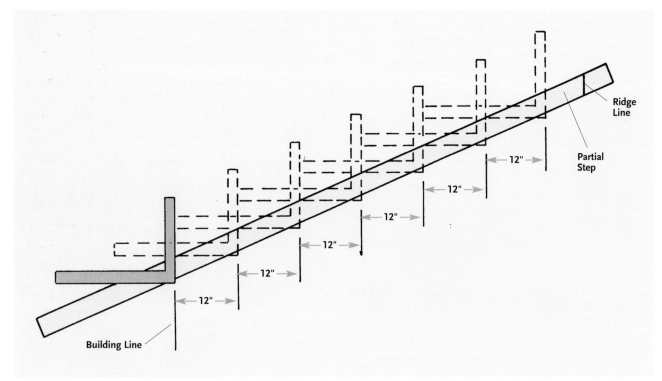

3 STEP OFF RUN UNITS. **Unless** you're building a birdhouse, your framing square won't be large enough to make a rafter layout in one setting. That leaves two options: either learning how to read and work with rafter tables, or stepping off the units. In the latter method, the stock is "stepped off" in 12-in. units of run until the desired number of steps, or units, is reached. You'll discover that as long as your pencil is sharp and you measure carefully, the second technique is accurate and will eliminate the need to do any major calculations.

Let's work with that same 8-in-12 roof with a run of 6 ft. 8 in. Starting from the partial step mark, continue stepping off, to your right, by marking the stock on the outside of the blade and shifting the square until the outside of the tongue aligns with that mark. Repeat this step five more times.

On the last step, mark a plumb line along the outside of the tongue. This plumb line, called the building line, should be directly above the outside of the cap plate.

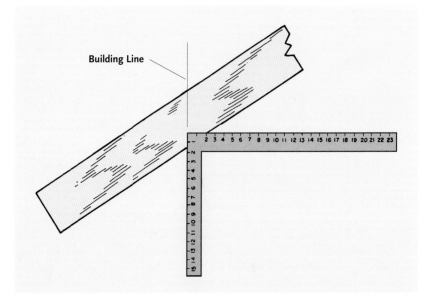

4 CUT THE BIRD'S MOUTH. **The** bird's mouth of the rafter is a combination level cut and plumb cut. The level cut rests on the top plate of the wall, and the plumb cut fits snugly against the outside edge of the cap plate.

Form the bird's mouth by measuring $1\frac{1}{2}$ in. up the building line. Bring the seat cut over to intersect this point. That will drop the rafter over the cap plate but not the top plate below the cap. To mark the seat cut, you will still be using your square, but you will have to flip it over and work from the other side. Mark along the blade for the level cut. Use a handsaw to cut out the mouth.

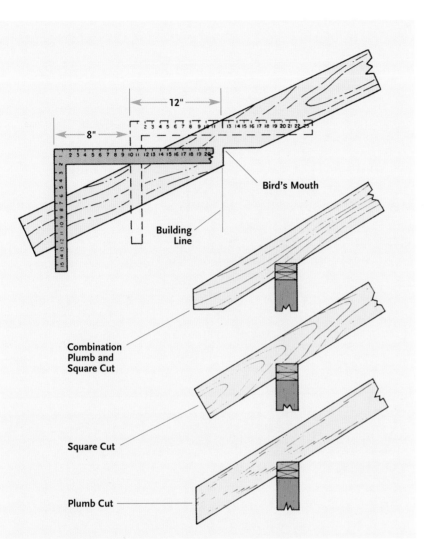

5 MEASURE THE TAIL. The rafter tail length is given in terms of a level measurement. To lay out the tail, simply add in the necessary amount of run (20 in., in this example), measuring from the plumb line of the bird's mouth. The tail cut is at the end of the rafter overhang and may be a plumb cut, a square cut, or a combination of cuts.

12"

8"

Bird's Mouth

Building Line

Combination Plumb and Square Cut

Square Cut

Plumb Cut

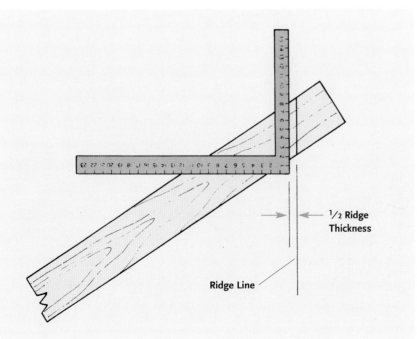

6 SHORTEN COMMON RAFTER FOR RIDGE. The length of the rafter has been calculated to the center of the ridge line. As a result, the rafter must be shortened to accommodate the ridge board. In the case of gazebos, where all the rafters come together at a key block, you need to shorten the rafters by one-half the width of the key block. To shorten a rafter, measure back a distance of one-half the thickness of the ridge board or key block, at a right angle from the ridge cut. Lay out another plumb line at this point for the actual length of the rafter.

¹/₂ Ridge Thickness

Ridge Line

FRAMING SQUARE STOPS

It's important that you keep the square at exactly the correct angle throughout the step-off process. One way to ensure this is to purchase special stops (sometimes called stair gauges) that clamp directly onto the blade and tongue.

Another way to do the same thing is to clamp a small straightedge across the tongue and blade of the square at the desired location to make sure that the square is kept in the same angle for every step.

Either way, make sure to measure and step carefully. Be sure your pencil is sharp. Any minute error will be multiplied with each step. A mistake of just ⅛ inch will become 1 inch in eight "steps."

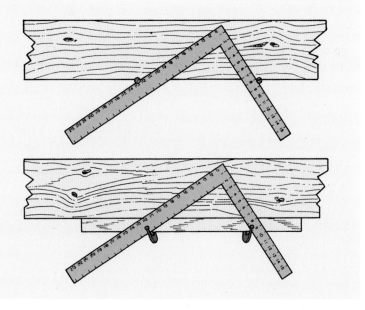

Creative framing can turn the underside of your roof into an attractive design feature.

LAYING OUT AND CUTTING THE HIP RAFTER

Draw a square with 12-inch sides, and you'll find that the diagonal is 16.97 inches long. Apply this to the geometry of a hip rafter, which runs diagonally to the corners of a building, and it's easy to see that for every 12 inches a common rafter runs, the hip rafter must travel 16.97 inches, or for practical purposes, 17 inches. So, if you are building a roof whose common rafters have a slope of 9 in 12, the hip rafters of the same slope will be laid out as 9 in 17. This means that hip rafters can be stepped off in the same way as common rafters. Just use the 17-inch mark on the blade instead of the 12-inch mark.

CUT THE HIP RAFTER

1 LAY OUT THE RIDGE CUT. This will be used as a pattern to mark the other hip rafters, so select the straightest piece possible. Say you are laying out an 8-in-17 hip rafter. Lay the square down on the stock at its extreme left end. Hold the tongue of the square with your left hand and the blade with your right. Move the square until the edge of the stock nearest you aligns with the unit rise mark (8 in., here) on the outside of the tongue and the 17-in. mark on the outside of the blade.

The major difference between a common and a hip rafter is the ridge cut. The ridge cut of a hip rafter is a compound angle; that is, the cut is made at an angle through its thickness and also across its side. This kind of cut is also referred to as a cheek cut. Depending on the design of the roof, the hip rafters may need a cheek cut on one or both sides (see drawing). For a single cheek cut (A), mark along the outside edge of the tongue for the ridge plumb line. Measure back at right angles from the plumb line, one-half the thickness of the rafter stock, and lay out another plumb line. This is your cut line. For a double cheek cut (B), use your square to wrap the cut line around to the other side of the rafter. Set your circular saw to cut at 45 deg., and make the cheek cut.

Cheek cuts are necessary for hip roofs where hip rafters intersect the ridge board at 45 deg. For projects such as the "Square Hip-Roof Gazebo" on page 132, cheek cuts aren't needed. The octagonal key block takes care of the 45-deg. angles for you (C).

Remember that hip rafters must be shortened just like commons to compensate for half the diagonal thickness of the ridge board or, in the case of a gazebo, half the width of the key block. When against common rafters, the hip is shortened by one-half the 45-deg. thickness of the common rafter (key blocks are the same thickness from any angle). Avoid any unnecessary work by including all of these measurements into the length of the rafter before making any cuts.

(continued on the next page)

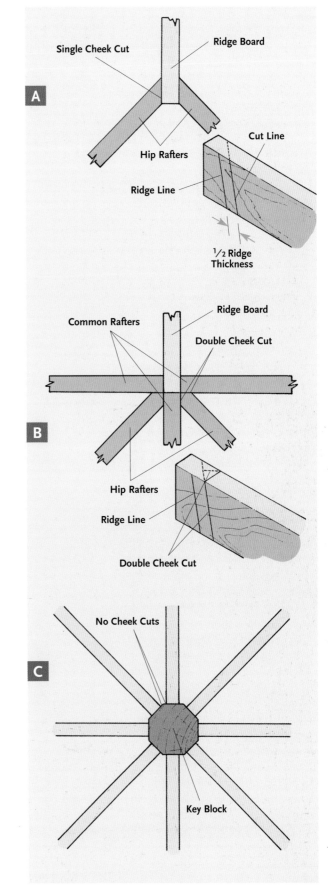

2 LAY OUT THE HIP RAFTER LENGTH. The length of the hip rafter is laid out in a manner similar to that used for the common rafter. Remember to start any layout for length from the original plumb line before any shortening is done.

In the step-off method, the number of steps is the same for the hip rafter length as for the common rafter in the same roof. The same rise is used, but the unit of run for the hip is 17 in. The odd unit must be adjusted for the 17-in. unit run. The length of the hip odd unit equals the diagonal of a square whose sides are the length of the common odd unit. If, for example, the common odd unit is 8 in., the hip odd unit is 11¼ in.

3 BACK OR DROP HIP. Imagine a line drawn down the center of the top edge of a hip rafter. At this line, the roof planes on both sides of the roof meet to form the hip. But because rafter stock is not just a theoretical line but a piece of wood with thickness, the corners of the top edge of the stock will protrude above the roof planes. You need to adjust for this so your roof sheathing or slats sit flat at the hip. There are two ways to make this adjustment. One, called backing the hip, involves planing off the projecting corners. Dropping the hip involves deepening the bird's mouth so that the entire hip is lowered.

To back the hip, create a bevel on each of the top edges with either a block plane or jack plane. Do not plane the bevel down to a point with a 45-deg. angle—all it takes is two or three strokes on each edge—too great an angle is almost as bad as no bevel at all. Try to work toward a 30-deg. bevel. The angle does vary somewhat, depending on the roof's pitch; but don't worry if it is not exact—the most important step in this operation is simply knocking off the corners.

A more accurate approach, and the most common, is to drop the hip. This involves adjusting the bird's mouth to bring the top edges of the hip rafter into the same plane as the common rafters. First, use your framing square to lay out the unadjusted bird's-mouth plumb cut in the same way as you did for common rafters, except that you are now using a unit run of 17 instead of 12. Next, align the outside of the square's blade perpendicular along the edge of the ridge's plumb cut, as shown in the illustration. Draw a line. The distance from that line to the peak is equal to twice the amount of drop. Measure this distance, divide the number in half, and add the required drop onto the seat cut of your bird's mouth.

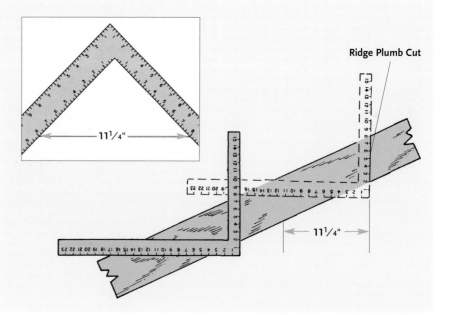

Ridge Plumb Cut

11¼"

11¼"

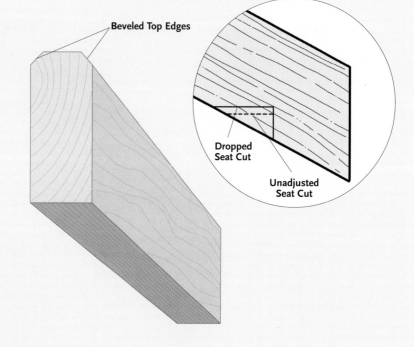

Beveled Top Edges

Dropped Seat Cut

Unadjusted Seat Cut

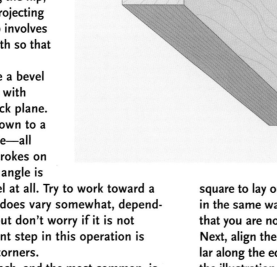

CUTTING THE PERFECT ROOF

If you have decided to use a slat-style roof, it is possible to cut the slat boards so that they perfectly match up with the angle of the roof. Nail your slats onto the rafters, and cut them in place so that each slat will match up with the next one right at the centerline of the rafter.

If you are cutting a slat that will butt up to a previously installed slat, you might find it easier to temporarily position it one slat-width above so that you can get the cutting angle and then install it in its correct location. Cut the other end once the cut end of the slat is fastened in place.

Hip-Rafter Tail

If you want to lay out the overhang of the hip rafter, use the same number of unit steps as used when laying out the overhang of the common rafter. Use 17 as the unit of run. The tail cut is usually a double cheek cut, to accommodate fascia trim that must come together to meet at the corner.

Hip-Jack Rafters

Hip-jack rafters are short rafters that run between the cap plate and hip rafter. Jack rafters run parallel to commons and are laid out in the same "X in 12" manner with your framing square. They have an identical bird's mouth and tail cut. (See "Laying Out and Cutting the Common Rafter" on page 99.) The two main differences between a jack and a common are that jack rafters require a single cheek where they meet the hip (commons are cut plumb), and as you travel down from the ridge line, jack rafters get shorter (commons are all equal in length because they all meet at the ridge or key block).

Jack rafters look a lot more difficult to lay out than they actually are. Assuming that you space the jacks equally along the hip rafter, the change in length from one rafter to the next will remain constant. This consistent change is called the common difference and is included on the rafter table printed on your framing square.

There's no trick to reading the rafter chart once you realize that it is already calculated to accommodate different roof pitches. The common difference for jacks on 16- or 24-inch centers can be determined on the third and fourth lines of the rafter table, respectively. Assuming you already know the pitch of your roof, look to that number on the outside edge of your square's blade. Simply read the numbers directly under the appropriate pitch.

For example, if you had a 6-in-12 roof, and wanted your jacks spaced 16 inches on center, you would look at the chart and learn that the common difference is 17$\frac{7}{8}$ inches. You would then cut the first jack 17$\frac{7}{8}$ inches shorter than the common rafter. Continue cutting each additional jack shorter by the same common difference.

To lay out jack rafters, lay out the bird's mouth and overhang from the common rafter pattern. Now lay out the line length of a common rafter. For the first jack rafter down from the ridge, subtract the common difference from the length. Finally, take off half of the 45-degree thickness of the hip. (This cheek cut is just like the one described in Step 1 on page 105.)

Remember that every hip jack on one side of a hip rafter must be opposed by a jack of the same length on the other side. Opposing jacks will be identical except that their cheek cuts will be on different sides. Label each set of jacks to make sure that you are cutting the angles correctly. Continue running jack rafters down from the hip until the remaining distance is less than the common difference.

HIP-JACK RAFTERS

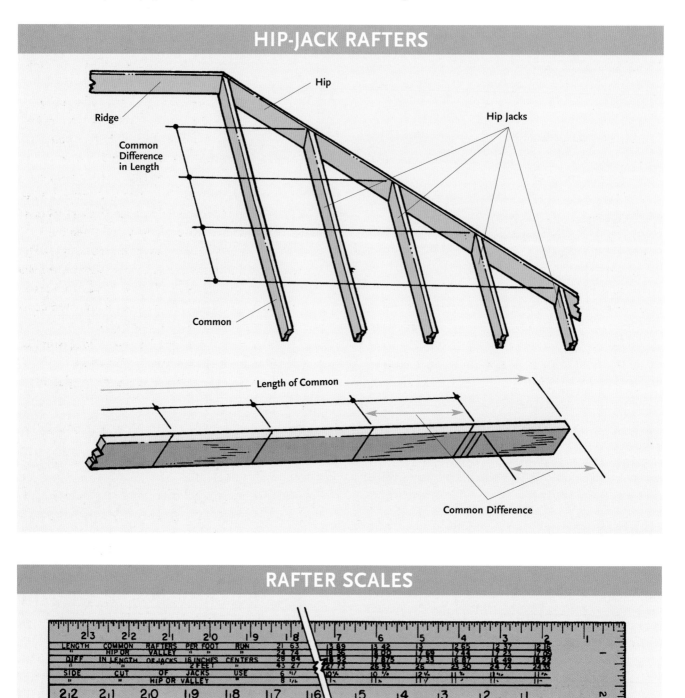

RAFTER SCALES

WOOD SHAKES AND SHINGLES

Once the roof frame is up, it's time to shingle it. You'll find that you have a lot of choices. The shingles on most house roofs are called asphalt or composite shingles. They're easy to install, readily available, and inexpensive. Slat roofing—boards with space between them—and lattice roofing let in the sun while providing shade. While they also let in the rain, this doesn't matter unless you're going to sit outside in a storm—your deck gets rained on all the time.

It's hard to beat the traditional elegance of a wood roof. Cedar shingles and shakes have been used for centuries, not just for appearance's sake but also because they have proven themselves as perfect roofing materials that can withstand many years of abuse. Cedar naturally resists decay much longer than other woods.

Although wood shakes and shingles have several things in common, don't confuse the two. They are made differently. There are four types of shakes: taper-split, hand-split, resawn, and straight-split. All but straight-split are thick at the butt end and taper to a thin end. Straight-split shakes are equally thick at both

Cedar shingles (left) are very different from cedar shakes (right).

ends and are too bulky for most roofs. Tapered resawn shakes give a roof an even profile, because one face is smooth and flat. Shingles are sawn on both sides. They are smaller, thinner, and lighter than shakes and will create the most uniform appearance.

Wood shingles generally last 15 to 30 years, but shakes can last quite a bit longer because they are split, rather than sawn from the wood. Wood's cellular structure consists of tiny pathways that carry water and minerals up the trunk to the leaves—similar to a bundle of straws. Splitting the wood along the grain leaves the straws intact so they remain open only at the ends of the face; sawing slices into the straws will create lots of openings on the face that suck up moisture. Because of this, shakes are more resistant to damage from moisture changes than shingles.

Shingles and shakes are graded from 1 to 3, with No. 1 being the highest quality. Number 1 is used on most homes, because the shakes and shingles are

● ROOFING MATERIALS

Type	Cost	Durability (years)	Sheathing	Install
Wood Shingles	Moderate to	15–30	Slat	Moderate
Wood Shakes	Expensive	25–75	Slat or Plywood	to Difficult
Asphalt (Composite)	Inexpensive to Expensive	12–25	Plywood	Easy
Slat	Inexpensive	*	None	Easy
Lattice	Inexpensive	*	None	Easy

*These wood roof options should last about as long as the rest of the project. Durability depends on various factors, including the type of wood used; the type of finish or paint, if any; and the weather conditions to which the structure is exposed.

RIGHT Asphalt shingles are the most commonly used roofing material. They are inexpensive, are easy to install, and lend a traditional look to any project.

ABOVE The cost of slate makes slate roofs a rarity, but vinyl shingles that look like slate are far more affordable.

RIGHT Wood shakes add texture and authenticity to the most visible part of your gazebo.

cut from heartwood and are knot-free. Lower-grade shingles (No. 2) are less expensive but are still more than adequate for use in a garden structure.

One obvious drawback of using a natural-wood roof is that unless properly treated, it's not fireproof. Shingles and shakes can be treated for fire resistance—some with a Class A rating—to fulfill most code requirements; however, this is an expensive option and may not be necessary. (This code may not apply for a garden structure; however, you still should check with your local building inspector just to make sure.)

ASPHALT SHINGLES

Asphalt, or composite, shingles are available in a wide variety of colors, weights, tab sizes, textures, and edge configurations. The simplest shingles to apply, and the most common, are the three-tab shingles, which measure 12 inches wide and 36 inches long. The slotting is designed to give the appearance of a roof made up of smaller shingles. Also available are fiberglass shingles. They last longer than other shingles and have a Class A fire rating (other com-

LEFT Stack unused shingles out of direct sunlight. Excessive heat will cause them to stick together or bend out of shape.

ABOVE Composite shingles are now available in hundreds of different colors. Some types are textured to mimic shake or cedar-shingle roofs.

posite shingles are Class C), which makes fiberglass a better choice wherever there is a risk of fire.

To prevent wind from lifting them, modern composite shingles are self-sealing. Strips of factory-applied roofing cement soften under the sun's heat to stick each shingle firmly to the course underneath. For this same reason, shingles should be stored in a cool location until they are to be installed.

Composite shingles come in different weights, from 215 to 390 pounds per "square" (100 square feet). The heavier the shingles, the more durable and more expensive. Thicker shingles can produce a roof with more texture. Some composite shingles are designed to mimic the random, rough-textured look of wood shakes.

There are dozens of manufacturers of asphalt and fiberglass shingles, and each calls its grades and styles by different names. However, the shingles are all basically made of the same material. Choosing between manufacturers is most often a matter of picking from what is available at the best price.

A slat-style roof is perfect for filtering out the worst of the summer sun.
For additional shade, consider climbing vines or flowers.

BUILDING LATTICE AND SLAT ROOFING

Lattice- and slat-style roofs cannot offer the same degree of protection as the other types, but their overall effect is hard to beat. These open-air roofs allow all of the summer breezes in while filtering out just the right amount of sunlight. They can also serve as a support for plants or flowering vines to grow on so that your project can completely blend in with the rest of your garden.

Although lattice and slat roofs are a more custom option, they can be easier and less expensive to construct than roofing your project with shakes or shingles. For example, you would essentially have to install a slat-style roof before you could start nailing on wooden shingles. By stopping at this step, you would save yourself the money that you would have spent on the additional material.

Estimating Roofing Materials

Roofing material is sold by the square; 1 "square" is equal to 100 square feet. To estimate the number of shingles you'll need, you must determine the number of squares in the roof's surface. The simplest way to do this is to climb up onto the roof and measure the area (length x width) of each surface, add those figures together, and divide the result by 100. Add 10 percent to allow for waste, and round up to the next highest figure. (At this point, it's better to overestimate what you will need. Unopened bundles can be returned, and because different pallets of the same shingle may have slightly different colors, you should order more than you need to finish the job on your first try.)

You will also have to include certain specialty shingles in your estimate. To approximate the number of hip and ridge shingles that you will need, measure the lengths of the hips and ridges, and divide the total by the exposure recommended for the shingles. For example, the "Eight-Sided Gazebo" (page 154) has eight hips, each about $7\frac{1}{2}$ feet long. The hips have a combined length of almost 60 feet, or 720 inches. Assuming that you want a 5-inch exposure, you would need 144 hip shingles (720/5 = 144), or 48 regular shingles cut in threes. Don't forget to measure the total length of eaves and rakes for drip-edge flashing.

With wood shingles, 1 square will cover about 240 lineal feet of double course; 1 square of shakes will cover about 120 lineal feet. One bundle of factory-produced ridge units will cover $16\frac{2}{3}$ lineal feet for both wood

T1-11 used under a shake or composite roof can create a finished slat appearance, unlike ordinary plywood sheathing.

shingles and shakes. On shake roofs you must also figure about one and a half rolls of 30-pound felt 18 inches wide, for each square of shakes at a 10-inch exposure.

For roofing nails, use $1\frac{1}{2}$ pounds per square of composite shingles and 2 pounds per square of wood shingles or shakes. You'll also need about 3 pounds of nails for the starter course and the hip and ridge shingles.

Sheathing with Plywood

Plywood sheathing is a perfect base for composite shingles or for shakes. Use $\frac{3}{4}$-inch exterior plywood, B-grade or better. Install the good side down, because you will be able to see it from inside your gazebo.

Run the panels perpendicular to the rafters. Use 8d hot-dipped galvanized nails every 6 inches along the ends and every 12 inches on the inside of each sheet. Leave ⅛-inch gaps at the edges to allow for expansion.

Texture 1-11 (T1-11) is a form of plywood made to resemble slat-style paneling. Typically it is used for exterior siding, but in this case, it can also be used effectively for roof work. Install the T1-11 so that the slat pattern is facing down into the gazebo. Make sure that the sheets are positioned so that the slats are oriented in the same direction.

Sheathing and Roofing with Spaced Slats

Spaced slats are simply 1x4s or 1x6s nailed directly to the rafters. They are used primarily with wood shingles and shakes because these materials need air to circulate on both sides to prevent moisture from rotting or cupping the wood.

The measurement for spaced sheathing depends on the exposure of the shingles, and it's easy to figure out. Start with the second sheathing board—this is where the first row of shingles must be nailed. For example, if the roof exposure is to be 5 inches, set the second board right next to the first board. Next measure from the second sheathing board, and set the third board on a 5-inch center from the second board. Now measure the space between the two boards and make a wooden gauge to space the rest of the sheathing. Solid-slat sheathing for the first 12 to 24 inches makes installing the first few courses much easier.

Many people prefer the open-air feeling of a slat-style roof. If you are concerned with letting in the sun more than keeping out the rain, you can stop right at this step. Obviously, you will not plan your slat width or slat spacing on shingle layout, but on the amount of light that you want inside your structure.

Felt Underlayment

Standard rolls of felt underlayment are 36 inches wide and 144 feet long. When used under asphalt or fiberglass shingles, plan on four standard rolls of 15-pound asphalt-saturated felt for every square of shingles. For a composite roof, lay each course of felt over the lower by at least 2 inches. Overlap each end by 4 inches. Lap the felt at least 6 inches over all hips and ridges.

Underlayment is used a little differently with cedar shakes. Shakes require 18-inch rolls instead of 36-inch rolls. The half-sized rolls are "woven" between each course to ensure a watertight roof. Plan on using approximately one and a half rolls of felt for shakes at 10-inch exposure. If 18-inch rolls are not available, you can cut pieces from a 36-inch roll in half with a utility knife.

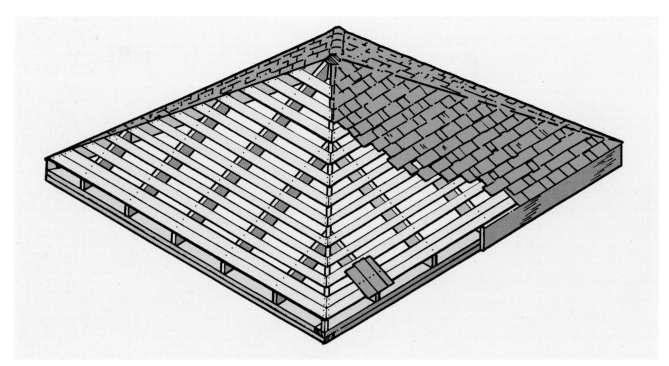

Spaced-slat sheathing allows wood roofs to dry quickly, preventing rot.

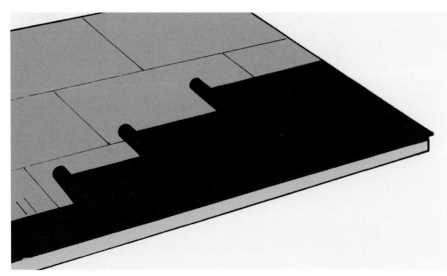

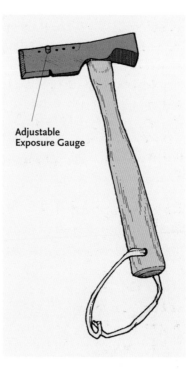

Adjustable
Exposure Gauge

ABOVE The preferred underlayment for cedar shakes and composite shingles is 15-lb. felt. Staple the felt in place.

RIGHT The roofer's hatchet is a specialized tool, suitable for installing only one material—wood shingles. Don't use it as a general-purpose hammer.

INSTALLING WOODEN ROOFING MATERIALS

With just a few simple tools, wood shingles and shakes can be applied by anybody with reasonable skills. This section will provide you with all the necessary fundamentals, but don't expect to be able to work at the rate of an accomplished wood shingler. Realistically, doing a job like this for the first time will demand some patience, but you will surprise yourself with professional-looking results.

Tools and Equipment

One tool that you will need is the roofer's hatchet. The hatchet has a nonskid head that prevents it from slipping off the rough galvanized nails, and a blade for cutting and splitting shingles; the better hatchets also have a shingle gauge. The gauge is important for spacing wood shingles. A peg fits into the gauge holes and is used to set shingles quickly to the correct exposure. If you use a hatchet with a sliding gauge, be careful—if it slips slightly, you'll wind up with misaligned shingles. You will also need a saw for cutting shingles across the grain and a block plane for beveling the edges so that you can ease in the shingles and clean up cuts.

RECOMMENDED EXPOSURES

Proper application starts with selecting the right shingles for the job. A good wood-shingle roof is never less than three layers thick. Consequently, the exposure of any given shingle must be slightly less than one-third its total length. The amount of shingle or shake exposed to the weather varies with the shingle's length and the roof's slope. Thinner wood shingles should be installed in a straight line like composite shingles. Thicker wood shakes, on the other hand, look great when installed in a more random pattern.

See the table below, but again, it's a good idea to check with your local building department.

Shingle Size	3-in-12 Roof	4-in-12 and Steeper Roofs
16"	3¾"	5"
18"	4½"	5½"
24"	5¾"	7½"

Choosing Nails

The nails are the second most important part of a wood shingle or shake roof. Use only rust-resistant nails, either zinc-coated or aluminum. Figure a little over 2 pounds per square for both shingles and shakes. Use 3d nails for 16- and 18-inch wood shingles, and 4d for 24-inch wood shingles. Hand-split shakes require 6d roofing nails. A rule of thumb is to make sure that the nail penetrates at least $\frac{1}{2}$ inch into the sheathing.

INSTALLING WOOD SHINGLES

Do not use a felt underlayment with wood shingles. Nail them directly over spaced sheathing. Take a little extra time getting started—the rest of the roof will be gauged from your beginning course.

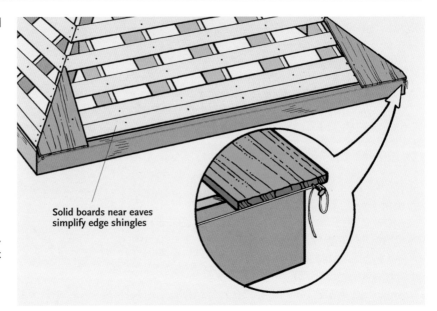

Solid boards near eaves simplify edge shingles

1 LAY OUT THE FIRST COURSE. Begin by nailing a shingle at each end of the eaves so that they overhang the eaves by 1 in. and the rake by $\frac{1}{4}$ to $\frac{3}{8}$ in. Drive a nail into the butt of each shingle and stretch a line between them to help align the rest of the starter course.

Right handers normally start in the left corner and apply enough shingles that they are able to sit down on the job. If you're a lefty, start on the right corner.

2 RUN THE COURSE. Leave a $\frac{1}{8}$- to $\frac{1}{4}$-in. gap between shingles. Double the first course of shingles, staggering gaps by at least $1\frac{1}{2}$ in.

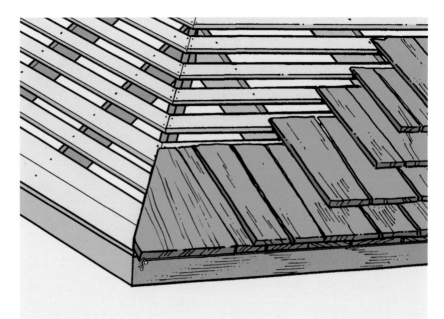

3 **START SECOND COURSE.** Start the second course of shingles at the recommended exposure, positioning it with the exposure gauge on your hammer, as shown above left. Two nails are required per shingle, regardless of width, to prevent the shingle from cupping. Always nail within 3/4 in. (1 in. for shakes) of the side edge of the shingle. Nail high enough so that the nails will be covered by the next course. On wood shingles with a 5-in. exposure, nail about 7 in. from the bottom edge of the shingle. On shingles with a 10-in. exposure, nail about 12 in. from the bottom edge. If you nail too high or too far in from the edge, the shingles will be able to curl up.

To locate the correct placement for each nail, measure up from the butt of the shingle you are nailing to a distance equal to the exposure plus 1 or 2 in. For a quick guide, mark the handle of your hammer with tape or a notch. Nail carefully: pounding too hard can break the wood fibers. If a shingle is crooked, pull it out and replace it.

Stagger gaps between shingles at least 1 1/2 in. between courses. Gaps should not line up over gaps two courses below.

If the shingle splits while you are nailing it, and the crack offsets the joint in the shingle below by at least 1 1/2 in., place a nail on each side of the split. You can treat the split shingle as two shingles. If the crack does not offset the joint in the shingle below, remove the split shingle and apply another.

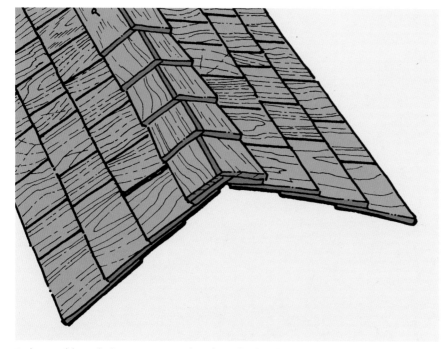

Ridge and hip shakes are mitered and applied with alternating overlaps.

Shingling the Ridge

You will not have to deal with valleys in any of the projects in this book, but you will have to know how to roof a ridge. The gazebos in this book all have hips, which are treated just like ridges. The appearance of your project (and its ability to shed water) depends on the neatness of the ridge. Factory ridge units are available and will make the job easier, because the two pieces are already fastened together and offset mitered joints are stacked alternately to speed installation. However, it's not too difficult to cut the ridges yourself.

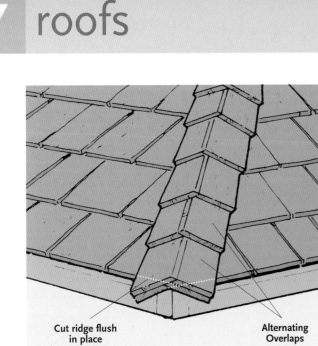

Cut ridge flush
in place

Alternating
Overlaps

ABOVE Alternating overlaps ensure that water cannot run through hip and ridge shingles. Double the first course of each run.

Cutting Your Own Ridge and Hip Shingles

Set your table saw's blade to a 35-degree angle and the fence to 4 inches (this measurement may vary according to the roof pitch). Cut two shingles at a time—one butt first, the other tail first. The top piece of ridge will come out about $1/4$ to $3/8$ inch wider than the bottom piece. The next piece will be reversed, giving you the same alternating mitered joints as the factory-made ridge pieces. For the next set, flip the pair—if the first pair was cut with the top shingle tail first, make the second ridge unit with the top shingle butt first.

Each ridge unit must have two nails on each side, placed 6 to 7 inches above the butt edge. Make sure that you offset ridge joints so that water will not seep through the joints as the roof ages. Give each ridge the same exposure as the roof shingles. For additional protection, it wouldn't hurt to lay a narrow strip of 30-pound felt over the ridge before installing the shingles. And always use a chalk line to make sure that the lines remain straight.

When starting a ridge run, start with a double course, as you did with the regular shingle courses. At those spots where the ridge meets the peak, you may have to trim the shingles to make a tight fit. Make the ridge in the middle and build a saddle by reversing two units on top of each other. Trim back the tail ends and leave about 8 inches of the butt portion. Use longer nails to apply the ridge to ensure that the nails penetrate the sheathing.

Shakes vs. Shingles

Shakes work best on roofs with at least a 6-in-12 slope, particularly in wet, humid climates. Shakes measuring 18 inches are overlapped $10 1/2$ inches, leaving an exposure of $7 1/2$ inches. Shakes measuring 24 inches are overlapped 14 inches, exposing 10 inches. This amount of overlapping provides standard 2-ply coverage. You can get even better coverage by using a 3-ply roof; in this case you need a $12 1/2$-inch and $16 1/2$-inch overlap, respectively. Nail shakes with 6d box nails in the same way as you would for wood shingles, allowing $1/2$ inch of space between shakes.

Preparing for Shakes

Shakes are usually installed over spaced sheathing, either 1x4s or 1x6s. However, because shakes are irregularly shaped, enough air can still circulate under them—even when using a solid-plywood sheathing—so that neither rotting nor cupping is a problem. If you decide to use plywood sheathing, you should not use any felt underlayment. The extra layer of underlayment will create a condensation problem; moisture under the shakes will affect your roof's life expectancy.

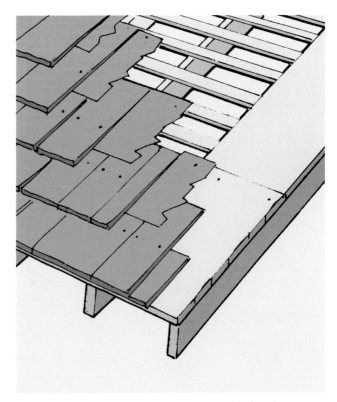

Shakes are applied over 1x4 or 1x6 spaced sheathing.

Except for a few minor considerations, shakes are installed exactly like shingles. When used to roof homes, wood shingles require 18-inch-wide strips of 30-pound roofing felt interwoven between the courses of shakes. This underlayment ensures that any water that penetrates under the shakes will quickly be carried back out to the roof surface. If you want a completely watertight roof and cannot locate 18-inch-wide felt in your area, cut a 36-inch-wide roll in half with a utility knife. Either apply the felt as you install each course of shakes, or else felt only the area you plan to install in a single day.

There is a disadvantage to using felt in this particular application: those black felt strips will be visible from the underside of your gazebo. You can choose to omit the felt entirely, but you may have to put up with a few leaks.

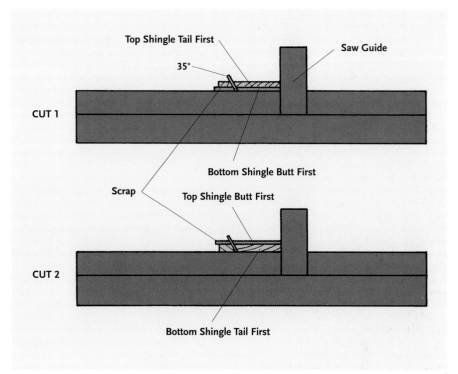

ABOVE Ridge and hip shakes are mitered and applied with alternating overlaps.

Applying Hip and Ridge Shakes

Cut and fit shakes at hip lines so that they end at the center of the hip. Shakes for covering hips and ridges are made with mitered edges. They require 8d nails or longer. Position shakes at the bottom and top of the hip, and snap a chalk line between them along one edge to serve as a guide. Apply a double hip shake at the eaves, cutting the first one so that its top edge butts against the next course of shakes. Proceed up the hip, alternating the overlaps of the mitered corners.

● SPLITTING SHINGLES

Because of their pronounced grain, shingles are surprisingly easy to split accurately along the grain. To split a shingle to width, embed the blade of a roofer's hatchet into the tapered end of the shingle, then strike down. To fine-tune a cut, shave the shingle with a utility knife.

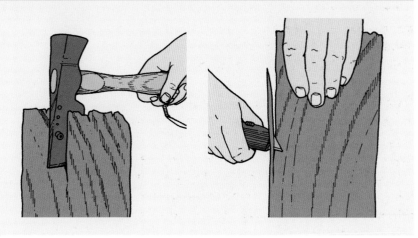

APPLYING SHINGLES

Asphalt (composite) shingles cut down dramatically on the time it takes to install a roof. They're uniform, they're bigger, and they require fewer nails than cedar shingles.

Because they are so uniform, though, you need to measure often when installing them. A crooked row looks bad enough on a regular roof. On an eight-sided roof, where the last shingle of the row needs to line up with the first shingle of the same row, it can be a disaster.

INSTALLING COMPOSITE SHINGLES

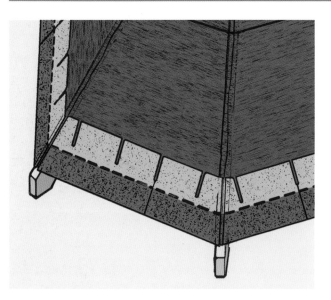

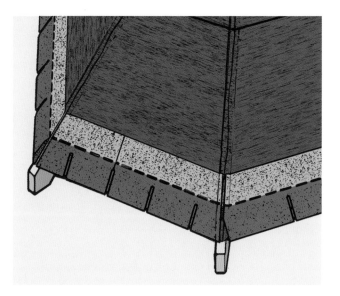

1 INSTALL STARTER COURSE. After installing the felt underlayment and metal drip edge, begin with a row of solid roofing along the eaves, using either starter-strip material or three-tab shingles turned upside down. Snap a chalk line to keep the top edges straight. Install the shingles so they overhang the edge of the roof by ³⁄₈ in.

2 START INSTALLING ROWS. Next apply the first row directly on top of the starter strip. Make sure the ends do not line up over the gaps below. Work from one end toward the other as far as you can reach; then begin the next course without changing your position. Start as many courses as you can reach before moving.

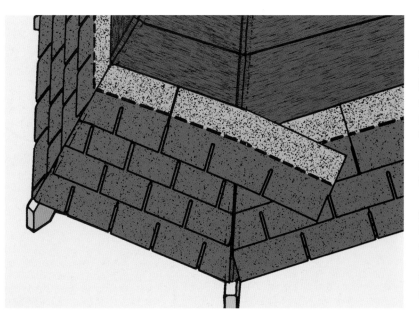

3 MAINTAIN CONSISTENT SPACING. The weather exposure for composite shingles is 5 in. Keep the courses from drifting out of line by measuring up from the eaves at several points along the course being applied. Stop and check your progress from the ground to make sure your lines remain straight.

Nail each three-tab shingle using four nails, each about ³⁄₄ in. above the top of the keyways.

When working on a six- or eight-sided gazebo, concentrate on installing the shingles in rows parallel to the bottoms of each panel. On the ridges that separate the panels, overlap the shingles, and cut them away in place. The ridge caps will cover up this unsightly overlap.

4 INSTALL RIDGE SHINGLES. Install the ridge shingles with the same amount of exposure. Fasten these shingles to the roof with two nails, one on each side of the ridge. Where the shingles meet the key block, fill the seam and cover the remaining exposed nailheads with roofing compound.

smart tip

HOW TO CUT SHINGLES You'll save a lot of wear and tear on your knife by cutting asphalt and fiberglass shingles from the back. Use your knife to mark the top and bottom edges of the shingle from the front. Flip the shingle over, and cut through the marks. Save the larger pieces for use on the opposite rake.

APPLYING HIP AND RIDGE COMPOSITE SHINGLES

Although hip and ridge shingles can be bought, it is easy to cut the required 12-inch squares from standard shingles, using a sharp utility knife. To shingle a hip, begin with a double layer of shingles at the bottom and work up to the peak. Leave a 5-inch exposure. Nail 1 inch in from the edge just below the self-sealing strip.

When shingling a ridge, begin at the end opposite from the prevailing wind. Apply roofing in the same way as hip shingles, caulking the exposed nailheads of the last shingle.

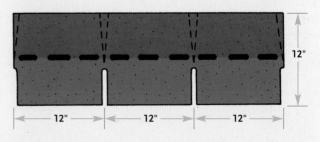

ABOVE Three shingles for use on a hip or ridge can easily be cut from one three-tab shingle.

LATTICE ROOFS

Installing a lattice roof is more like installing trim than any of the other roofing options. The lattice roof offers little in the way of structural strength; subsequently, you'll need to take special care during installation—you can't just climb on top to set the last screw.

BUILDING A LATTICE ROOF

1 INSTALL BOTTOM CLEATS. Rip 1-in. strips off a piece of 1-by stock, and fasten them on both sides of the opening that you plan to install lattice in. Nail or screw the cleat 1¾ in. down from the top of the rafter.

It's not necessary to surround the lattice completely on all four sides. The lattice will not have any load resting on it, nor are the spans in the projects in this book that great to justify the extra support. On the six- and eight-sided gazebos, for example, there's no need to worry about cleating around the point. Leaving the base open emphasizes the stepped pattern of the lattice.

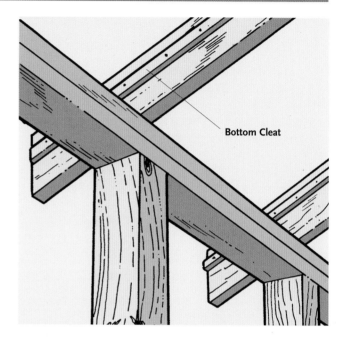

Bottom Cleat

2 MEASURE AND CUT LATTICE. Measure each opening individually, just in case they differ. Mark the measurements on each piece of lattice. Use a chalk line to ensure straight cut lines.

When cutting the lattice, rest the entire panel on a scrap of plywood. Make a straight-edge jig by screwing a narrow board to a wider board. Trim the wider board by running the base of your saw against the narrow board. Clamp the jig along the chalk line. Adjust the depth of your saw's blade so that it cuts through the lattice and just barely scores the plywood underneath.

Install each cut panel on top of the backing cleats, and tack them in with a few brads.

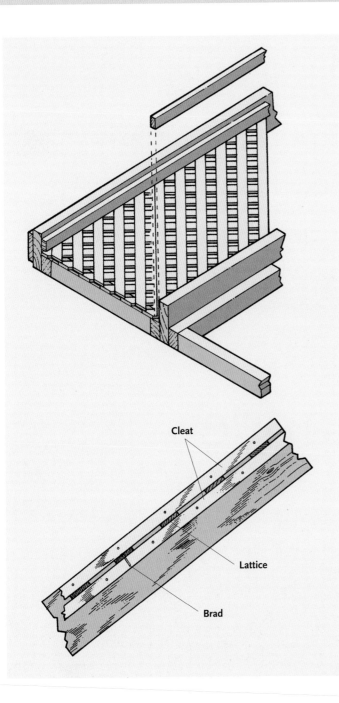

Cleat

Lattice

Brad

3 INSTALL THE TOP CLEAT. **Cut the top cleat out of 1-by stock just as you did for the bottom cleat. Nail this cleat in to secure the panel.**

FINISHING AND MAINTENANCE

Red cedar does not need any finishing or preservatives under ordinary weather conditions. It will weather naturally to a silver-gray color. Over a long period, it will become almost black. In year-round warm, humid areas such as the U.S. Southeast, or in any site below overhanging trees, you should use a fungicide to control mildew and fungus growth. Some shingles may come pretreated; you can also apply a wood preservative and water repellent after installation. Wood shingles and shakes may also be colored. Use a penetrating wood stain—not paint—for this job. (Paint will seal the shingles or shakes so moisture can't escape.) Composite shingles require no special attention.

Clean wood roofs periodically to remove accumulated debris and to prevent moisture buildup. Use a stiff broom or brush to keep the joints clear between the shingles.

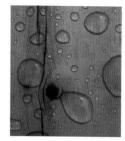

8 maintenance

Your project will begin its battle with the forces of nature the moment you set the first post. Sunlight will bake it. Rain and snow will attack it. Insects and fungus will eat it. The most effective defense is a judiciously maintained paint job. But if you have invested in the natural beauty of redwood, cedar, or even teak, painting is not an option and staining may not be your first choice. There are other defense strategies. You can use water repellents, wood preservatives, clear penetrating finishes, or any combination of the three to add years to a structure's useful life and keep it looking good. Before deciding what preservatives to use on your project, it helps to understand the natural forces that will work to destroy it.

INSECTS AND FUNGUS

Like all living organisms, wood-eating insects and rot-causing fungus have four basic needs: food, water, air, and warmth. Remove any one of these elements and a well-built structure will last indefinitely. Of course, it's not possible to keep air or warmth away from an outdoor structure, so that leaves you the options of removing the water and removing the food.

Remove the Food

Wood preservatives work by poisoning the food. Some woods, including redwood and cedar, have natural rot- and insect-repelling toxins. But no natural toxin is as effective as pressure-treating wood.

Wood that has been pressure-treated does not rot, because organisms will not eat it. For this reason, pressure-treated wood is an excellent choice for wood that will be in contact with the ground, a situation that makes it nearly impossible to eliminate moisture.

An advantage of pressure treatment is that the poison cannot leach out to harm animals, plants, or the environment. Of course, you release these dangerous chemicals whenever you saw the wood. Also, you should never sand or burn pressure-treated wood, because these practices will release large amounts of toxic chemicals.

There are other chemicals that you can apply to wood on your own. These chemicals are safer than the older types of preservatives, but they still cannot provide the

smart tip

TOXIC COMPOUNDS ALTHOUGH THEY WERE ONCE HIGHLY REGARDED AS EFFECTIVE CHEMICAL PRESERVATIVES, THE EPA HAS LABELED SEVERAL COMPOUNDS HIGHLY TOXIC TO HUMANS: CREOSOTE, INORGANIC ARSENIC COMPOUNDS, AND PENTACHLOROPHENOLS. THESE CHEMICALS HAVE BEEN PROVEN TO BE POISONOUS TO YOU AND YOUR GARDEN. AND IMPROPER DISPOSAL OF THESE PRODUCTS WILL CREATE STILL MORE PROBLEMS. SIMPLY STATED, DON'T USE THESE CHEMICALS AT ALL.

ground-contact protection of pressure-treated wood. This difference is due to the methods of application. These chemicals are applied only on the surface and not injected into the wood. Both will keep fungus and termites at bay reasonably well, as long as the wood is not constantly wet. In areas of prolonged exposure, pressure-treated wood is still your best choice.

Copper napthenate is a fungicide that has been used safely for many years. This heavy-duty green preservative is designed to protect any wood that will be in contact with soil or water. It can be applied by brushing, dipping, or spraying. Because it is nontoxic to plants and animals, it is especially ideal for treating garden structures. This preservative can also be used to treat the

Regular application of preservative can keep your project looking new, like the left part of these decking boards.

ends of freshly sawn pressure-treated boards to ensure uniform weather resistance.

Zinc napthenate is another type of preservative that also has been used safely for many years. It is designed to protect wood above ground from rot and mildew while allowing the surface to weather naturally. This preservative is traditionally used on fences, outdoor furniture, and wood house siding. It can be applied by brushing, dipping, or spraying.

Both copper and zinc napthenates typically include water repellents (such as paraffin) in their formulations to help prevent wood warping and cracking. It should also be noted that although the EPA considers these two chemicals "safe," proper precautions should be taken, because both are toxic in the concentrations used during application.

REMOVING THE MOISTURE

Fortunately, removing the moisture doesn't mean you must keep the wood dry. It just means the wood must be able to dry out before mildew and mold get a chance to do any damage. That's why wood siding and roof shingles don't rot, even though they get wet with every rain. A deck in direct sunlight is probably safe from rot, especially if you have thwarted termites by building the understructure out of pressure-treated wood. But decking under shade trees is particularly susceptible to rot. Not only is there no sun to dry out the wood, but leaves and other bits of tree debris that accumulate on your deck retain additional moisture.

Although mold and mildew limit their activities to the wood's surface, they can attract other microorganisms and insects that feed on the cellulose cell structure of the wood. Wood-eating insects such as termites, carpenter ants, and bees will bore through the wood, leaving a riddled shell with little structural strength.

One surprisingly effective way to thwart rot is simply to keep your outdoor structure clean. A regular thorough sweeping will keep moisture-retaining debris from collecting in the cracks.

EFFECTS OF RAIN

Moisture can attack outdoor wood in a way that has nothing to do with rot. Wood swells when it's wet, and shrinks when it's dry; this natural tendency is exacerbated by freeze-thaw cycles. Cycling through these conditions will really take a toll on boards, especially at all the points where boards are fastened. Following a good rain, the underside of a decking board will retain moisture, while the sun-drenched surface will quickly dry. The difference in moisture will create stresses that can eventually lead to cupping, cracking, and splitting. Boards may even begin to pop free from their fasteners. These cracks and other nailholes will serve as new spots for water to seep into, creating even more water damage down the line.

Pressure treatment and other chemical preservatives are not designed to provide defense against this kind of moisture damage. Moisture will move in and out of a treated board just as readily as if the board had not been treated. Either way, the board will have the same tendency to crack, split, and warp.

In general, heavier woods (for example, southern pine, the most common pressure-treated wood) will suffer

smart tip

BEAUTIFUL MILDEW? MANY PEOPLE PREFER THE SILVERY GRAY COLOR THAT OFTEN DEVELOPS ON A PROJECT AFTER A FEW YEARS OF EXPOSURE. SOME EVEN APPLY A SIMILARLY COLORED STAIN TO CREATE A MORE ESTABLISHED LOOK. WHAT MOST PEOPLE DON'T KNOW IS THAT THIS MELLOW GRAY COLOR IS CAUSED BY A MILDEW THAT GROWS ON THE SURFACE OF THE WOOD.

YOU CAN REMOVE THIS GROWTH QUITE EASILY WITH EITHER A FUNGICIDE OR A BLEACH SOLUTION. HOWEVER, BECAUSE THIS NATURAL GRAYING AFFECTS ONLY THE TOP LAYER OF THE WOOD AND DOES NOT AFFECT THE STRUCTURAL STRENGTH OF YOUR PROJECT, THERE'S REALLY NO REASON TO WORRY ABOUT IT.

more from moisture movement than will lighter woods. Heavier woods are denser, and so they have more internal tension. Lighter woods, such as redwood and cedar, are more spongelike: moisture can pass through them with much less effect.

The only defense against water movement is to reduce it by using a water repellent. An excellent water repellent is a good coat of paint. The alternative is a clear repellent often marketed as a sealer. The most common clear repellents on the market are little more than paraffin wax dissolved in mineral spirits. When you apply the repellent, the solvent evaporates, leaving the wax in the pores of the wood. The wax impedes the flow of water vapor in and out of the wood, and this decreases the rate of expansion

and contraction. As a result, the wood is less likely to cup. You can buy water repellents that also contain fungicides. Exterior stains often contain paraffin and fungicide.

Some clear penetrating finishes are formulated with linseed oil, tung oil, or alkyds, like many paints or varnishes; but instead of acting as a film-forming agent, the resin will act as a sealer. A limited amount of resin can help seal the wood and will accent the grain pattern. But some care should be taken with these finishes, because multiple coats could create a buildup.

To a gazebo, a sunny day means parching sun and temperature extremes. Add in a bit of bad weather, and maintenance becomes crucial.

EFFECTS OF THE SUN

Sunlight, or more specifically ultraviolet (UV) light, is the single most pervasive weathering factor on any exterior structure. Fortunately, the effect is cosmetic, not structural. UV radiation breaks down the lignin (the binding agent that holds the cells together) in exterior wood cells, but only penetrates to a depth of about $1/100$ inch. The damaged cells will block out any further degradation, unless the loose fibers are washed away by either wind or rain. Don't worry too much—the combined effects of these two weathering agents is, on average, about $1/4$ inch per century.

Absorbers, Blockers, and Inhibitors

If you want to prevent the weathering effect of the sun, look for a finish that contains either UV absorbers or UV blockers. Absorbers and blockers are particles that either absorb or reflect UV light to minimize its effect on the wood. There are also more expensive finishes that contain UV inhibitors. These compounds are designed to actually disrupt the normal chemical action caused by UV light. Sealers containing UV inhibitors are more expensive than sealers containing either absorbers or blockers, but are not that much more effective in the long run. UV inhibitors disrupt the chemical reaction caused by UV light, but they break down in the process and become less effective. In comparison, the particles in the other two compounds do not degrade under UV radiation, and they provide more consistent protection. Read the label on the container to find out what's in your finish.

All of these finishes will need to be reapplied, typically every other year.

FILM-FORMING FINISHES

You might think that by using a clear polyurethane or other similar film-forming finish (such as clear varnish), you would be able to achieve a more durable finish while still preserving the appearance of the wood. Clear film-forming finishes such as these are not generally recommended for extended outside wear.

Polyurethane is generally not suitable for sealing decks or other outdoor structures, because it is hard and inflexible. It tends to crack and flake, rather than moving with the wood through natural changes in temperature or moisture.

The other problem with a clear polyurethane finish is that it still allows UV rays through to the wood. The UV light destroys the lignin in the cells as if the wood were unfinished. When the surface cells have been broken down, the polyurethane has nothing left to adhere to and will start flaking off in sheets.

Reapplying a new coat on top of a cracked one is extremely difficult; the first coat has to be completely stripped. Stick with penetrating finishes or paint for outdoor structures.

Polyurethane can be used effectively on portable projects such as outdoor furniture that you want to protect yet still show off the wood. Make sure you use polyurethane formulated for exterior use. You can extend the life of the finish (and the project) by bringing it inside for the winter.

For those who insist on using polyurethane, there are mixes available that contain powdered iron oxides. These formulas are not perfectly clear. They will add a tint of orange or red to the overall color, but these particulates make the project completely opaque in the UV spectrum. They can extend the useful life of the finish from one to three years.

APPLICATION

The thing to remember when applying a penetrating finish is that you want the wood to absorb as much as it can. By its very nature, you will not be able to notice brush marks, and any finish that isn't absorbed can be wiped off. The most common mistake when applying finish is not using enough to saturate the wood fibers. Remember that the end grain of a dried piece (such as the ends of posts or railings) will absorb sealer almost as quickly as you can brush it on. Check these spots during application, and reapply as necessary.

Avoid breathing vapors or spray mists. Work outside.

Wear rubber gloves and long-sleeved garments during application to reduce exposure and minimize the chance of skin irritation. Always wear goggles or safety glasses to protect yourself from any backspray or drips.

APPLYING A FINISH

1 PREPARE THE WOOD. Sanding cedar, redwood, or cypress will increase the sealant's penetration and give you a cleaner-looking surface. Do not sand pressure-treated wood—sanding will release the toxins bonded to the wood's cells and could make you sick. The best way to clean the wood before finishing without exposing yourself to any toxins is to use a power washer.

The timing of your application is not that critical. Two dry, windy days should be an adequate amount of time for your project to dry sufficiently to accept a finish.

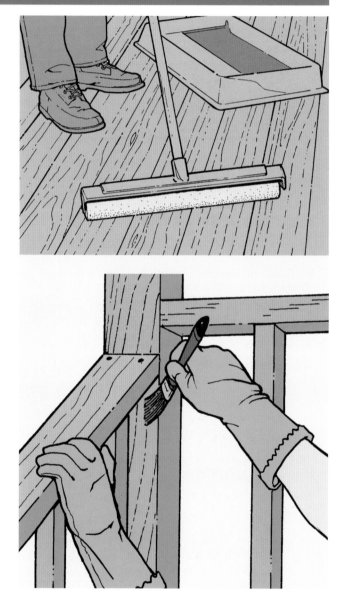

2 APPLY THE FINISH. Horizontal decking boards can be coated with a roller or spray equipment. (Small pump-pressured sprayers can be purchased inexpensively at most hardware stores.) Follow the sprayer with a brush to spread out the finish. Apply the sealer to the underside of decking and to joists, beams, and posts. For posts, railings, and stair stringers, brush application is best. Remember that visible end grain will absorb more sealer than the flat surfaces.

3 REMOVE EXCESS FINISH. With a clean rag, wipe off excess finish that isn't absorbed after half an hour. Be sure to dispose of all rags properly, because the heat generated from the evaporating finish can cause rags to burst into flames. Allow used rags to dry completely, outside, before disposing of them.

● DIPPING

Short of pressure-treating, dipping is the most thorough way of applying sealant after a piece has been cut to size. In this kind of treatment, the wood is immersed in a bath of sealant for several minutes, and then allowed to air-dry. This maximizes coverage and penetration.

There are some drawbacks to this method, however. Logically, the dip treatment can be done with lumber only before it is nailed in place. And it is time-consuming because you must allow each piece to soak. The size of the trough also limits the size of the members that you will be able to dip.

While it may not be practical to dip decking boards, you might consider the dip treatment for balusters or shorter parts of the project that can benefit from complete coverage. For instance, if you are using the more-expensive turned balusters, you might want to give them extra protection to prevent them from cracking or splitting.

One way to make a dip treatment trough is to place a seamless plastic sheet in a wooden frame. The frame should rest on a flat surface. Use a heavy-duty sheet (6-mil), and make sure that its edges are well away from the edges of the frame. Including a

drying rack in your trough will enable your pieces to dry while funneling back excess sealant.

Any excess sealant can be reused. Filter out the wood and debris through a piece of cheesecloth, and store the remaining sealant in a tightly sealed container.

9 square hip-roof gazebo

This basic gazebo plan offers many advantages. First of all, it is square, so the need for the many special-angle cuts that you would find with six- or eight-sided gazebos is eliminated. The 8-foot-square design is modular, so standard-length lumber can be used with minimal cutting.

The roof in this roof-over-deck design is supported by 4x4 posts. The deck size is 8 feet across, with a deck-to-roof distance of 78 inches. These proportions create an intimate, cozy structure, but read this entire chapter as well as "Roofs" and "Customizing Options" before finalizing your design.

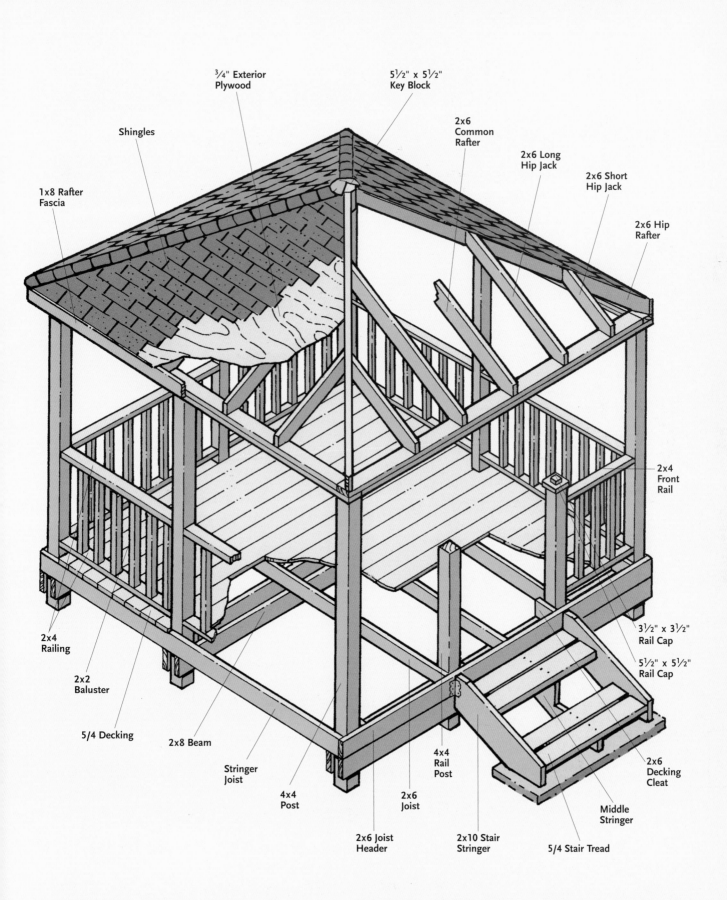

¾" Exterior Plywood

5½" x 5½" Key Block

2x6 Common Rafter

2x6 Long Hip Jack

2x6 Short Hip Jack

2x6 Hip Rafter

Shingles

1x8 Rafter Fascia

2x4 Front Rail

2x4 Railing

2x2 Baluster

5/4 Decking

2x8 Beam

Stringer Joist

4x4 Post

2x6 Joist Header

2x6 Joist

4x4 Rail Post

2x10 Stair Stringer

3½" x 3½" Rail Cap

5½" x 5½" Rail Cap

2x6 Decking Cleat

Middle Stringer

5/4 Stair Tread

OVERALL VIEW

SQUARE HIP-ROOF GAZEBO

Name	Qty.	Size
Gazebo Deck Framing		
Posts (Roof Support)	7	4" x 4" x 8'
Posts (Rail)	2	4" x 4" x 54"
Beams	6	2" x 8" x 8'
Stringer and Intermediate Joists	4	2" x 6" x 93"
Header Joists	2	2" x 6" x 8'
Center Joist	1	2" x 6" x 89$\frac{1}{2}$"
Decking Cleats	8	2" x 6" x 5"
Decking Cleats (Middle)	2	2" x 6" x 6$\frac{1}{2}$"
Stair Stringers	3	2" x 10" x 30"
Stair Treads	4	$\frac{5}{4}$ x 6" x 33"
Decking	18	$\frac{5}{4}$ x 6" x 10'
Roof Framing		
Top and Cap Plates	8	2" x 4" x 89$\frac{1}{2}$"
Key Block	1	5$\frac{1}{2}$" x 5$\frac{1}{2}$" x 8"
Common Rafters	4	2" x 6" x 59"
Hip Rafters	4	2" x 6" x 74$\frac{1}{4}$"
Long Hip Jacks	8	2" x 6" x 39$\frac{3}{4}$"
Short Hip Jacks	8	2" x 6" x 20$\frac{1}{2}$"
Rafter Fascia	4	1" x 8" x 94$\frac{1}{2}$"
A/C Exterior-Grade Plywood Sheathing	4	$\frac{3}{4}$" x 4' x 8'
15-lb. Roofing Felt		100 sq. ft.
Metal Drip Edge	4	8' lengths
Composite Shingles		100 sq. ft.
Composite Hip and Ridge Shingles		Needed to cover approximately 26'

Name	Qty.	Size
Railing		
Rails	12	2" x 4" x 41$\frac{1}{4}$"
Front Rails	4	2" x 4" x 20$\frac{1}{2}$"
Rail Cap Pieces	2	1$\frac{1}{2}$" x 5$\frac{1}{2}$" x 5$\frac{1}{2}$"
	2	1$\frac{1}{2}$" x 3$\frac{1}{2}$" x 3$\frac{1}{2}$"
Balusters	48	2" x 2" x 30"
Nails and Fasteners		
Carriage Bolts	18	$\frac{3}{8}$" x 8"
Nails		
16d Common		
12d Common		
10d Common		
8d Common		
10d Finishing		
Roofing		
Post Anchors	9	
Stair Angles	4	
Framing Angles	2 for stair stringers	
Premixed Concrete		As required to set post and step footings below frost line

DECK FRAMING PLAN

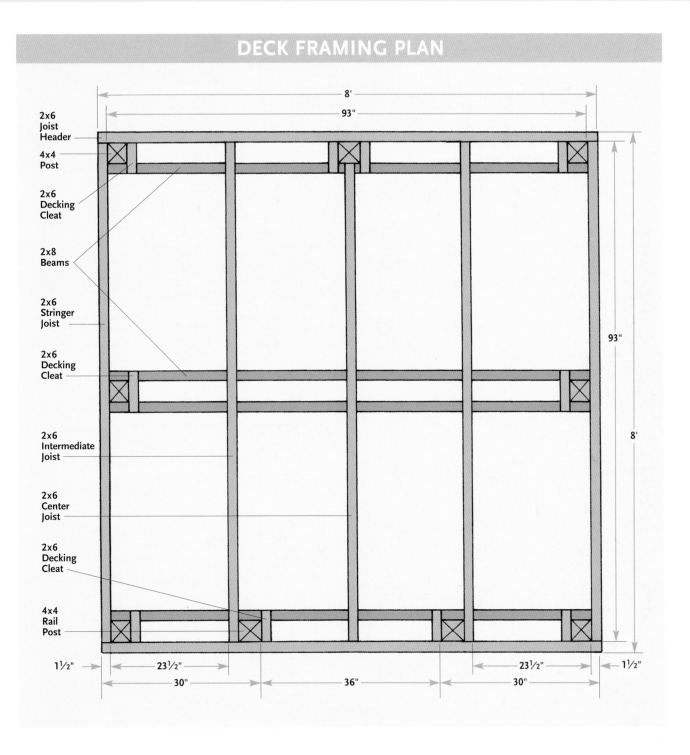

CONSTRUCT THE DECK

The basic structural components of the gazebo deck are 4x4 posts that support the deck beams and roof headers; 2x8 beams that bolt to the posts and support the floor joists; and 2x6 joists, stringer joists, and joist headers that fasten to the beams and support the 1-inch-thick decking. Decking of this dimension is commonly known as

$5/4$ (pronounced "five-quarter") stock. The gazebo must be square, level, and built to exact dimensions. All sides of the deck should measure 8 feet. The corner posts are located $1\frac{1}{2}$ inches inside the outside corners of the layout so that standard 8-foot lumber can be used for beams, joists, and decking. Note that accurate post placement is critical.

135

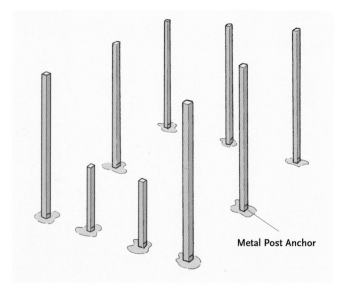

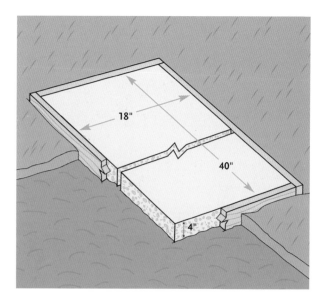

Metal Post Anchor

1 INSTALL POSTS. Cut the posts to the sizes listed in the materials list. Pour footings to the depth required by the building department, and install anchors as described in "Techniques" on page 72. Adjust the post length as needed. Make sure you position the footings so the outside edges of the corner posts will be no more than 93 in. apart.

2 PLACE STEP FOOTING. Pour a 4-in.-thick concrete slab where the gazebo stairs will meet the ground. Make the slab 18 x 40 in., with the front edge 26 in. out from the edge of the deck.

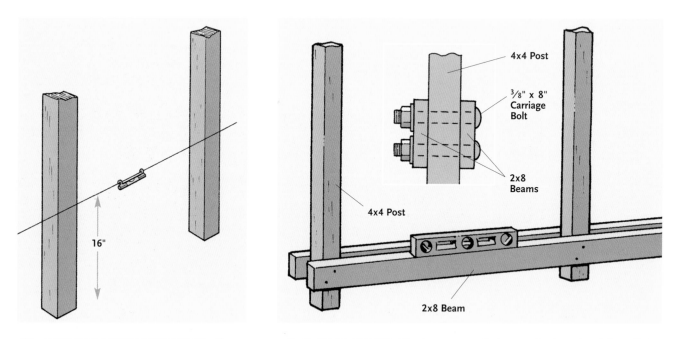

3 ESTABLISH DECK HEIGHT. The finished deck is 16 in. above grade. Mark the 16-in. height on one of the posts, and transfer this dimension to all other posts using a level or line level. Once the deck height is marked, measure down 1 in. and draw a line marking the top of each joist. Measure down an additional 5½ in. to locate the top of the beams.

4 INSTALL BEAMS. The beams are 2x8s attached to the sides of the posts. Temporarily clamp a 2x8 to one of the posts at the marks you drew. Level it, and nail it temporarily in place. Temporarily attach the rest of the beams, leveling them with the first beam. Lay a straight 2x4 diagonally across the beams, check for level, and make any necessary adjustments. Drill ⅜-in.-dia. holes all the way through the beams at each post, and bolt them in place with 8-in.-long, ⅜-in.-dia. hex-head bolts, with nuts and washers.

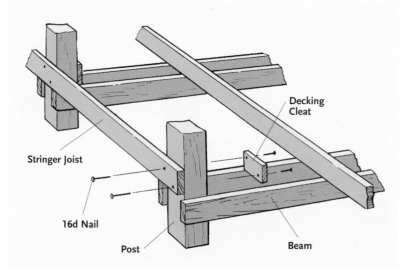

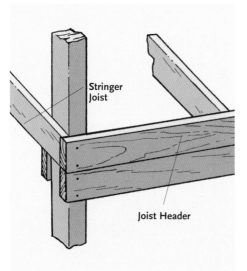

5 INSTALL JOISTS. Rest two joists, called stringer joists, across the beams against the outside posts. Nail them to the posts with two 16d nails. Face-nail two more joists, called intermediate joists, to the front posts and toenail them to the beams. Cut the center joist to length. Toe-nail each side of the joist to the back center post. Cut cleats for the ends of the decking, which is unsupported whenever it meets the post. Nail the cleats to posts as shown to provide the necessary support.

6 INSTALL JOIST HEADERS. Nail joist headers to the exposed ends of the joists you've installed and to the ends of the cleats and to the posts.

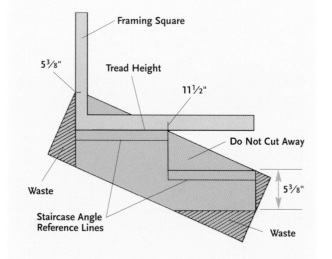

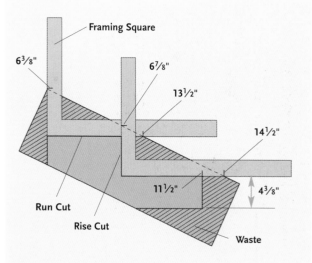

7 LAY OUT END STRINGERS. Cut the end stringers from two 30-in.-long 2 x 10s. Place a framing square on a stringer as shown so that the 5³⁄₈-in. mark on the outside of the square's tongue and the 11¹⁄₂-in. measurement on the outside of the square's blade both align with the top edge of the stringer, and trace along the square. Extend the rise line to the bottom of the stringer. Lay out the lower step the same way, then measure down 1¹⁄₄ in. from each of the treads and draw layout lines for the stair angles. Make cuts at the back, front, and bottom of the stringer. Do not cut notches for the stairs.

8 LAY OUT MIDDLE STRINGER. You will need a middle stringer to support the stair tread. Start by marking out the top step with the outside edge of the tongue of the square at 6³⁄₈ in. and the blade at 13¹⁄₂ in. For the second step, put the tongue at 6⁷⁄₈ in. and the blade at 14¹⁄₂ in. Make a mark at 11¹⁄₂ in., too, and draw a 4³⁄₈-in. line as shown to lay out the front of the stringer. Cut the back, front, and bottom, as in Step 7. Cut along each rise and each run using a circular saw to cut notches for the stairs. Finish using a handsaw.

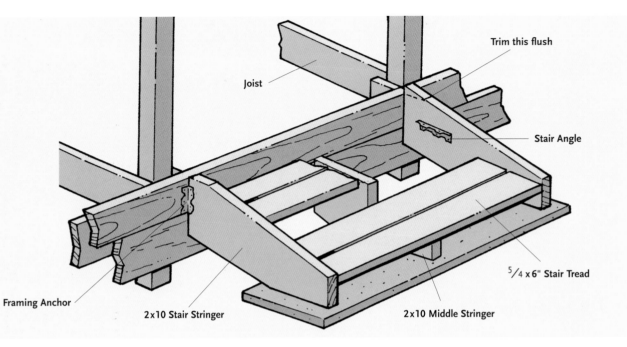

Joist

Trim this flush

Stair Angle

5/4 x 6" Stair Tread

Framing Anchor

2x10 Stair Stringer

2x10 Middle Stringer

9 ASSEMBLE STAIRS. Nail the stair angles to the stringers with heavy-duty joist-hanger nails. Attach the stringers to the joist header with framing anchors, spacing them 33 in. apart and equidistant from the rail posts. Nail the middle stringer to the front beam, centering it between the two outer stringers. When the bottoms of the stringers sit flat on the concrete slab, the top points of the stringers will extend about 1 in. higher than the header joist and will get in the way later on. Cut the top of the stringers flush with the header, using a handsaw. Cut the treads 33 in. long. Attach the front tread pieces flush with the front of the stringers. Leave 1/2 in. of space between the front and back treads for drainage.

10 INSTALL DECKING. Install the decking boards perpendicular to the floor joists, starting at the front of the gazebo and working toward the rear. Let the boards overhang the stringer joists. You'll trim them to length later. Align the first board so it overhangs the header by 1/2 in., and notch the deck boards as needed to fit around the posts. When cutting the notches, leave about 1/8 in. of clearance around the post. Nail the decking to each joist with two 8d nails driven at a slight angle. Put a 10d nail between boards to space them properly. After every three or four boards, measure to make sure the boards are running parallel with the back joist header. As you near the opposite end of the deck, lay the last few deck boards in place before nailing them. If the last board doesn't overhang the back header by about 1/2 in., adjust the spacing so that it will. Snap chalk lines across the ends of the deck boards 1/2 in. from the outside faces of the stringer joists. Tack a board to the deck as a guide for the saw, and make the cuts. Make the cuts by hand where the posts get in the way.

ROOF FRAMING PLAN

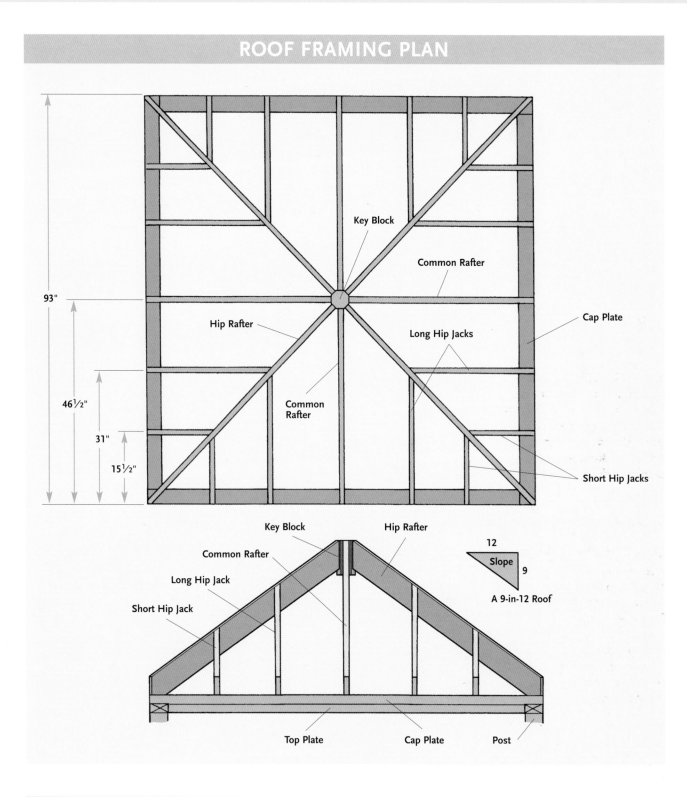

93"

46½"

31"

15½"

Key Block

Common Rafter

Cap Plate

Hip Rafter

Long Hip Jacks

Common Rafter

Short Hip Jacks

Key Block   Hip Rafter

Common Rafter

Long Hip Jack

Short Hip Jack

12
Slope
9

A 9-in-12 Roof

Top Plate   Cap Plate   Post

FRAME THE ROOF

This square hip roof has four types of rafters, all made of 2x6 stock. As shown in the "Roof Framing Plan," there are four common rafters, four hip rafters, eight short hip jacks, and eight long hip jacks. The rafters don't have bird's-mouth cuts or tails that overhang the cap plate. Instead, they have a seat cut and a tail plumb cut. If you are not an experienced roof builder, refer to "Roofs" on page 96.

139

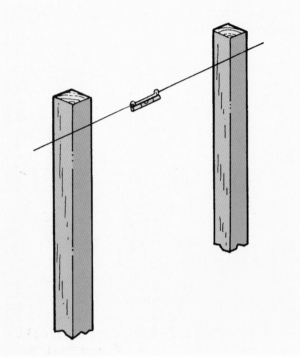

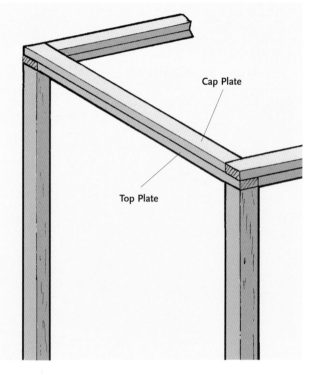

1 CUT POSTS. Measure up one post 78 in. from the deck floor. Mark this height, and then use a line level to transfer this to the other posts. Cut the posts at the marks.

2 INSTALL TOP PLATES. Cut the top plates and cap plates to overlap at the corners as shown. Nail cap plates to top plates with 8d nails. Nail one of these assemblies atop the front posts and another atop the back posts with 12d nails. Install the remaining two assemblies.

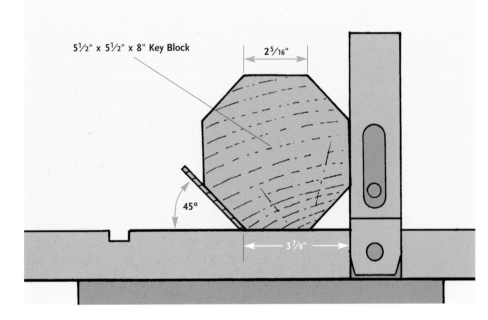

5½" x 5½" x 8" Key Block

2⁵⁄₁₆"

45°

3⁷⁄₈"

3 MAKE THE KEY BLOCK. At the peak of the roof, the rafters meet an 8-in.-long octagonal key block made from a 6x6. For safety, cut the block on a table saw from a piece about 20 in. long. Set the table saw rip fence 3⅞ in. from the blade. Set the blade at 2¾ in. high and tilt it 45 deg. Remove the four corners.

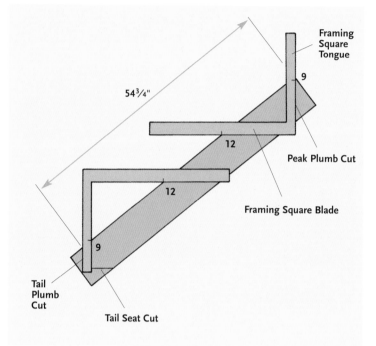

4 CUT COMMON RAFTERS. The common rafters and the hip jack rafters have a rise of 9 in. per 12 in. of run. If the corner posts are all 93 in. apart, as planned, cut your rafters to the lengths given in the materials list. If not, see "Roofs" on page 96. Use a framing square to lay out the tail plumb cut, the seat cut, and the peak cut as shown.

5 INSTALL COMMON RAFTERS. Toenail two opposing common rafters to the key block with two 8d nails on each side of each rafter. Position the rafters to land exactly on the middle of opposing cap plates. With a helper, lift the two-rafter assembly onto the gazebo. Toenail it to the cap plates with 8d nails. Install the two remaining common rafters.

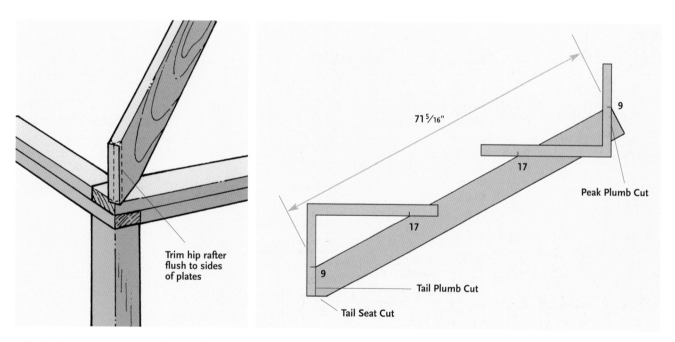

6 CUT AND INSTALL HIP RAFTERS. A gazebo whose common rafters have a rise of 9 in. per 12 in. of run will have hip rafters with a rise of 9 in. per 17 in. of run. Use the 9- and 17-in. marks on the framing square blade, as shown in the drawing. Put the hip rafters in place, toenailing them to the plates and the key block. The rafters will overlap the corners of the cap plates slightly as shown. After the rafters are installed, use a handsaw to cut them off flush with the sides of the plates.

141

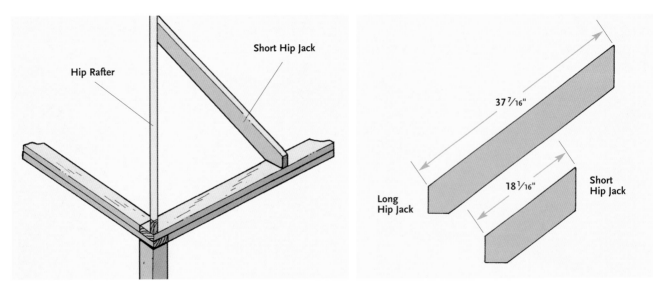

7 **CUT AND INSTALL HIP JACKS.** The hip jacks have the same 9-in-12-pitch run as the common rafters. Measure between the plates and hip rafters before cutting to make sure the lengths are right. Lay out the plumb and seat cuts in the same way you did for the common rafters. Make the tail plumb cut and the seat plumb cut just as you did for the common rafters. To make the peak plumb cut, set your saw blade to 45 deg. Note that four long hip jacks and four short hip jacks are beveled to the left, while the rest are beveled to the right. Toenail the hip jacks to the cap plate with 8d nails, and nail them through the bevel into the hip rafters with 10d nails.

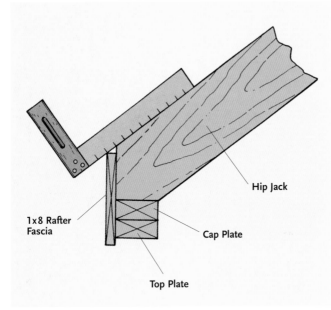

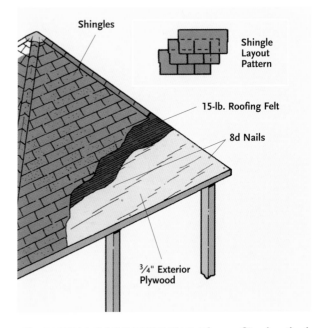

8 **INSTALL RAFTER FASCIA.** The 1x8 roof fascia covers the ends of the rafters. Measure between the ends of the hip rafters and cut the fascia to fit, mitering the ends. Attach the fascia to the ends of the rafters with 8d nails. Use a square as shown to keep the fascia boards low enough so the plywood roof sheathing can go over it.

9 **INSTALL ROOF COVERING.** The roof is sheathed with 3/4-in. exterior-grade plywood. Each roof pitch requires two pieces of plywood—a trapezoid below a triangle. Cut the plywood to size, and nail it to the rafters with 8d nails every 8 in. Put the better side of the plywood facing down, where it will be seen as the gazebo ceiling. Cover the sheathing with 15-lb. roofing felt. Install an aluminum drip edge, and then install the shingles. Complete shingling instructions are given in "Roofs" on page 96.

INSTALL THE RAILING

Cut the rail support posts to their final height of 35 inches.

Build and install the railing using 2x4 top and bottom rails with equally spaced 2x2 balusters. Space the balusters as shown. Lay out the top of the upper rail at 33 inches above the deck. Measure and cut each top and bottom rail section separately to ensure a snug fit between the posts, but don't install them yet. Cut the balusters to 27 inches long. Lay out the baluster positions on the rails, spacing them as shown. Attach the balusters to the rails using 8d nails. Nail through the bottom rail into the balusters, but carefully toenail the top of the baluster to the top rail from below so there are no exposed nailheads on the top rail. Attach the assembled section to the post using railing hangers or by toenailing with 10d nails.

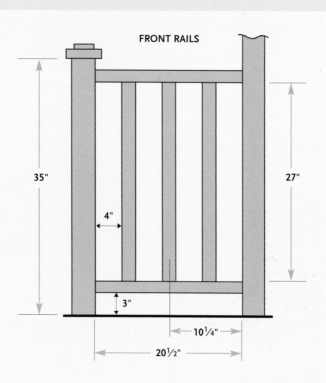

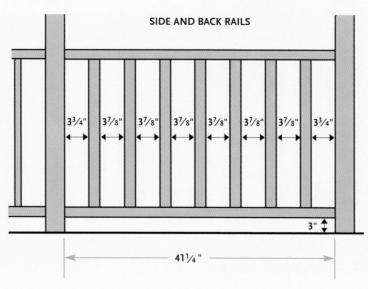

10 six-sided gazebo

A six-sided gazebo is the classic design. It requires careful planning and accurate angle cutting; but for those with patience and skill, the results are well worth it. With six identical rafters, the roof of this gazebo is simpler to build than the roof on the "Square Hip-Roof Gazebo" on page 132. You can make the roof framing even easier by using hardware specifically designed for attaching rafters on a six-sided gazebo. You also can substitute a concrete deck for a raised wood deck foundation or add permanent benches or seating to your gazebo. Measure and cut your stock to fit as you work. The angles involved in most gazebo construction make precutting lumber risky, so take the extra time, and give yourself the opportunity to correct slight errors before they become big ones.

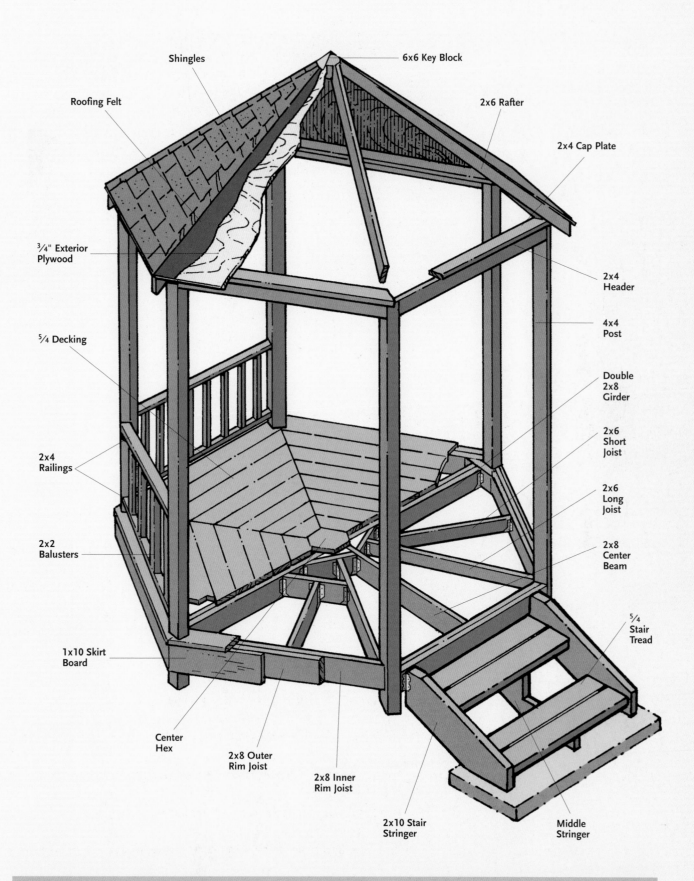

Shingles

Roofing Felt

6x6 Key Block

2x6 Rafter

2x4 Cap Plate

3/4" Exterior Plywood

2x4 Header

4x4 Post

5/4 Decking

Double 2x8 Girder

2x6 Short Joist

2x6 Long Joist

2x8 Center Beam

2x4 Railings

2x2 Balusters

5/4 Stair Tread

1x10 Skirt Board

Center Hex

2x8 Outer Rim Joist

2x8 Inner Rim Joist

2x10 Stair Stringer

Middle Stringer

OVERALL VIEW

SIX-SIDED GAZEBO

cutting & materials

Name	Qty.	Size
Gazebo Deck Framing		
Posts	6	4" x 4" x 8'
Center Post	1	4" x 4" x 48"
Inner Rim Joists	6	2" x 8" x $52\frac{1}{2}$"
Outer Rim Joists	6	2" x 8" x $54\frac{1}{4}$"
Diagonal Girder Support	2	2" x 8" x cut to fit
Girders	2	2" x 8" x 8' $8\frac{1}{2}$"
Center Beams	2	2" x 8" x $46\frac{15}{16}$"
Inner Diagonals	4	2" x 8" x 11"
Outer Diagonals	4	2" x 6" x $12\frac{5}{16}$"
Long Joists	4	2" x 6" x $47\frac{5}{16}$"
Short Joists	4	2" x 6" x $34\frac{1}{2}$"
Skirt Boards	5	1" x 10" x $59\frac{1}{16}$"
Stair Stringers	3	2" x 10" x 30"
Stair Treads	4	$\frac{5}{4}$ x 6" x $47\frac{1}{2}$"
Center Hex	1	$\frac{5}{4}$ x 6" x 6"
Decking	24	$\frac{5}{4}$ x 6" x 10'
Roof Framing		
Headers	6	2" x 4" x $54\frac{1}{4}$"
Cap Plates	6	2" x 4" x $52\frac{3}{4}$"
Key Block	1	6" x 6" x 8"
Rafters	6	2" x 6" x $81\frac{3}{4}$"
A/C Exterior-Grade Plywood Sheathing	8	$\frac{3}{4}$" x 4' x 8'
15-lb. Roofing Felt		100 sq. ft.
Composite Shingles		100 sq. ft.
Metal Drip Edge	3	10' lengths
Composite Hip and Ridge Shingles		Needed to cover approximately 40'

Name	Qty.	Size
Railing		
Rails	10	2" x 4" x $54\frac{1}{4}$"
Balusters	40	2" x 2" x 30"
Nails and Fasteners		
Nails		
20d Common		
16d Common		
10d Common		
8d Common		
Roofing		
Post Anchors	7	
Joist Hangers	4	Single 8" (for beams)
	16	Single 6" (for joists)
	2	Double 8" (for girder)
Roof-Peak Gazebo Ties	1 set	
Plate-Rafter Gazebo Ties	6	
Stair Angles	4	
Framing Angles	3 for stringers	
Premixed Concrete		As required to set post and step footings below frost line

DECK FRAMING PLAN

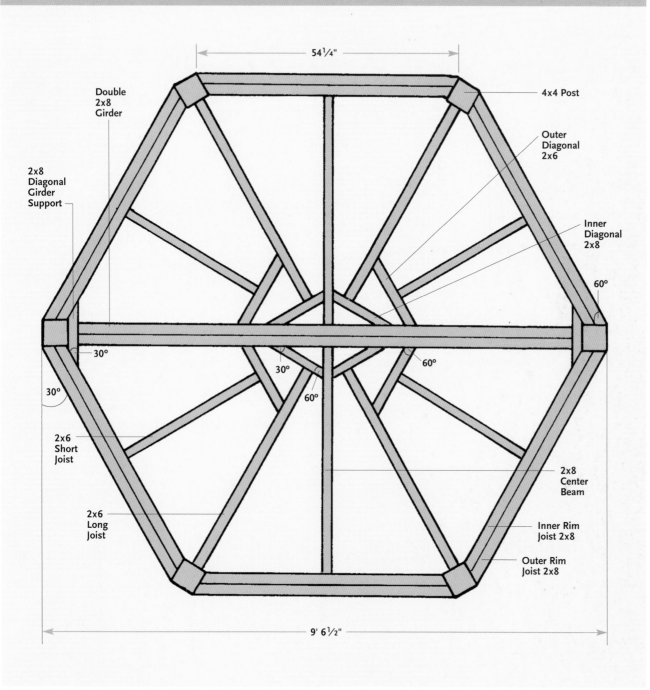

54¼"

Double
2x8
Girder

4x4 Post

Outer
Diagonal
2x6

2x8
Diagonal
Girder
Support

Inner
Diagonal
2x8

60°

30°

30°

60°

30°

60°

2x6
Short
Joist

60°

2x8
Center
Beam

2x6
Long
Joist

Inner Rim
Joist 2x8

Outer Rim
Joist 2x8

9' 6½"

CONSTRUCT THE DECK

A big job is made up of several smaller ones. It's only when you think of this gazebo as more than one project that it begins to make sense. Look at the floor framing: it's intricate and confusing until you realize that it's based on joists running from the posts to the center of the building. The spider's web in the middle is only there to avoid some very fancy, very crowded joinery. Try to understand the job piece by piece—stairs, floor, posts, and roof. Once you do, you may decide it's not for you. But you will have learned a lot of carpentry in the process.

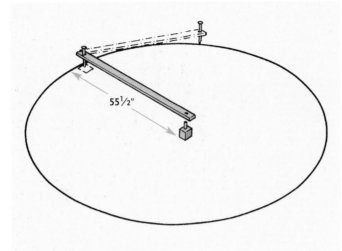

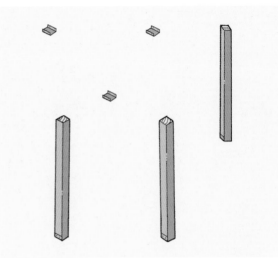

1 LAY OUT POSTS. Level the site. Select the center of the gazebo, and drive a stake into the ground. Drive a nail into the top of the stake, letting the head protrude an inch or so. Cut a piece of straight lumber about 5 ft. long, and drill two holes 55½ in. apart on center. Fit one of the holes over the nail in the stake, and scribe a circle on the ground by rotating this measuring stick. Lay out six equidistant points along the circle, 55½ in. apart, to locate the center of the posts.

2 SET POSTS. Check with your local building department about proper footing depth, and adjust the post length as needed. Dig holes for the footings at the center and six perimeter locations. Pour the concrete footing in the center posthole, and position the bolt for the adjustable post anchor. Pour the remaining footings, and place the anchor bolts. After the concrete sets, slip the post base anchor over the bolt and install the washer and nut. Turn the anchor to the required 30-deg. angle between posts. When the concrete has set and the post bases are properly positioned, nail the post on the base, using heavy-duty galvanized post-hanger nails.

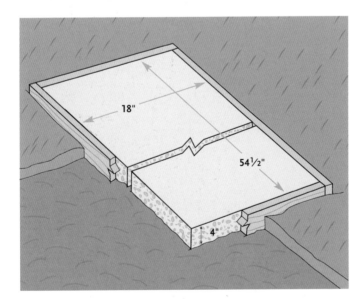

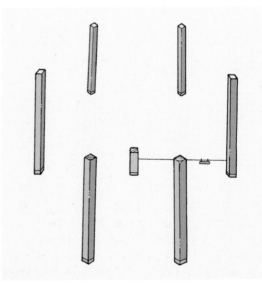

3 PLACE STEP FOOTING. Pour a 4-in.-thick concrete slab where the gazebo stairs will meet the ground. Make the slab 18 x 54½ in., with the front edge 26 in. out from the edge of the deck.

4 ESTABLISH DECK HEIGHT. The finished deck is 16 in. above grade, but the deck boards are 1 in. thick, so the top of the joists will be 15 in. from the ground. Mark this height on one of the posts, and use a line level to transfer this dimension to all other posts.

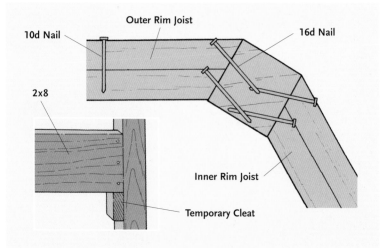

5 INSTALL RIM JOISTS. All the joists are mitered to fit between the posts. Measure and cut the joists to fit with a 60-deg. angle on each end. Then measure down $7\frac{1}{4}$ in. from the marks you made in Step 4, and lay out the bottom of the rim joists on each outer post. Put the top of a temporary cleat along each line and nail in place. Set the inner rim joists on the cleats. Turn the post anchor to match the angle on the end of the joists, and then tighten the anchor. Check for level, and tack the joists in position. Double-check for level, and nail each to the posts with three 16d nails. Repeat to install the outer joists, and then join the joists together with 10d nails every 12 in.

6 TRIM CENTER POST. Cut the center 4x4 post to final height using a portable circular saw. The top of the post is at the same height as the bottom of the rim joists and main girder beam.

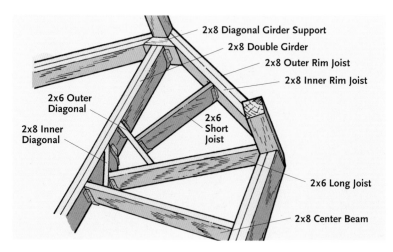

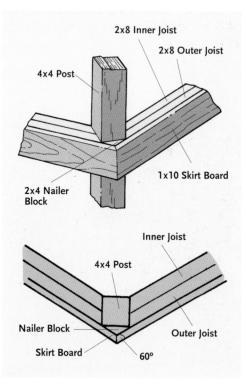

7 INSTALL FLOOR FRAMING. Cut 30-deg. miters in the ends of the diagonal girder supports so that they fit snugly against the posts and rim joists. Nail in place with 20d nails. Nail a metal double-hanger to the girder supports, and nail the girders in their hangers. Nail the girders together with 10d nails. Toenail them to the center post. Attach joist hangers for the beams at the midpoint of the girder and midway across the inner rims. Miter and install 11-in. inner diagonals between the girder and the beams. Nail joist hangers to the posts that support joists. Cut the long joists to fit, and use them to position the hangers on the inside diagonals. Nail hangers and joists in place. Miter the outer diagonals to fit, and nail them in place. Cut the short joists to fit, and nail in place.

8 INSTALL SKIRT BOARDS. Measure and cut 1x10 skirt boards to fit over the outer rim joists. Cut the ends at 60-deg. angles to meet at the middle of the outside face of the posts. Cut a small scrap of 2x4 to fit between the skirt and post to serve as a nailer block. Don't put a skirt board between posts where the stairs will be installed.

149

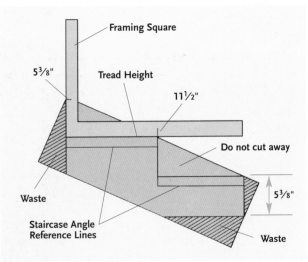

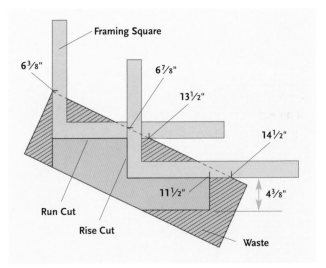

9 LAY OUT END STRINGERS. **Cut the end stringers from two 30-in.-long 2x10s.** Place a framing square on a stringer as shown so that the 5³⁄₈-in. mark on the outside of the square's tongue and the 11¹⁄₂-in. measurement on the outside of the square's blade both align with the top edge of the stringer, and trace along the square. Extend the rise line to the bottom of the stringer. Lay out the lower step the same way; then measure down 1 in. from each of the treads, and draw layout lines for the stair angles. Make cuts at the back, front, and bottom of the stringer. Do not cut notches for the stairs.

10 LAY OUT MIDDLE STRINGER. **You will need a middle stringer to support the tread.** Mark out the top step with the tongue of the square at 6³⁄₈ in. and the blade at 13¹⁄₂ in. For the second step, put the tongue at 6⁷⁄₈ in. and the blade at 14¹⁄₂ in. To lay out the bottom rise, start from the 11¹⁄₂-in. mark on the blade and draw a 4³⁄₈-in.-long perpendicular line as shown.

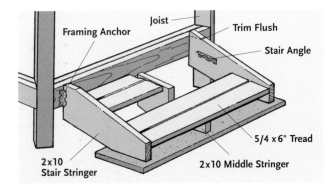

11 ASSEMBLE STAIRS. **Nail the stair angles to the stringers with heavy-duty joist-hanger nails.** Attach the stringers to the joist header with framing anchors, spacing them 47¹⁄₂ in. apart and equidistant from the posts. Nail the middle stringer to the front beam, centering it between the two outer stringers. When the bottoms of the stringers sit flat on the concrete slab, the top points of the stringers will extend about 1 in. higher than the header joist and will get in the way later on. Cut the top of the stringers flush with the header, using a handsaw. Cut the treads 33 in. long. Attach the front tread pieces flush with the front of the stringers. Leave ¹⁄₂ in. of space between the front and back treads for drainage.

12 INSTALL DECKING. **Cut a hex piece from a 6 x 6-in. scrap of clear deck board.** Strike chalk lines centered along the length of each joist that runs to a post. Make a mark on each line 2³⁄₄ in. from where they intersect. Align the center hex with these marks. Add blocking as needed, and nail the center hex piece in place. Use it as a guide to measure and cut the first row of decking. End joints should fall along the chalk lines that run at angles from the center hex. Nail the decking to the joists, driving two 8d nails through the boards and into each joist. Put a 10d nail temporarily between boards to space them. Trim the last row of decking so it extends ³⁄₄ in. or so beyond the skirt board. Notch the last row of deck boards to fit around the posts.

FRAME THE ROOF

The six-sided gazebo has six identical common rafters that meet the posts at 90-degree angles. The rafters have a rise of 9 inches per 12 inches of run. If you are not an experienced roof builder, read "Roofs" on page 96 to learn about laying out rafters and cutting plumb and bird's-mouth cuts. This is important if your gazebo is not exactly the same size as the one described. You can avoid these cuts by using special peak and plate ties designed for roofs on six-sided gazebos. The instructions below explain how to frame the roof with and without this hardware.

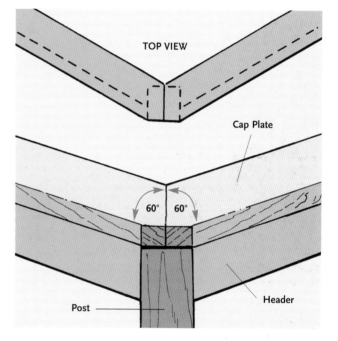

TOP VIEW

Cap Plate

60° 60°

Post

Header

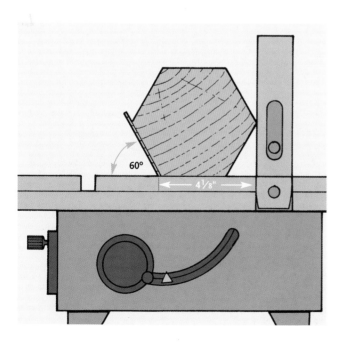

1 CUT POSTS. Mark one of the posts 78 in. from the deck floor. Use a line level or carpenter's level to transfer this height to the other five posts. Cut the posts.

60°

4⅛"

2 INSTALL ROOF HEADERS. Cut the 2x4 headers to the same length as you cut the outer rim joists, with the same 60-deg. angle on each end. Nail the headers to the posts with 10d nails. Make sure the tops of the headers are level with the post tops. If you will be using peak and plate ties, cut the cap plates now so they meet each other over the posts with 60-deg. miters on each end. Make sure the sides of the plates are flush with the faces of the headers. Nail the plates to the headers with 10d nails. The mitered corners of the plates will overlap the posts a little. You'll need to cut the ends flush with the posts to allow for the plate ties. If you will not be using plate and peak ties, do not cut or install the top plates yet.

3 MAKE THE KEY BLOCK. Make the block only if you are not using peak ties. Make the block on the table saw from a 20-in.-long 6x6. Set the fence 4⅛ in. from the blade, and tilt the blade to 60 deg. When you've cut the sides, cut the block so that it's 8 in. long.

4 CUT RAFTERS. If you use peak and plate ties, the roof will be a few inches higher than if you don't, but the rafter length and tail plumb cuts will be the same. To lay out the tail plumb cuts, align the top edge of the rafter to the 9-in. mark on the inside of the framing square tongue. Align the 12-in. mark on the inside of the square's blade to the top edge of the rafter. If you are not using ties, slide the square up 12 in. to lay out the bird's-mouth plumb cut. Now lay out a 3 1/2-in. seat cut perpendicular to the plumb cut as shown. Flip the square over to lay out the peak plumb cut. Align the 12-in. mark on the outside of the blade and the 9-in. mark on the outside of the tongue with the top of the rafter. Cut the rafters to size.

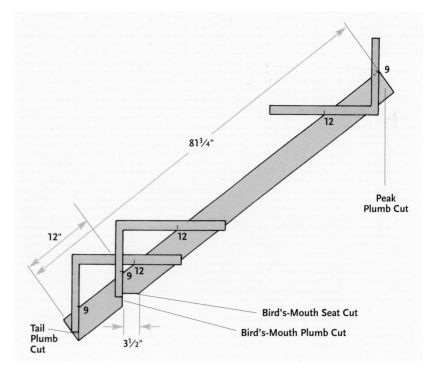

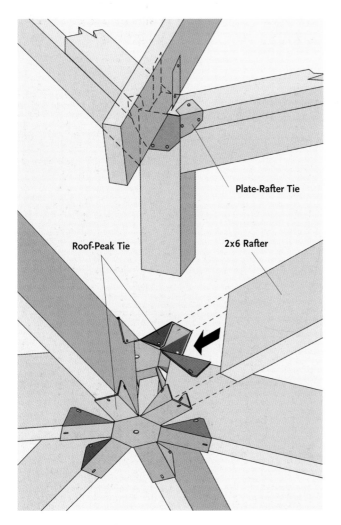

5 INSTALL RAFTERS. If you are using plate ties, nail them to the cap plates and posts as shown at left, using the heavy-duty galvanized hanger nails. The peak ties consist of a top plate and a bottom plate that hold the rafters as shown. Bend the legs of the plates down to accommodate the roof pitch. If you are not using ties, nail two opposing rafters to the key block, above. Then, with a helper, lift the assembly onto the header with the bird's-mouths seated on top of opposing posts. Toenail the rafters to the posts with 8d nails. Assemble the remaining rafters.

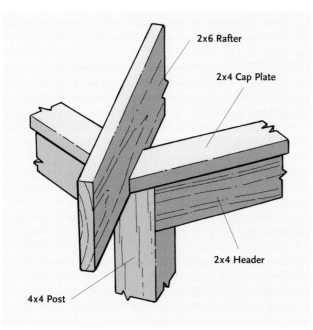

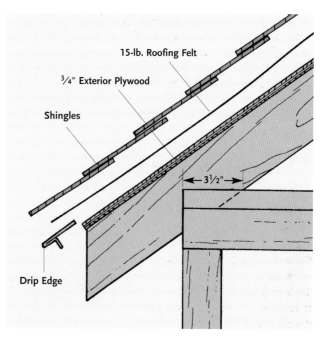

6 INSTALL THE CAP PLATES. **If you are not using ties, install the cap plates. Measure and cut them with a 30-deg. angle at each end to fit snugly between rafters. Nail the cap plates to the headers with 10d nails. Use 8d nails to toenail the cap plates to the rafters.**

7 COMPLETE THE ROOF. **Cut the plywood triangles to size, and install them over the rafters using 8d common nails spaced 12 in. apart. Complete the shingling. Instructions for installing shingles and other roofing alternatives are in "Roofs" on page 96.**

● INSTALL THE RAILING

Build and install the railing, using 2x4 top and bottom rails with equally spaced 2x2 balusters. Lay out the top rail height 33 inches above the deck. Measure and cut each top and bottom rail section separately to ensure a snug fit between the posts. Cut the balusters to 27 inches long and spaced 5 inches on center. Miter the ends of the rails at 30 degrees. Attach the balusters (eight per section) to the rails. Nail through the bottom rail into the balusters, but carefully toenail the top of the balusters to the top rail from the underside so there are no exposed nailheads on the top rail. Attach the assembled section to the posts, using railing brackets or 2x4 cleats, or by toenailing with 10d nails.

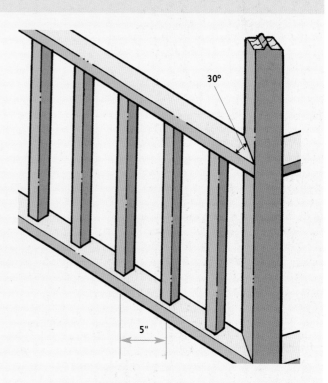

153

11 eight-sided gazebo

T his eight-sided gazebo gets a special touch of elegance from its high, gracefully curved roof. The roof is created with curved rafters sheathed with slats. Of course, you can simplify construction by using straight rafters instead. As with any project, careful planning and precise layout are essential, so take your time. This eight-sided building will require some fairly complex cutting and joinery; time invested now will eliminate the need to do any time-consuming alterations later.

Don't let the complexity of the octagonal shape discourage you. The layout and foundation work required for this project are basically the same as in the less complex projects. You can incorporate any of the custom options into this project. Just be sure you understand how these changes could affect the structure.

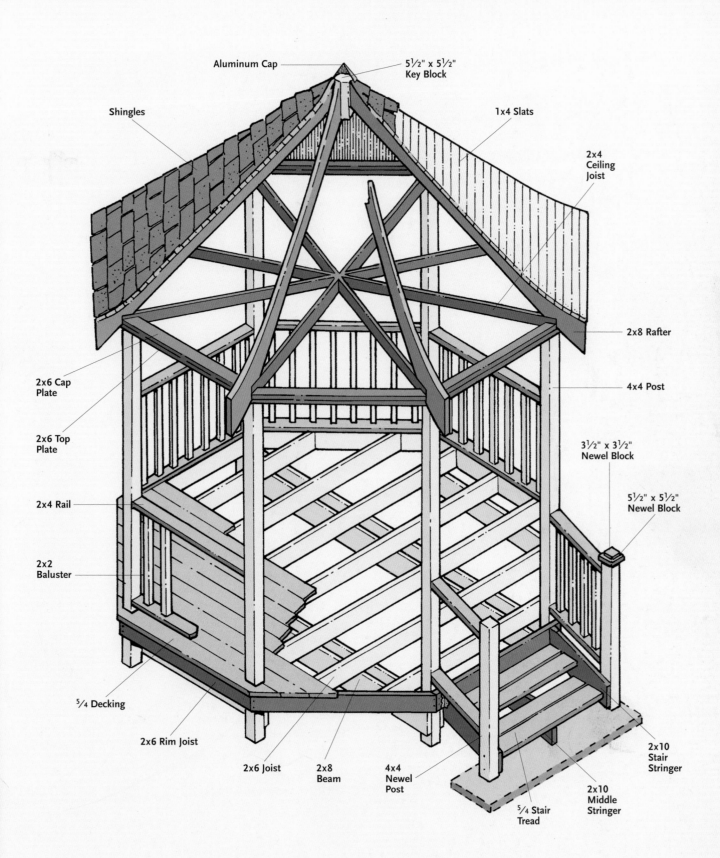

Aluminum Cap

5½" x 5½" Key Block

Shingles

1x4 Slats

2x4 Ceiling Joist

2x8 Rafter

2x6 Cap Plate

4x4 Post

2x6 Top Plate

3½" x 3½" Newel Block

5½" x 5½" Newel Block

2x4 Rail

2x2 Baluster

⁵/₄ Decking

2x6 Rim Joist

2x6 Joist

2x8 Beam

4x4 Newel Post

⁵/₄ Stair Tread

2x10 Middle Stringer

2x10 Stair Stringer

OVERALL VIEW

EIGHT-SIDED GAZEBO

Name	Qty.	Size
Gazebo Deck Framing		
Roof Posts	8	4" x 4" x 12'
Long Beams	4	2" x 8" x 93"
Short Beams	2	2" x 8" x 45$\frac{3}{4}$"
Square-End Rim Joists	4	2" x 6" x 42$\frac{3}{4}$"
Decking Cleats	4	2" x 6" x 5"
Decking Cleats	4	2" x 6" x 4$\frac{3}{8}$"
Mitered Rim Joists	4	2" x 6" x 37$\frac{11}{16}$"
Long Joists	3	2" x 6" x 93"
Short Joists	2	2" x 6" x 51$\frac{1}{2}$"
Mid-Length Joists	2	2" x 6" x 78$\frac{1}{8}$"
Stair Stringers	3	2" x 10" x 30"
Stair Treads	4	$\frac{5}{4}$ x 6" x 32$\frac{3}{4}$"
Newel Posts	2	4" x 4" x 41$\frac{1}{4}$"
Stair Rails	4	2" x 4" x 24$\frac{3}{4}$"
Large Newel Block	2	1$\frac{1}{2}$" x 5$\frac{1}{2}$" x 5$\frac{1}{2}$"
Small Newel Block	2	1$\frac{1}{2}$" x 3$\frac{1}{2}$" x 3$\frac{1}{2}$"
Stair Balusters	8	2" x 2" x 27$\frac{5}{8}$"
Decking	14	$\frac{5}{4}$ x 6" x 10'
Roof Framing		
Top Plates	4	2" x 6" x 39$\frac{3}{4}$"
Top Plates	4	2" x 6" x 37$\frac{11}{16}$"
Ceiling Joists	2	2" x 4" x 8' 5$\frac{1}{8}$"
Ceiling Joists	2	2" x 4" x 49$\frac{13}{16}$"
Ceiling Joists	2	2" x 4" x 49$\frac{1}{2}$"
Cap Plates	4	2" x 6" x 39$\frac{3}{4}$"
Cap Plates	4	2" x 6" x 37$\frac{11}{16}$"
Key Block	1	5$\frac{1}{2}$" x 5$\frac{1}{2}$" x 12"
Rafters	8	2" x 8" x 8' 2$\frac{5}{8}$"
Roof Slats	32	1" x 4" x 10'
15-lb. Roofing Felt		100 sq. ft.

Name	Qty.	Size
Roof Framing (continued)		
Metal Drip Edge	4	8' lengths
Composite or Wood Shingles		100 sq. ft.
Composite Hip and Ridge Shingles		Needed to cover approx. 60'
Aluminum Cap	1	
Railing		
Square-End Rails	6	2" x 4" x 32$\frac{3}{4}$"
Mitered Rails	8	2" x 4" x 37$\frac{11}{16}$"
Balusters	46	2" x 2" x 27"
Nails and Fasteners		
Metal Post Anchors	8	
Nails		
16d Common		
10d Common		
8d Common		
6d Common		
8d Galvanized Finishing		
Roofing		
Carriage Bolts	8	$\frac{3}{8}$" x 8"
Lag Screws	8	$\frac{3}{8}$" x 3"
3" Galvanized Deck Screws		
2$\frac{1}{2}$" Galvanized Deck Screws		
Stair Angles	4	
Framing Angles	2 for stringers	
Premixed Concrete		As required to set post and step footings below frost line

FRAMING PLAN

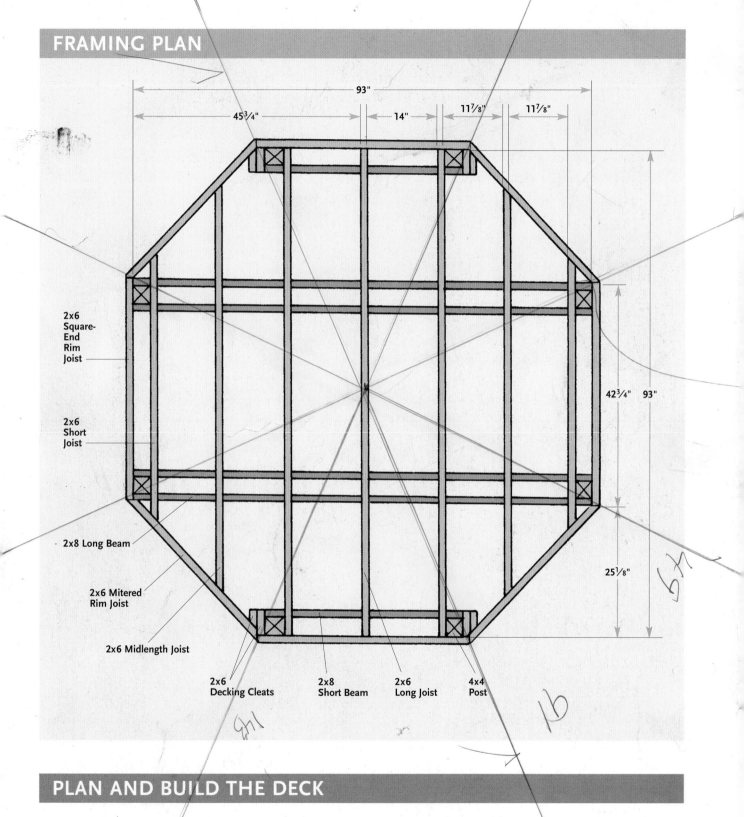

93"

45³⁄₄" **14"** **11⁷⁄₈"** **11⁷⁄₈"**

2x6
Square-
End
Rim
Joist

2x6
Short
Joist

2x8 Long Beam

2x6 Mitered
Rim Joist

2x6 Midlength Joist

2x6
Decking Cleats

2x8
Short Beam

2x6
Long Joist

4x4
Post

42³⁄₄" 93"

25¹⁄₈"

PLAN AND BUILD THE DECK

This gazebo is supported by 2x8 beams bolted to 4x4 posts. The beams support 2x6 rafters, which are covered with ⁵⁄₄ decking boards. The deck is 8 feet across. The materials list and the illustrations for this project provide more detail and specific lengths for each part. They would be accurate if all lumber were perfect and if you managed to locate all the posts with pinpoint accuracy. But the real world isn't like that, so measure as you go, and adjust as necessary.

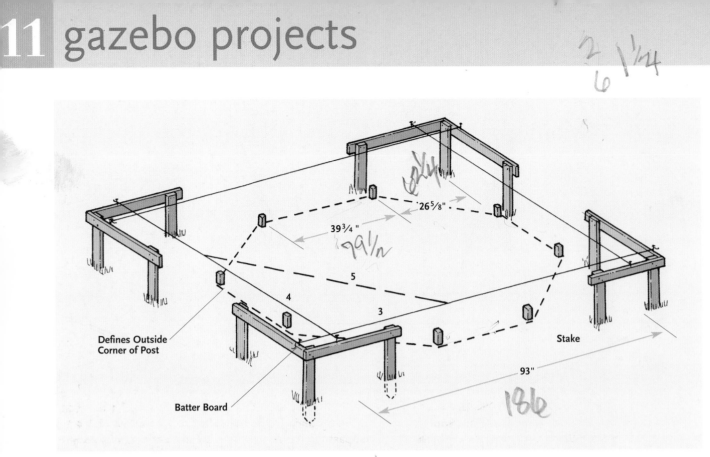

Defines Outside Corner of Post

Batter Board

26⁵⁄₈"

39³⁄₄"

5

4

3

Stake

93"

1 LAY OUT POSTS. Construct batter boards with strings to lay out a 93-in. square. See "Laying Out the Site" on page 84 for instructions. Use a felt-tipped pen to mark the string 26⁵⁄₈ in. from each corner. From these points, locate the center of each post. This will be the center of your postholes.

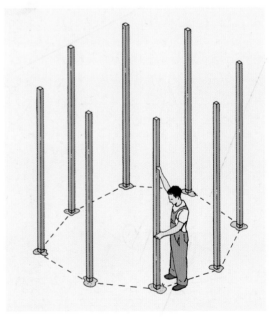

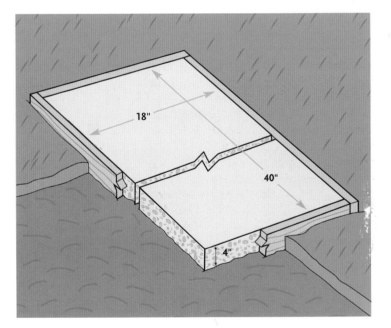

18"

40"

4"

2 INSTALL POSTS. Pour footings to the depth required by the building department, adjusting post length as needed. Install anchor bolts as described in "Techniques" on page 72. Install the anchor hardware and posts when the concrete has set.

3 PLACE STEP FOOTING. Pour a 4-in.-thick concrete slab where the gazebo stairs will meet the ground. (See "Laying the Groundwork" on page 88.) Make the slab 18 x 40 in., with the front edge 26 in. from the outside rim joist.

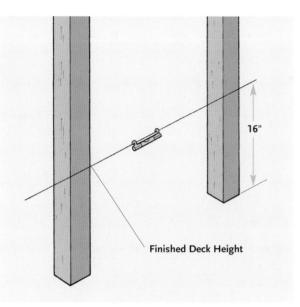

Finished Deck Height

16"

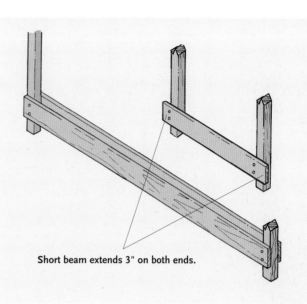

Short beam extends 3" on both ends.

4 ESTABLISH DECK HEIGHT. **Mark the 16-in. finished deck height on one of the posts, and transfer this dimension to all other posts using a line level or water level. Once the deck height is marked, measure down 1 in., and draw a line marking the top of each joist. Measure down an additional 5½ in., and draw a line marking the top of the beams.**

5 INSTALL BEAMS. **The joists are supported by four long beams and two short beams. The short beams extend 3 in. past the posts on each end. Cut these beams to length. Through-bolt the long beams to the posts with two ⅜ x 8-in. carriage bolts at each post location. Attach the two short beams to the inside of the posts with two ⅜ x 3-in. lag screws into each post.**

6 INSTALL JOISTS. **Measure and cut the square-end rim joists, and attach them to the posts with 16d nails. Measure and cut the decking cleats with a 45-deg. miter on the end of the outer cleats, as shown in the drawing. Place the cleats on the short beams, and nail them to the posts and the short beam. Measure and cut the mitered rim joists, and attach them to the ends of the square-end rim joists with two 8d nails at each connection. Measure and cut the three long joists. Place them across the long and short beams. Attach the two outer long joists to the inside of the posts and to the square rim joists with 16d nails. Center the middle long joist between the first two, and nail it to the rim joists. Toenail the long joists to the beams with one 8d nail on each side of each connection. Measure and cut the two short joists with 45-deg. miters at each end. Nail the short joists to the posts and to the mitered rim joists. Measure and cut the midlength joists to fit between the mitered rim joists, centered between the short joists and long joists. Nail the mitered ends of the midlength joists to the rim joists, and toenail them to the long beams.**

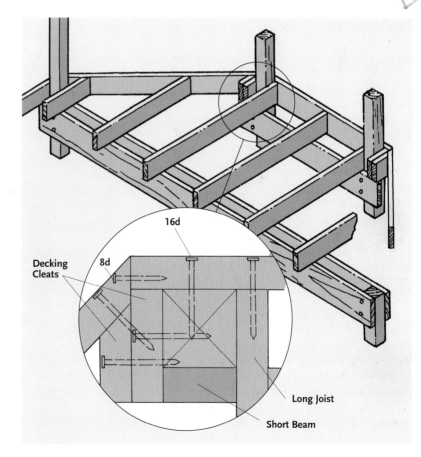

16d

8d

Decking Cleats

Long Joist

Short Beam

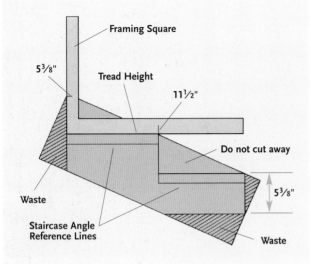

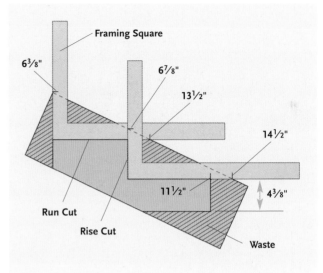

7 **LAY OUT END STRINGERS.** The stair has a rise of 5³⁄₈ in. and a run of 11¹⁄₂ in. Start with two pieces of 2x10, each about 30 in. long. Place a framing square on a stringer as illustrated, and trace around the square. Extend the rise line to the bottom of the stringer to lay out the upper end of the stringer. Move the square down to lay out the second step, as shown in the drawing. Use the square to lay out the cuts for the front and bottom of the stringers. Measure down 1 in. from the top of the treads, and draw layout lines for the stair angles. Lay out the other end stringer. Cut away the waste on both stringers.

8 **LAY OUT MIDDLE STRINGER.** The middle stringer keeps the tread from flexing. It's designed so that the treads overhang the risers by 1 in. Use the framing square to lay out the rise and run cuts and the bottom cut, positioning it as shown. For the second step, put the tongue at 6⁷⁄₈ in. and the blade at 14¹⁄₂ in. To lay out the bottom rise, start from the 11¹⁄₂-in. mark on the blade and draw a 4³⁄₈-in.-long perpendicular line as shown in the illustration. Cut along the layout lines using a circular saw, stopping when the blade reaches another layout line. Finish cutting using a handsaw.

9 **ASSEMBLE STAIRS.** Nail metal stair angles to the stringers with heavy-duty nails known as "hanger nails." Working with the stringers upside down, nail the stair angles to the bottom of the treads. Attach the front tread pieces flush with the front of the stringers. Leave ¹⁄₂ in. of space between the front and back tread pieces to improve drainage. Nail the middle stringer to one of the square-end joists, centering it between posts. Put the stair assembly in place over the middle stringer. Attach it to the front rim joist with framing anchors. Nail the treads to the middle stringer with two 8d nails at each connection. When the bottom of the stringer sits flat on the concrete slab, the top point of the stringer should extend about 1 in. above the header joist. The decking will overhang the header slightly. To allow for this, use a handsaw to cut the top of the stringer flush with the header after you install the stringers. Cut the two newel posts 41¹⁄₄ in. long. Attach them to the bottom of the stringers with two 16d nails at each side connection. Nail through the stringers into the posts.

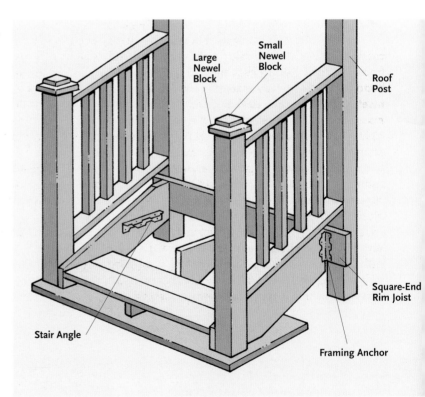

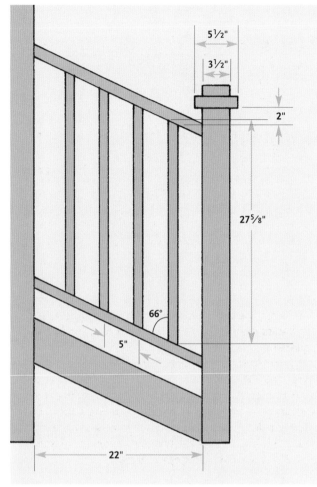

10 ASSEMBLE STAIR RAILS. Mark the front roof posts 34$\frac{1}{4}$ in. from the top of the rim joist, indicating the top of the top rails. Make another mark 5$\frac{3}{4}$ in. from the top of the rim joist, indicating the top of the bottom rails. Now mark where the tops of the rails will meet the newel posts, 10$\frac{3}{4}$ in. from the ground and 2 in. from the top of the post. Cut the four stair rails to about 30 in. long; align the rails to the marks; and scribe the angle cuts at each end. Make the cuts. Screw the rails to the posts with two 3-in. galvanized deck screws at each connection. Screw the small newel block on top of the large newel block with two 3-in. deck screws. Toenail the blocks to the newel post top with 8d galvanized finishing nails. Cut the eight 2 x 2-in. balusters to 27$\frac{5}{8}$ in. long with 66-deg. angles on each end. Attach the balusters with 3-in. galvanized deck screws through the bottom rails, spacing the balusters 5 in. apart on center, as shown. Toe-screw the balusters into the top rails.

11 INSTALL DECKING. Install $\frac{5}{4}$ x 6-in. deck boards perpendicular to the joists, using two 8d nails at each joist location. Position the first deck board so that its side overhangs a rim joist by $\frac{1}{2}$ in. Leave it a couple of inches long on each end; you'll trim the deck boards to length after all are in place. Use a 10d nail as a gauge to space the deck boards. When you get within a few boards of the opposite side, check the remaining distance. You may be able to adjust your spacing slightly to avoid ripping the last board to width. If you do have to rip the last board, make sure it remains wide enough to screw or nail it down without splitting. Snap a line around the perimeter of the deck, leaving the $\frac{1}{2}$-in. overhang. Cut the boards.

FRAME THE ROOF

1 **CUT POSTS. Measure** up one post 78 in. from the deck floor; mark it. Use a line level to transfer this height to the other posts. Mark and cut the posts at the line.

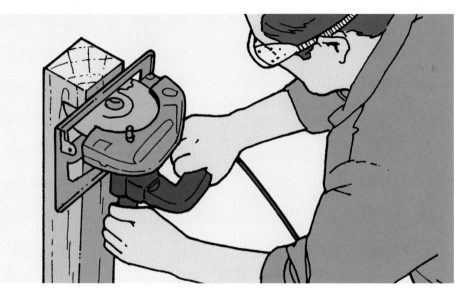

2 **INSTALL TOP PLATES.** As shown in the drawings, the top plates are two different lengths, are mitered at 67$\frac{1}{2}$ deg., and are flush with the outside corner of each post. Measure between the outside corners at the tops of your posts; your distances could be different than the dimensions in the drawings and in the materials list on page 156. Cut the top plates with opposing 67$\frac{1}{2}$-deg. angles on each end to meet over the posts. Nail the top plates in place with 16d nails.

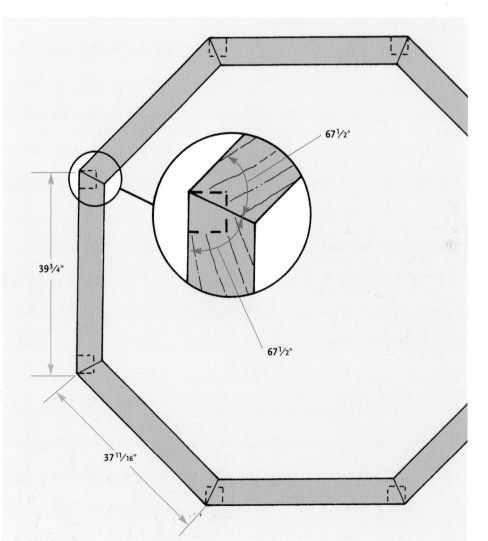

39$\frac{3}{4}$"

37$\frac{11}{16}$"

67$\frac{1}{2}$°

67$\frac{1}{2}$°

3 INSTALL CEILING JOISTS. Two long ceiling joists span the width of the gazebo. Measure from the outside corners of opposing posts to get the joist length. Make a 1½-in.-wide by 1¾-in.-deep notch in the center of each, so they form a lap joint as shown. Toenail the joists to the posts with 8d nails. Shorter joists meet the installed joists with 45-deg. bevels on both sides of the ends. Toenail these joists into the long joists and the top plates with 8d nails. Cut cap plates to fit between the ceiling joists. Fasten them to the top plates with 10d nails, and toenail them to the ceiling joists with 8d nails.

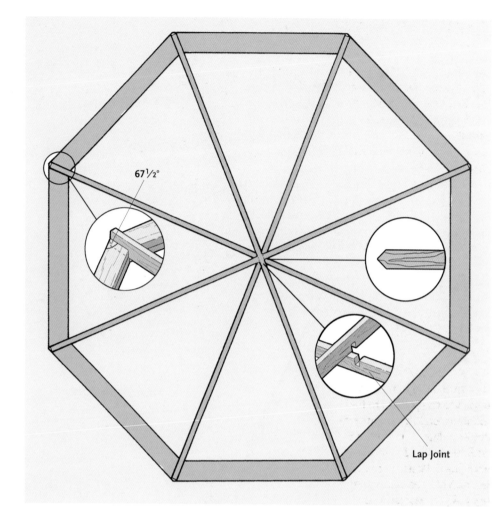

67½°

Lap Joint

4 MAKE THE KEY BLOCK. At the peak of the roof, the rafters meet an eight-sided key block made from a 12-in.-long piece of 6x6. Cut the block on the table saw, using a 15- to 20-in. piece for safety. Set the rip fence 3⅞ in. from the blade. Set the blade about 3 in. high and tilt it to 45 deg. Remove the four corners, and then cut it to length.

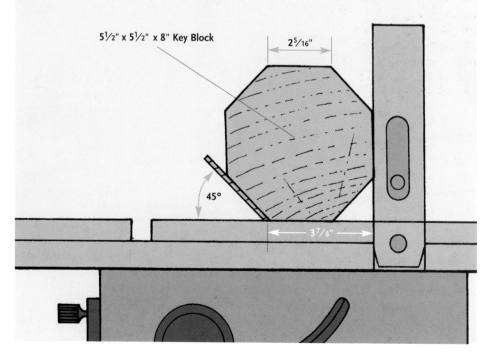

5½" x 5½" x 8" Key Block

2⁵⁄₁₆"

45°

3⁷⁄₈"

5 MAKE PATTERN RAFTER. The eight curved rafters have a rise of 15 in. per 12 in. of run. If the perimeter of your gazebo came out exactly as planned, use the rafter dimensions shown in the drawing. If not, see "Roofs" on page 96 for information on determining rafter length. Then make a pattern rafter from a 10-ft.-long 2 x 8. Lay out and cut the bird's-mouth and plumb cuts before laying out the curve. Begin by aligning the 15-in. mark on the framing square blade and the 12-in. mark on the tongue with the top of the rafter as shown. Mark the tail plumb cut along the blade. Slide the square 12 in. up the rafter to lay out the bird's-mouth plumb cut. The bird's-mouth seat cut is a 2³⁄₄-in. line square to the plumb cut. To lay out the peak cut, place the framing square on the rafter as shown. Mark the peak cut on the inside of the blade. Make the cuts.

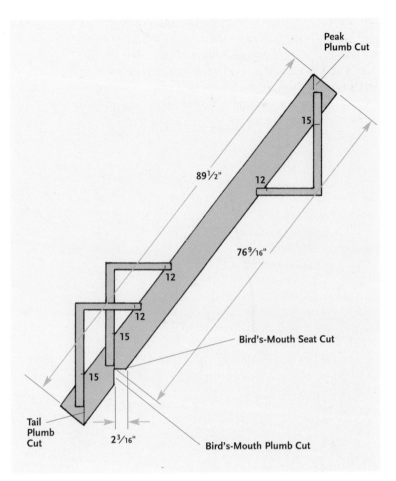

6 CUT RAFTER CURVES. Lay out the rafter curves using a ¹⁄₄-in.-thick batten of clear wood cut from a piece of 2-by lumber. Drive seven 4d finishing nails halfway into the pattern rafter at the points shown in the drawing. All distances are measured square with the top of the rafter. Bend the batten around the center nail as shown in the drawing. Draw a line along the length of the batten on the side closest to the top of the rafter. Remove the batten and nails. Cut the curve using a saber saw. Use this rafter to lay out the remaining rafters.

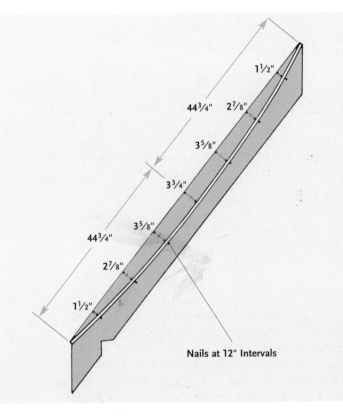

7 INSTALL RAFTERS. Toenail two rafters to opposing sides of the key block. With a helper, position the assembly on the ceiling joists. Toenail the rafters through their bird's mouths into the top of the ceiling joists with 8d nails. Put the other rafters in position one at a time, toenailing them to the key block and joists.

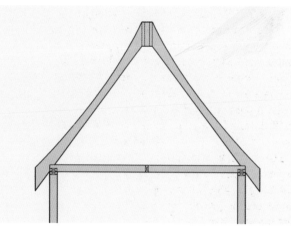

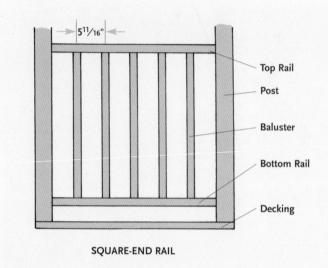

SQUARE-END RAIL

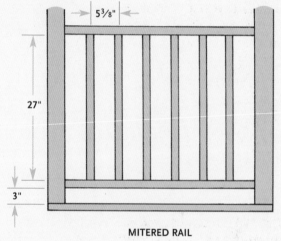

MITERED RAIL

8 INSTALL RAILINGS. Three of the rail assemblies meet the posts squarely, and four meet the posts with 45-deg. miters. The deck railings are assembled and installed in the same way as the stair railings except: (1) the balusters are cut square at the end and (2) the deck balusters are spaced $5^{11}/_{16}$ in. on center for the square-end rails and $5^{3}/_{8}$ in. on center for the mitered rails.

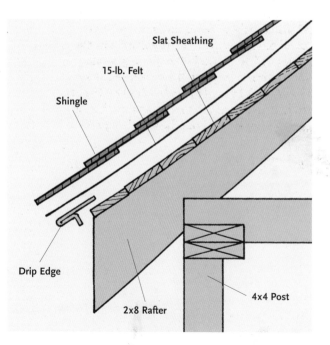

9 COMPLETE THE ROOF. The roof is sheathed with 1x4 slats nailed to the rafters with 6d nails. Size the slats for one section of the roof at a time, and fit them carefully in place. The roof isn't sturdy until all the slats are nailed in place, so do not climb on it until they are. Cover the slats with 15-lb. roofing felt, and shingle the roof. Detailed roofing options are given in "Roofs" on page 96.

12 pavilion with gable roof

This pavilion features a gable roof supported by four trusses, each of which is supported by two posts anchored to a concrete deck. As an alternative to the concrete deck, you can install the posts directly in the ground and use another deck scheme such as bricks set in sand.

The roof of this pavilion has a 6-in-12-in. slope, for a moderately steep roof that will shed rain and melting snow. As shown, it's made with plywood sheathing covered with composite (asphalt) shingles. It would also be a great opportunity to try your hand at a cedar shingle or shake roof, or you might just decide to opt for a more open lattice-style roof.

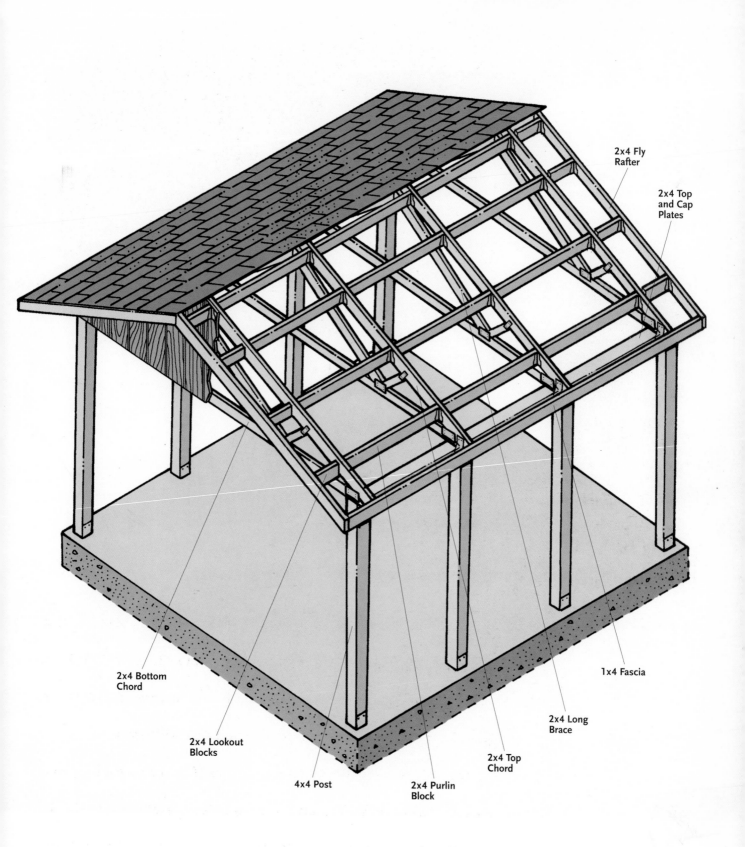

2x4 Fly Rafter

2x4 Top and Cap Plates

2x4 Bottom Chord

2x4 Lookout Blocks

4x4 Post

2x4 Purlin Block

2x4 Top Chord

2x4 Long Brace

1x4 Fascia

OVERALL VIEW

PAVILION WITH GABLE ROOF

cutting & materials

Name	Qty.	Size
Pavilion Framing		
Posts	8	4" x 4" x 8'
Top Plates	2	2" x 4" x 12'
Cap Plates	2	2" x 4" x 12'
Roof Framing		
Top Chords	8	2" x 4" x 94"
Bottom Chords	4	2" x 4" x 12"
Long Braces	8	2" x 4" x 41"
Short Braces	8	2" x 4" x $18\frac{3}{16}$"
Purlin Blocks	24	2" x 4" x 46"
Plywood Siding	2	$\frac{1}{2}$" x 4' x 8'
Fly Rafters	4	2" x 4" x $94\frac{11}{16}$"
Lookout Blocks	16	2" x 4" x 8"
Plywood Sheathing	7	$\frac{3}{4}$" x 4' x 8'
Fascia	2	1" x 4" x 13' 5"
15-lb. Roofing Felt		200 sq. ft.
Metal Drip Edge	3	8' lengths
Composite Shingles		200 sq. ft.

Name	Qty.	Size
Nails and Fasteners		
Nails		
16d Common		
12d Common		
10d Common		
8d Common		
6d Common		
Roofing		
Post Anchors	8	
Purlin Clips	80	
Storm or Hurricane Clips	8	
Truss Clip Packs	4	Sized for 2x4 truss system
Premixed Concrete		As required to set post footings below frost line
Ready-Mix Concrete		As required for 4"-thick slab

FRAMING PLAN—FRONT

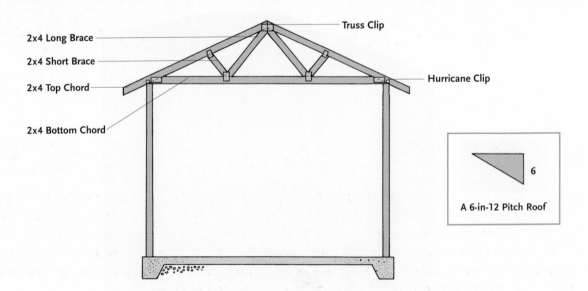

2x4 Long Brace
2x4 Short Brace
2x4 Top Chord
2x4 Bottom Chord
Truss Clip
Hurricane Clip

A 6-in-12 Pitch Roof

FRAMING PLAN—TOP

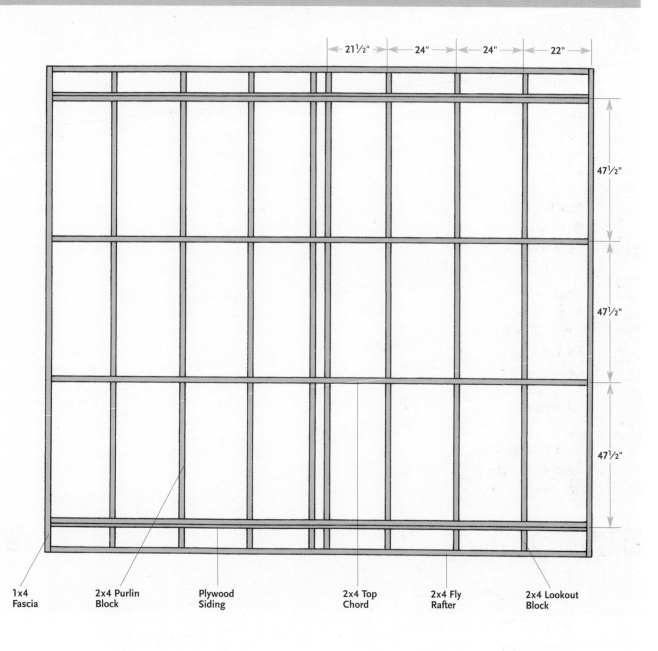

CONSTRUCT THE PAVILION

The roof is the central feature of this pavilion and presents the greatest building challenge. Simplify construction by assembling the trusses on the ground and then lifting them into position. If you like, you can save some work by ordering trusses from a lumberyard.

The trusses are fastened together with four rows of blocking, called purlins, on each pitch. The purlins also provide nailing surfaces at the edges and center of the plywood roof sheathing panels.

Study the project drawings for the pavilion until you understand all dimensions and the relationship of all major components.

1 CUT POSTS. If you build the pavilion on a slab, you can cut the posts to length before they are installed. Measure and cut each post to 93 in. You will have to cut from both sides to make it through the $3\frac{1}{2}$-in.-thick posts. If you opt not to use a slab, you will cut the posts in place, after installation.

2 LAY OUT AND INSTALL POSTS.

If you use a concrete slab foundation, the eight post anchors must be set in the wet concrete when the slab is placed and finished. To do this, construct batter boards at each corner. (See "Laying the Groundwork" on page 88.) Mark out the exact locations of the post anchor locations and slab borders on string lines strung between the batter boards. Use a plumb bob to transfer the points to the surface of the slab so the anchors can be placed in wet concrete with a minimum of shifting. If the posts will be set in the ground or anchored to individual footings, stake out locations using the 3-4-5 triangle method. (See "Laying Out the Site" on page 84.) When finished, the posts should stand 93 in. above grade. Check with your local building department on footing requirements.

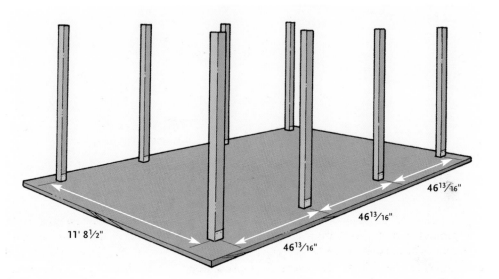

11' 8½"
46^{13}/$_{16}$"
46^{13}/$_{16}$"
46^{13}/$_{16}$"

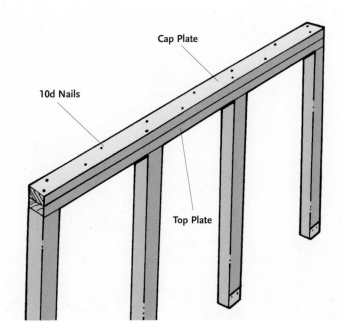

Cap Plate

10d Nails

Top Plate

3 INSTALL TOP AND CAP PLATES. Nail the top plates to the posts with 16d nails. Then nail the cap plate to the top plate with 10d nails.

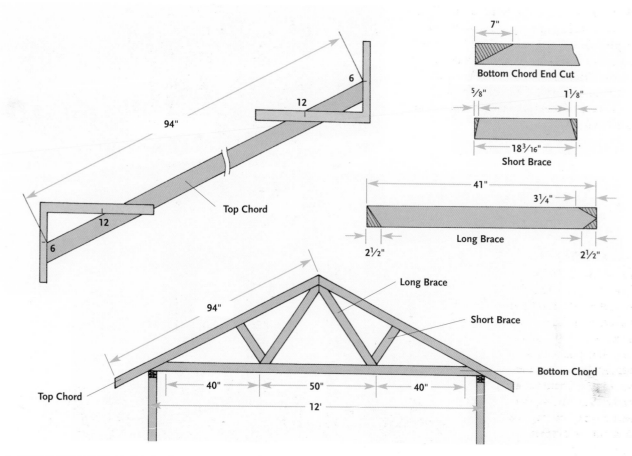

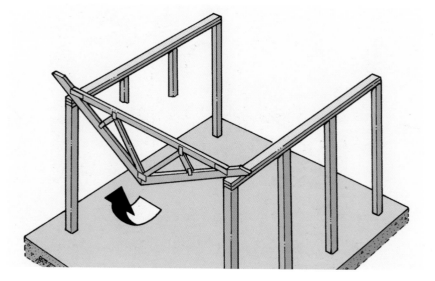

4 BUILD TRUSSES. Build the four trusses on the ground, and lift them into place one at a time. Start by cutting all the parts for one truss. Lay the pieces out on the slab to check for fit. Use these pieces as patterns to cut the parts for the remaining trusses. Use a framing square as shown to lay out the plumb cuts on both ends of the top chords. Align the 6-in. mark on the inside of the rafter square tongue and the 12-in. mark on the square's blade with the top of the chord. The drawing shows the measurements you'll need to cut the angles on the bottom chords and braces. Assemble the pieces using properly sized truss clips. Position a truss clip over the joint, and hammer the barbed tips into the wood. Nail through the clips as specified by the manufacturer. Clips must be installed on both sides of the truss at each joint.

5 RAISE TRUSSES. Enlist a helper or two for raising and securing the trusses. Have a ladder and worker on each side. Position the truss in between the headers at the post positions. The truss can hang peak-down until you are ready to swing it up into position.

6 FASTEN TRUSSES. Raise the end trusses so that they are plumb and flush to the outside of the end posts. You may need to brace the trusses in place before you can secure them to the cap plates and posts with hurricane clips or storm clips. Position the two middle trusses directly above the center of the middle posts.

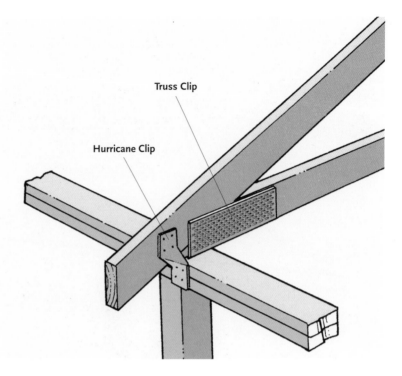

Truss Clip

Hurricane Clip

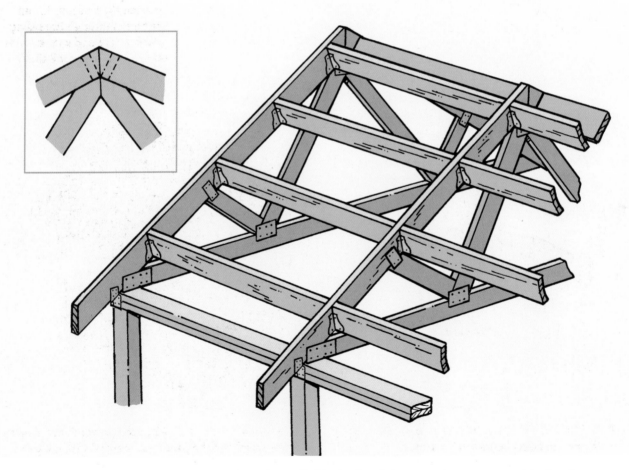

7 INSTALL PURLIN BLOCKS. Measure and cut the purlin blocks that fit between the trusses, positioning them as shown in the "Framing Plan" on page 169. Install the blocks using purlin clips, or toenail the blocking using 12d nails.

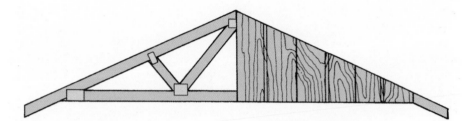

8 INSTALL GABLE PANELS. Size and cut the triangular gable panels from plywood siding such as Textured 1-11 (called T1-11). Fasten the panels to the end trusses with 6d nails.

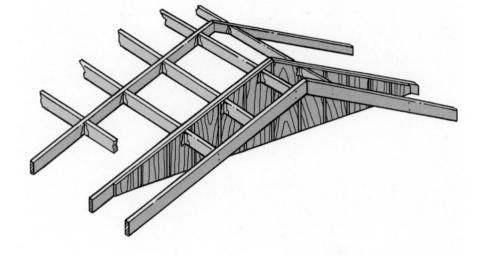

9 INSTALL LOOKOUTS. The lookouts are the pitched overhangs on the gable ends. Each consists of blocks and fly rafters. Make the fly rafters the same way as the truss top chords, but $^{11}/_{16}$ in. longer to cover the end of the fascia. Cut the lookout blocks to length, and use 12d nails to fasten to the fly rafters. Space the blocks to line up with the blocking between the trusses. Fasten the blocks through the siding panels to the end trusses with purlin clips, or toenail them in place.

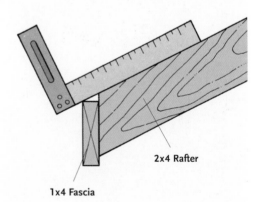

2x4 Rafter

1x4 Fascia

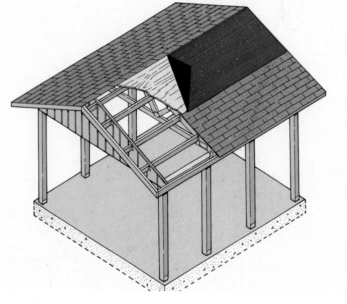

10 INSTALL FASCIA. Use 12d nails to fasten the fascia boards to the ends of the rafters. Use a square to position the fascia so that the sheathing can cover it.

11 INSTALL ROOF COVERING. Place the plywood roof sheathing so the lengths of the panels run parallel with the peak. Trim the sheets so all joints butt over a truss. Install the sheathing using 8d nails spaced 12 in. on center. Cover the roof with 15-lb. felt. Install metal drip edge and shingles.

13 freestanding pavilion

This pavilion is constructed using the standard post, beam, and joist design. The overall roof area is 14 x 16 feet. The floor is a concrete deck floor, with the posts attached to adjustable post bases set in the concrete. If you would like to use another type of floor treatment, such as brick set in sand or simply in grass, you can either set the posts into the ground or attach them to individual concrete footings. The brick-in-sand base can then be laid around the posts. See "Laying the Groundwork" on page 88 and "Customizing Options" on page 22 for details on setting posts and alternative floor treatments.

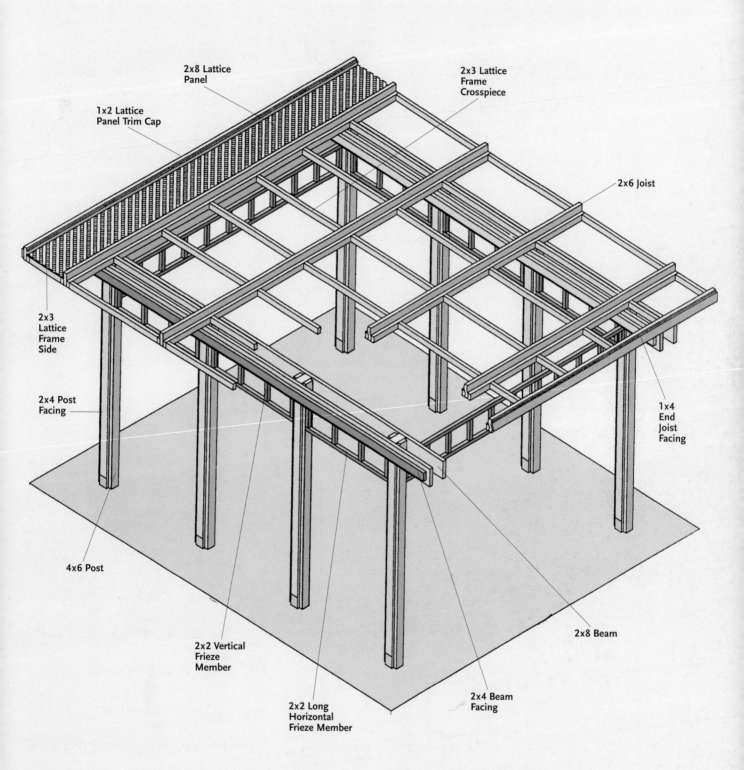

2x8 Lattice Panel

1x2 Lattice Panel Trim Cap

2x3 Lattice Frame Crosspiece

2x6 Joist

2x3 Lattice Frame Side

2x4 Post Facing

1x4 End Joist Facing

4x6 Post

2x2 Vertical Frieze Member

2x2 Long Horizontal Frieze Member

2x4 Beam Facing

2x8 Beam

FREESTANDING PAVILION

cutting & materials

Name	Qty.	Size
Pavilion Framing		
Posts, pad construction	8	4" x 6" x 8'
Posts, posthole construction	8	4" x 6" x 13'
Post Facing, pad construction	16	2" x 4" x 8'
Post Facing, posthole construction	16	2" x 4" x 13'
Beam Facing	4	2" x 4" x 15' 8"
Beams	4	2" x 8" x 16'
End-Joist Facing	2	1" x 4" x 14'
Joists	6	2" x 6" x 14'
Lattice Frame Sides	10	2" x 3" x 14'
Lattice Frame Crosspieces	24	2" x 3" x 45"
	16	2" x 3" x 16½"
Roof Lattice		
Lattice Panels	4	2' x 8'
	6	4' x 8'
Lattice Panel Trim Cap	10	1" x 2" x 14'
Frieze Members		
Long Horizontal	4	2" x 2" x 9' 6½"
Short Horizontal	12	2" x 2" x 43"
Rungs	46	2" x 2" x 9"

Name	Qty.	Size
Nails & Fasteners		
Post Anchors	8	4" x 6"
2¼" Galvanized Deck Screws		
Nails		
16d Common		
10d Common		
10d Finishing		
8d Common		
6d Common		
Adjustable Post Bases	8	4" x 6"
2½" Galvanized Deck Screws		
Threaded rod with washers and nuts	16	⅜" x 13"
Premixed Concrete		As required to set post footings below frost line
Ready-Mix Concrete		As required for 4"-thick slab

FRAMING PLAN

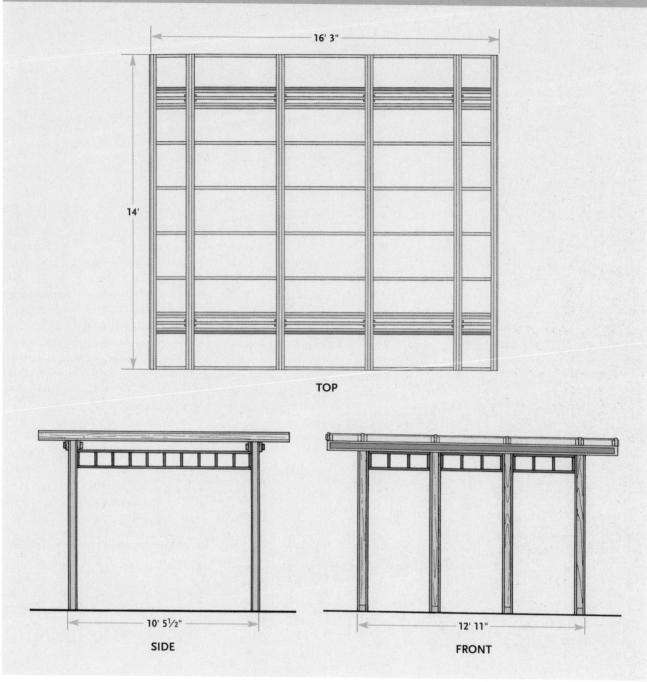

TOP

SIDE

FRONT

KEEPING IT SIMPLE

This may be the simplest structure in this book: posts, beams, and joists—eight posts, two sets of beams, and six joists. At heart, it is a pole building, a roof supported by 4x6s. But simple isn't always plain. Facings on the posts turn them into stepped columns. The frieze across the top is inspired by Japanese shoji screens. The roof is lattice, a nice break from the more functional—and more expensive—plywood. And if lattice doesn't provide the best protection from rain, it doesn't need shingling, either. But it all comes back to the posts. Whether you bury them in concrete or mount them on footings, getting this pavilion right means getting the posts right. Make sure you read "Post Footings" on page 85 before you start digging.

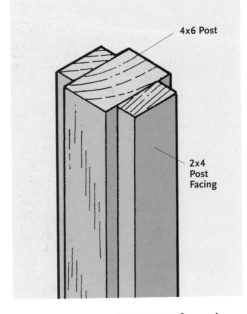

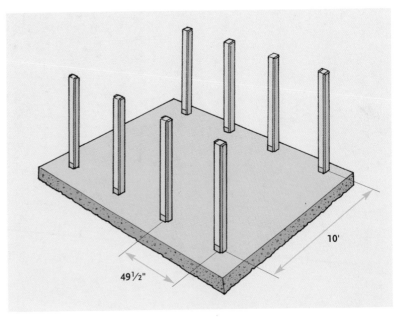

1 ATTACH POST FACINGS. If you plan to set the posts in the ground, use pressure-treated wood. Nail the post facings to the posts with 10d finishing nails before anchoring or setting the posts.

2 INSTALL POSTS. If you use a concrete slab foundation, position the post anchors before the concrete sets. Lay out the post anchors with line and batter boards; transfer to the surface of the slab with a plumb bob. Because the posts will rest on a flat surface, you can cut them to length before installation and proceed to Step 4. For posthole construction, check with your local building department for proper depth, and adjust the post length as needed. Lay out footings as described in "Laying Out the Site" on page 84, and pour as described in "Setting Posts" on page 85.

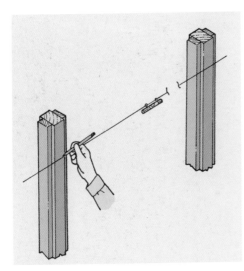

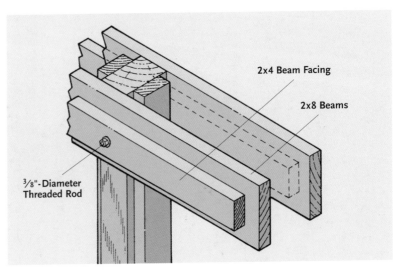

3 TRIM POSTS TO SIZE. Mark 8 ft. up from the ground on one post, and transfer the mark to all other posts using a line level. Cut the posts at the line.

4 ASSEMBLE AND INSTALL BEAMS. Cut the 2x4 beam facings to length. Center the facings on the beams and fasten with 10d finishing nails. Lift the beams to the tops of the posts, resting them temporarily on 16d nails partially driven 7¼ in. from the top of the posts. Check that the tops of the beams are flush with the post tops. At each post, drill two ⅜-in. holes through the beams and post, and attach the beams to the post with two 13-in. pieces of ⅜-in.-dia. threaded rod. Use washers and nuts on both ends of each rod. Remove the 16d nails.

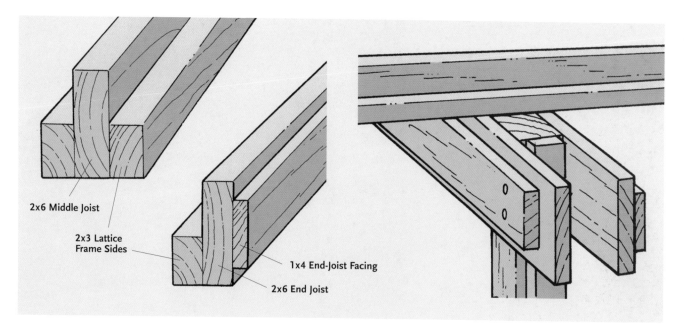

2x6 Middle Joist

2x3 Lattice
Frame Sides

1x4 End-Joist Facing

2x6 End Joist

5 ASSEMBLE AND INSTALL JOISTS. Nail the 1x4 end-joist facing to the outside end joists with 10d nails. Use 10d nails to attach the lattice frame sides to the inside face of the end joists and to both faces of the other joists. Position the joists exactly 4 ft. apart over the posts to allow room for the lattice panels. Toenail the joists to the posts with 16d nails.

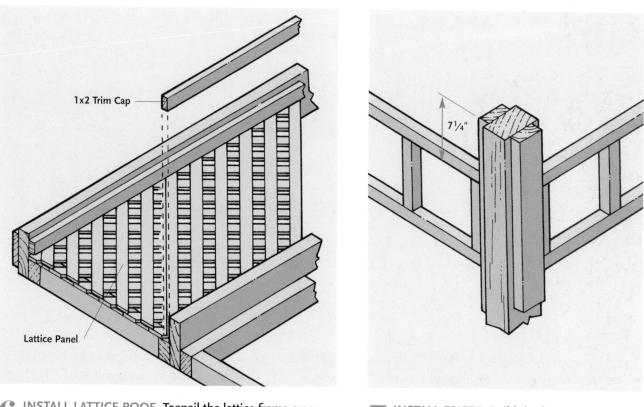

1x2 Trim Cap

7¼"

Lattice Panel

6 INSTALL LATTICE ROOF. Toenail the lattice frame crosspieces to the lattice frame, spacing the crosspieces 24 in. on center. Install the crosspieces for one section of the roof at a time. Then install the lattice with 6d nails, and nail the trim cap over the lattice with 8d nails. Do not climb on or lean against the crosspieces or lattice.

7 INSTALL FRIEZE. Build the friezes before you install them, screwing the rungs in place with 2½-in. galvanized deck screws. Nail the end rungs of each section to the posts with 10d nails.

14 open-air arbor

An arbor like this is building at its simplest. It uses the ground as a floor, and vines for a roof. It's a pleasant place to sit in the afternoon—breezes can come in from any direction, and harsh overhead light is filtered out by the vines. Unfinished rot-resistant lumber—be it cedar, redwood, or pressure-treated lumber—is perfect for this project. The wood will weather and require almost no maintenance. Painting or staining the structure gives the arbor a more finished appearance and won't hinder plant growth. But paint and stain need to be reapplied periodically—not an easy task when the arbor is covered by roses or grapes. Plant annual vines instead, so you can repaint in the late fall or early spring without having to kill the vines.

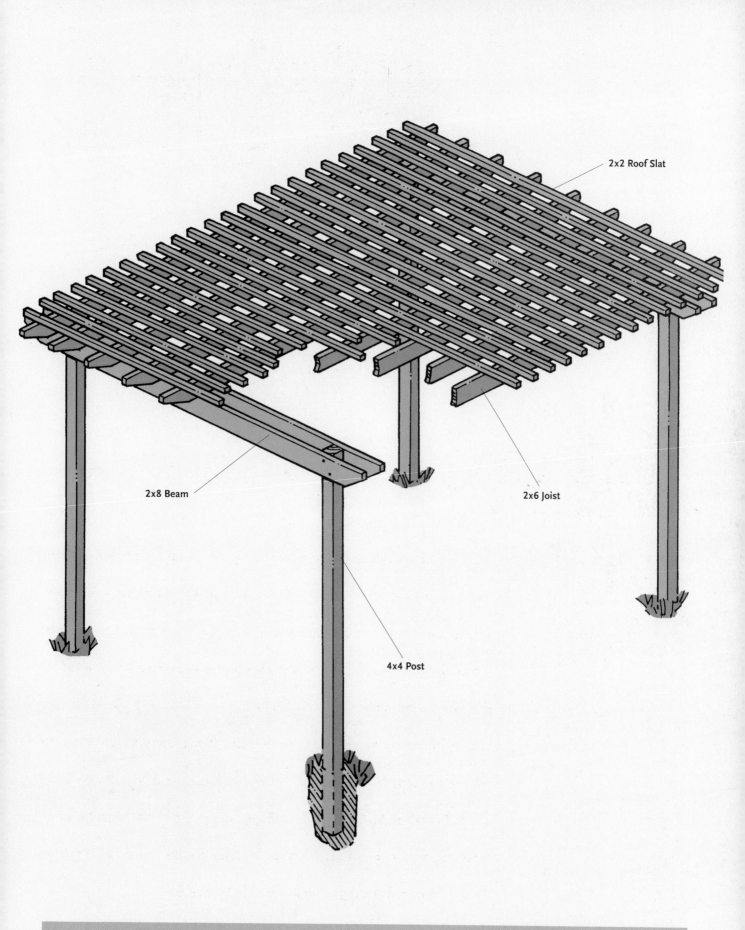

2x2 Roof Slat

2x8 Beam

2x6 Joist

4x4 Post

OPEN-AIR ARBOR

cutting

Name	Qty.	Size
Arbor Framing		
Posts	4	4" x 4" x 12'
Beams	4	2" x 8" x 12'
Roof Joists	9	2" x 6" x 12'
Roof Slats	24	2" x 2" x 12'

& materials

Name	Qty.	Size
Nails and Fasteners		
Nails		
16d Common		
10d Common		
8d Common		
Carriage Bolts	8	$3/8$" x 8"
Premixed Concrete		As required to set post footings below frost line

FRAMING PLAN—FRONT

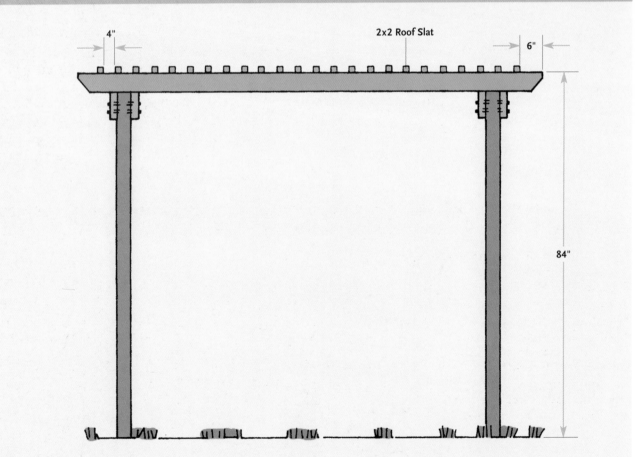

4"   2x2 Roof Slat   6"

84"

FRAMING PLAN—TOP

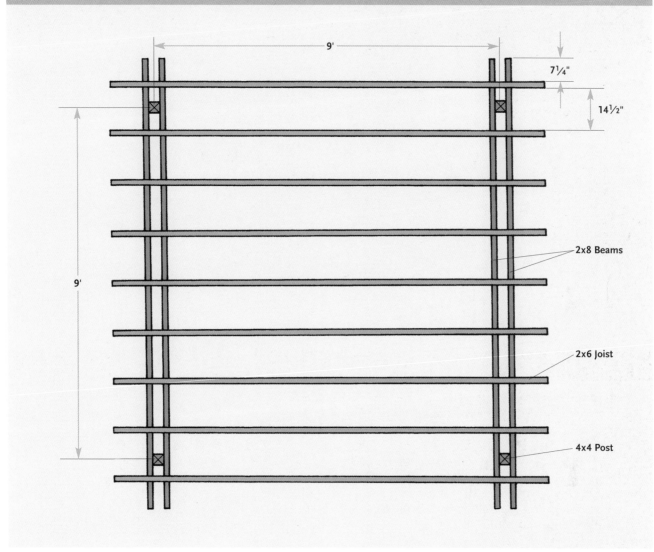

9'

7¼"

14½"

2x8 Beams

2x6 Joist

4x4 Post

9'

CONSTRUCT THE ARBOR

1 INSTALL POSTS. Set the posts in concrete to the depth required by your building department. Before the concrete hardens, brace the posts on two adjacent sides using stakes and furring strips, checking that the posts are plumb on adjacent sides. Run string past the bottom of the posts to see that they are aligned. Allow the concrete to set up overnight.

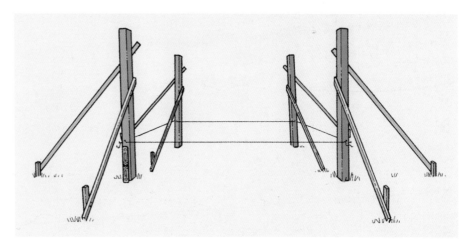

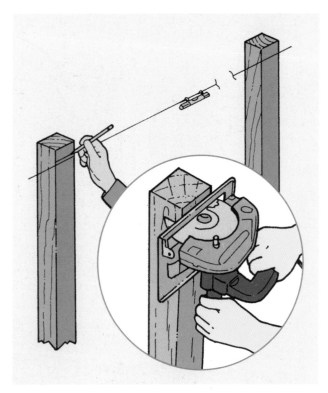

END CUT OPTIONS

2 TRIM POSTS TO SIZE. Measure up one post 7 ft. and draw a line. Use a line level to transfer this height to the other posts. Cut the posts at the lines.

3 INSTALL BEAMS. Cut the beams and trim the ends to one of the patterns shown. Lift the beams onto the tops of the posts, resting them temporarily on 16d nails partially driven $7\frac{1}{4}$ in. from the top of the posts. Check for level. At each post, drill two $\frac{3}{8}$-in.-dia. holes through beams and post, and attach the beams to the post using two $\frac{3}{8}$ x 8-in. carriage bolts.

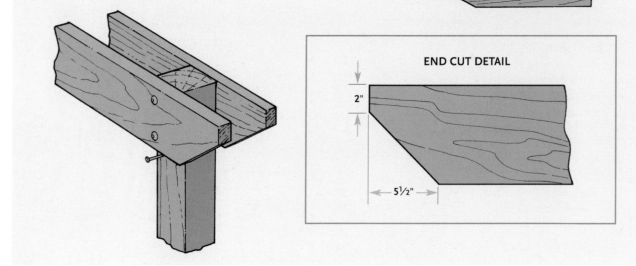

END CUT DETAIL

2"

$5\frac{1}{2}$"

4 INSTALL JOISTS. Cut and trim the joists. Place the last joist on each side 7$\frac{1}{4}$ in. from the ends of the beams. Make sure there is an equal overhang on both sides of the beams. Toenail the joists to the beams with 10d nails. Position the joists 16 in. on center on top of the beams, centering the middle joist between its neighbors.

5 INSTALL ROOF SLATS. Cut the roof slats to 12 ft. long. Place a slat 6 in. from one end of the joists, with an equal overhang on both sides. Nail the slat to the joist with 8d nails. Repeat on the other end. Space the remaining slats 4 in. apart, and nail them in place.

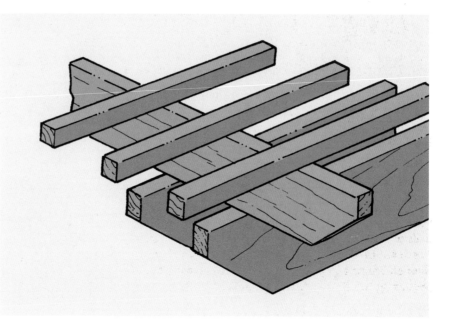

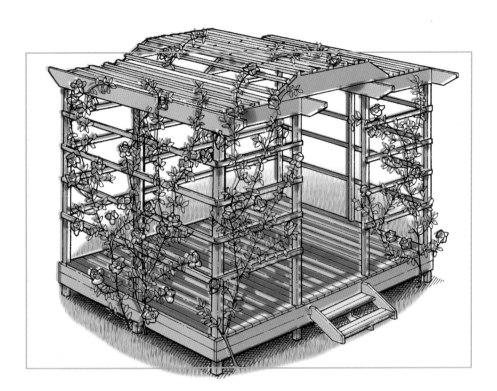

15 arbor with deck

T his arbor with deck is a wonderful way to create a private retreat in your own backyard. You'll enjoy the convenient, clean, flat surface of a deck while surrounded by the natural shade and privacy provided by growing vines. The deck shown is 8 x 12 feet, a cozy structure that still provides plenty of room for entertaining. The walls of the arbor use widely spaced 1x4 slats to support vines. If you want a more open look, you can omit the slats on one or more sides of the arbor.

Before you start building your arbor with deck, study the "Overall View," opposite, and the "Framing Plan" on page 189. Measure and cut as you work. This will let you correct any slight measurement errors before they accumulate into big problems.

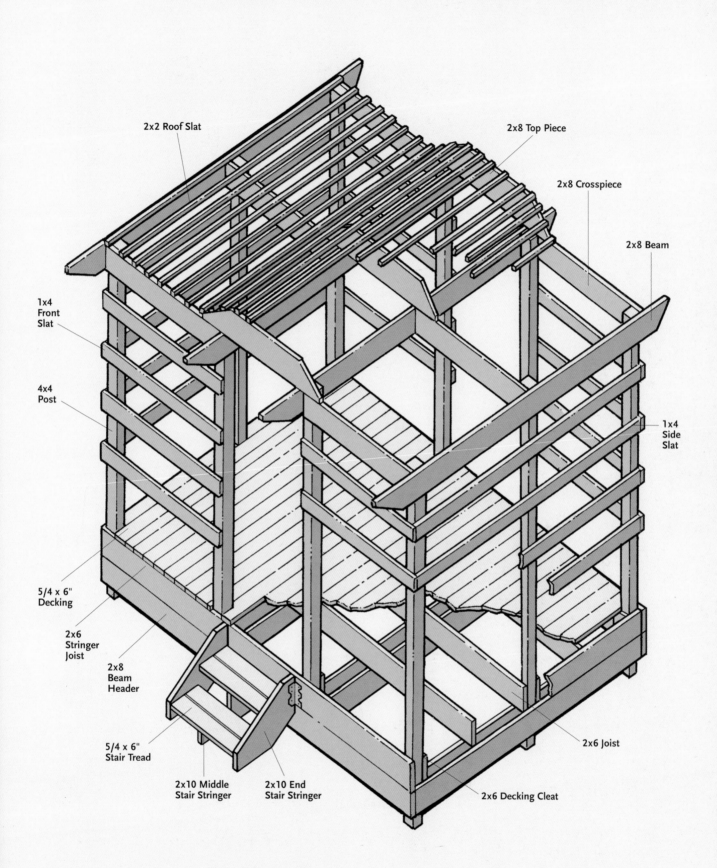

2x2 Roof Slat

2x8 Top Piece

2x8 Crosspiece

2x8 Beam

1x4 Front Slat

4x4 Post

1x4 Side Slat

5/4 x 6" Decking

2x6 Stringer Joist

2x8 Beam Header

5/4 x 6" Stair Tread

2x10 Middle Stair Stringer

2x10 End Stair Stringer

2x6 Decking Cleat

2x6 Joist

OVERALL VIEW

ARBOR WITH DECK

cutting & materials

Name	Qty.	Size
Arbor Deck Framing		
Posts	10	4" x 4" x 10'
Beams	8	2" x 8" x 93"
Beam Headers	2	2" x 8" x 12'
Stringer Joists	2	2" x 6" x 12'
Joists	3	2" x 6" x 11'9"
Decking Cleats	6	2" x 6" x 5"
Decking Cleats	4	2" x 6" x 6½"
Joist Headers	2	2" x 6" x 93"
Stair Stringers	3	2" x 10" x 30"
Stair Treads	4	5/4 x 6" x 36"
Decking	25	5/4 x 6" x 10'
Roof Framing		
Beams	4	2" x 8" x 10'
Crosspieces	6	2" x 8" x 51"
Top Pieces	3	2" x 8" x 62"
Roof Slats	28	2" x 2" x 96"
Side Slats	8	1" x 4" x 93"
Front and Rear Slats	16	1" x 4" x 51¾"

Name	Qty.	Size
Nails and Fasteners		
Machine Bolts	20	⅜" x 7½"
Nails		
16d Common		
10d Common		
8d Common		
8d Finishing		
Post Anchors	10	
Stair Angles	4	
Framing Angles		2 for stringers
Premixed Concrete		As required to set post and step footings below frost line

FRAMING PLAN

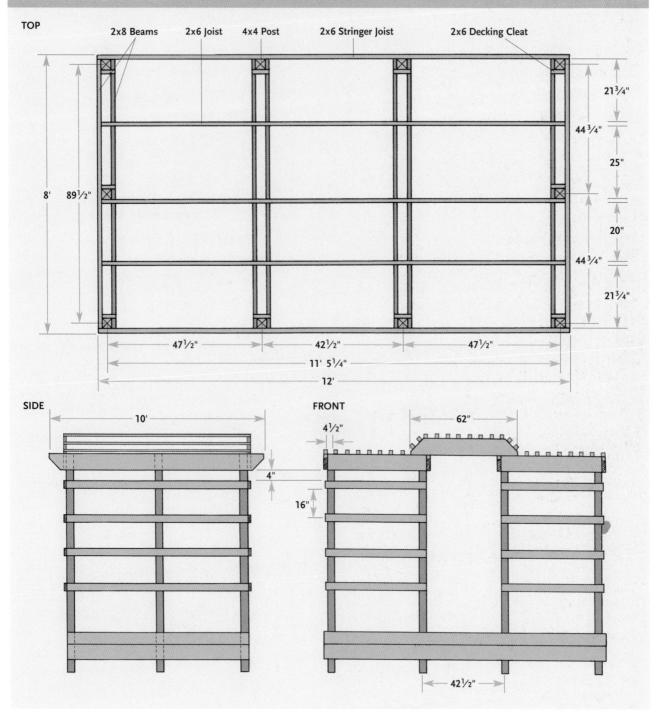

TOP

2x8 Beams   2x6 Joist   4x4 Post   2x6 Stringer Joist   2x6 Decking Cleat

21³/₄"
44³/₄"
25"
20"
44³/₄"
21³/₄"

8'   89¹/₂"

47¹/₂"   42¹/₂"   47¹/₂"
11' 5¹/₄"
12'

SIDE   FRONT

10'   62"

4¹/₂"

4"

16"

42¹/₂"

CONSTRUCT THE DECK

The basic structural components of the deck are 4x4 posts that support the deck beams and roof; 2x8 beams that bolt to the posts and support the floor joists; and 2x6 joists, stringer joists, and joist headers that fasten to the beams and support the 1-inch-thick decking. Lay out the locations for the 10 posts as shown in the "Framing Plan." It is essential that your post layout be square; use the 3-4-5 method described in "Laying Out the Site" on page 84.

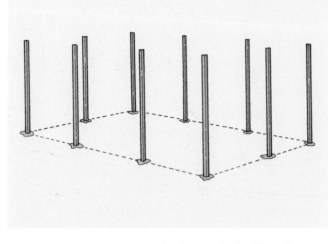

1 INSTALL THE POSTS. **Check with the building department, and pour footings to the proper depth as described in "Techniques" on page 72. If necessary, adjust the post length first. Put the anchor bolts in the wet concrete, and install the posts when the concrete has set.**

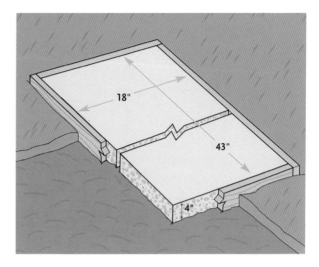

2 PLACE THE STEP FOOTING. **Pour a 4-in.-thick concrete slab where the arbor stairs will meet the ground. Make the slab 18 x 43 in., with the front edge 26 in. from the edge of the deck.**

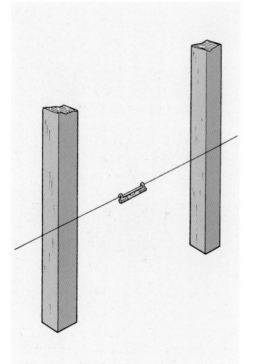

3 ESTABLISH THE DECK HEIGHT. **Mark the 16-in. finished height on one of the posts, and transfer this dimension to all other posts using a line or water level. Measure down 1 in. from this line, and mark the top of each joist. Measure down an additional 5 1/2 in., and draw a line marking the top of the beams.**

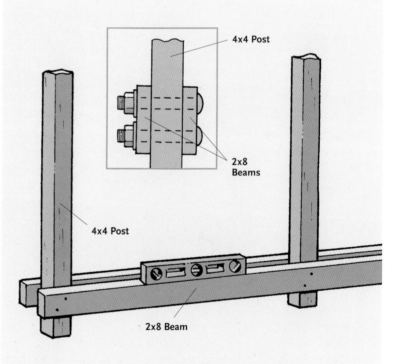

4 INSTALL THE BEAMS. **Temporarily tack a beam to each post at the line you drew, and check for level. Attach the remaining beams the same way, leveling them with the first beam. Lay a straight 2x4 diagonally across the beams and check for level. When all the beams are in position, drill two $3/8$-in.-dia. holes through each assembly and install the bolts, washers, and nuts. Nail on the two beam headers with 16d nails.**

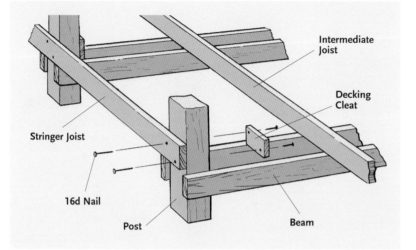

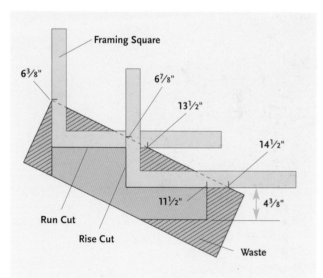

5 INSTALL THE JOISTS. Attach the stringer joists to the posts with two 16d nails at each connection. Position the remaining joists across the beams, spacing them as shown in the "Framing Plan" on page 189. Toenail in place. Attach the decking cleats to the posts with 16d nails.

6 INSTALL THE JOIST HEADERS. Use 16d nails to face-nail the joist header to the ends of the joist at the sides of the deck. Nail the headers to the posts.

MAKE THE STAIRS

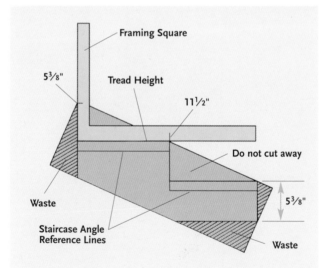

1 LAY OUT END STRINGERS. The stair has a rise of 5³⁄₈ in. and a run of 11¹⁄₂ in. Start with two pieces of 2x10, each about 30 in. long. Place a framing square on a stringer as illustrated, and trace around the square. Extend the rise line to the bottom of the stringer to lay out the upper end of the stringer. Move the square down to lay out the second step, as shown in the drawing. Use the square to lay out the cuts for the front and bottom of the stringers. Measure down 1 in. from the top of the treads, and draw layout lines for the stair angles. Lay out the other end stringer. Cut away the waste on both stringers.

2 LAY OUT THE MIDDLE STRINGER. You will need a middle stringer to support the tread. Mark out the top step with the tongue of the square at 6³⁄₈ in. and the blade at 13¹⁄₂ in. For the second step, put the tongue at 6⁷⁄₈ in. and the blade at 14¹⁄₂ in. To lay out the bottom rise, start from the 11¹⁄₂-in. mark on the blade and draw a 4³⁄₈-in.-long perpendicular line as shown.

3 ASSEMBLE THE STAIRS. Nail the stair angles to the end stringers with heavy-duty galvanized hanger nails. Cut the treads to 36 in. long. Working with the stringers upside down, nail the stair angles into the bottom of the treads. Attach the front treads flush with the front of the stringers. Leave ½ in. between the front and back for drainage. Center the middle stringer between the entry posts and toenail it to the front beam, with two 8d nails on each side. Put the stair assembly in place over the middle stringer. Attach the assembly to the stringer joist with framing anchors; then nail the treads to the middle stringer, using two 8d nails at each connection. When the bottoms of the stringers sit flat on

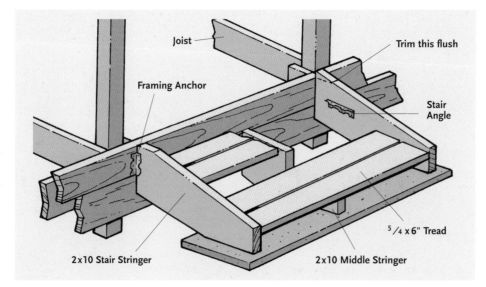

Joist

Trim this flush

Framing Anchor

Stair Angle

2x10 Stair Stringer

⁵/₄ x 6" Tread

2x10 Middle Stringer

the concrete slab, the top point of the end stringers should extend about 1 in. higher than the stringer joist. Cut the top of the end stringers flush with the joist after the stringers are installed.

COMPLETE THE DECK

1 INSTALL DECKING. Nail the decking to each joist with two 8d nails driven at an angle. Let the board overhang the joist headers by ½ in., and leave them long over the stringer joists; you'll trim them to length later. Use a 10d nail as a spacer between boards. Notch the boards as needed to fit around the posts, leaving about ⅛ in. of clearance. After every three or four boards, measure to make sure that the boards are running parallel with the joist headers. As you near the opposite end of the deck, alter the spacing as needed to end the deck with a full-width board. Plan ahead by laying the last few deck boards in place before nailing them. Snap chalk lines across the ends of the deck boards ½ in. from the outside faces of the stringer joists. Cut the boards.

2 MEASURE AND CUT POSTS. Measure up 84 in. from the deck floor along one of the posts. Use a line level or a water level to transfer this height to all other posts. Cut the roof support posts at this height.

CONSTRUCT THE ARBOR

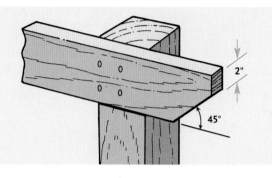

1 CUT AND INSTALL BEAMS. Trim the ends of the four beams as shown above. Nail the beams across the sides as shown in the "Overall View" on page 187, making sure they are flush with the tops of the posts. Use four 16d nails for each connection.

2 CUT AND INSTALL CROSSPIECES. Cut six crosspieces to fit between the beams, right. Drive 16d nails through the crosspieces into the posts and through the beams into the ends of the crosspieces. Use three nails at each connection.

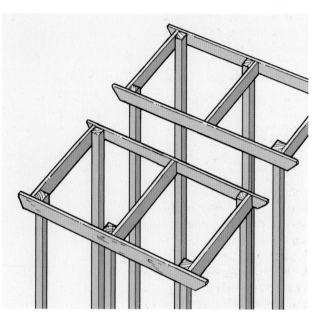

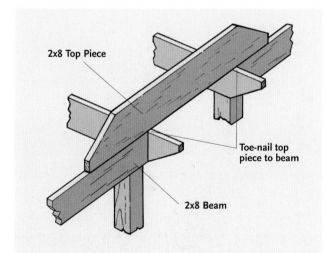

2x8 Top Piece

Toe-nail top piece to beam

2x8 Beam

3 CUT AND INSTALL TOP PIECES. Cut three 2x8 top pieces to 62 in. long. Give them the same decorative end cuts as the beams. Place the top pieces across the middle beams, aligning them with the crosspieces. Toe-nail the top pieces to the middle beams with 10d nails.

4 INSTALL SLATS. Measure from the outside faces of the front crosspieces to the outside faces of the rear crosspieces, and cut the roof slats to this length. Nail the slats in place with 8d nails, spacing them $4\frac{1}{2}$ in. apart. Cut 8 slats to fit across the sides of the arbor as shown in the "Framing Plan" on page 189. Measure down 4 in. from the beams and nail in the first slat. Space the remaining slats 16 in. on center, and nail in place with 8d finishing nails. Measure and cut 16 slats for the front and rear of the arbor, making them long enough to cover both the post and the end grain of the side slats. Nail in place with 8d nails.

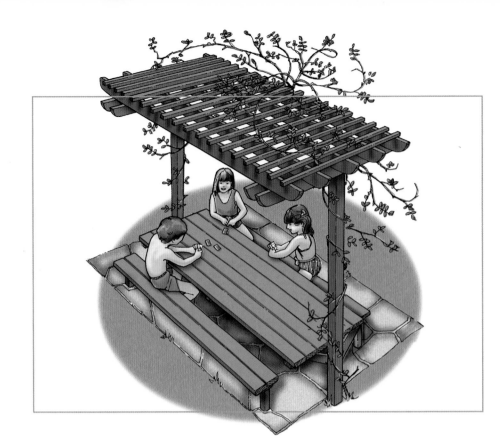

16 arbor with picnic table

This combination arbor and picnic table is perfect for yards where space is at a premium. Like the basic arbor, this arbor consists of beams, joists, and slats supported by posts. In this case, only two posts are used, and they support a table as well as the arbor. For your arbor, you want either a wood that is naturally rot-resistant, such as cedar or redwood, or a pressure-treated lumber, which is fine both for the table and for the plants. One option is to use pressure-treated posts, and cedar or redwood for the rest of the project. A word of advice: don't plant flowering vines on this arbor—the flowers will attract bees and make the table a dangerous place to eat.

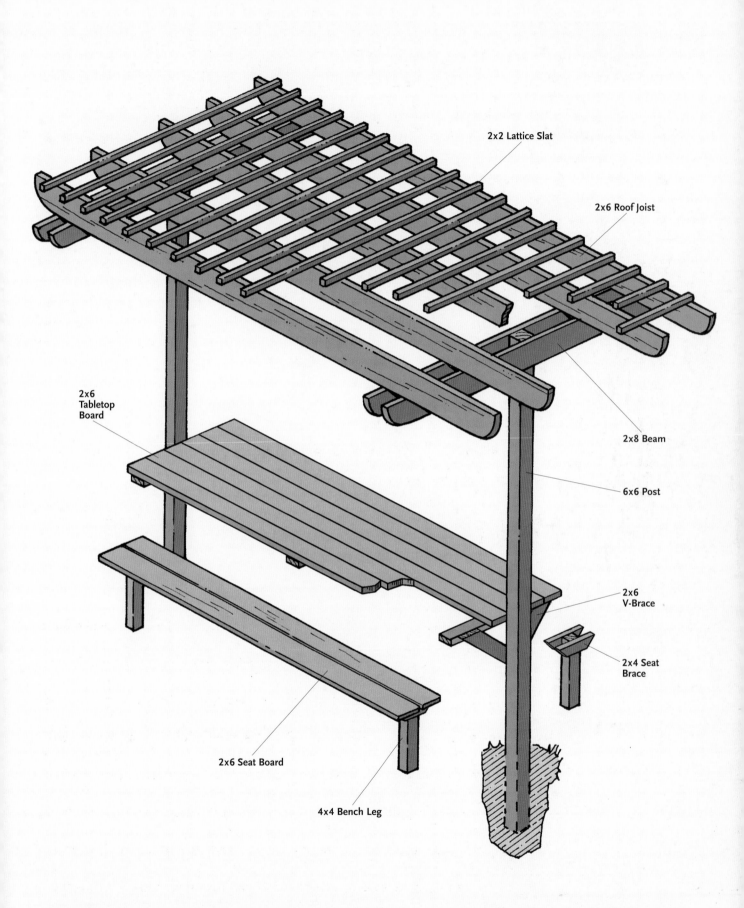

2x2 Lattice Slat

2x6 Roof Joist

2x6 Tabletop Board

2x8 Beam

6x6 Post

2x6 V-Brace

2x4 Seat Brace

2x6 Seat Board

4x4 Bench Leg

ARBOR WITH PICNIC TABLE

cutting

Name	Qty.	Size
Arbor Framing		
Posts	2	6" x 6" x 10'
Beams	4	2" x 8" x 63"
Roof Joists	5	2" x 6" x 9'
Lattice Slats	18	2" x 2" x 63"
Table Materials		
Tabletop V-Braces	4	2" x 4" x 18"
Tabletop	6	2" x 6" x 72"
Tabletop Support Ribs	3	2" x 4" x 33"

& materials

Name	Qty.	Size
Bench Materials		
Bench Legs	4	4" x 4" x 36"
Seat Boards	4	2" x 6" x 72"
Seat Braces	8	2" x 4" x 10"
Nails and Fasteners		
Nails		
16d Common		
10d Common		
Carriage Bolts	4	⅜" x 7"
3" Galvanized Deck Screws	8	⅜" x 7"
Premixed Concrete		As required to set posts and legs below frost line

FRAMING PLAN—TOP

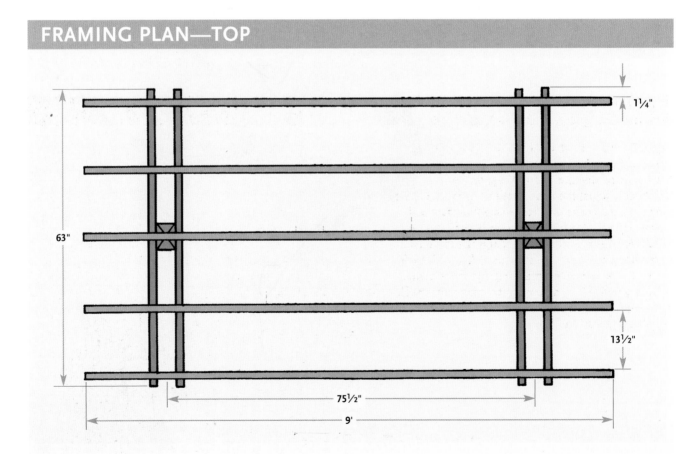

Dimensions shown: 1¼", 63", 13½", 75½", 9'

FRAMING PLAN—FRONT

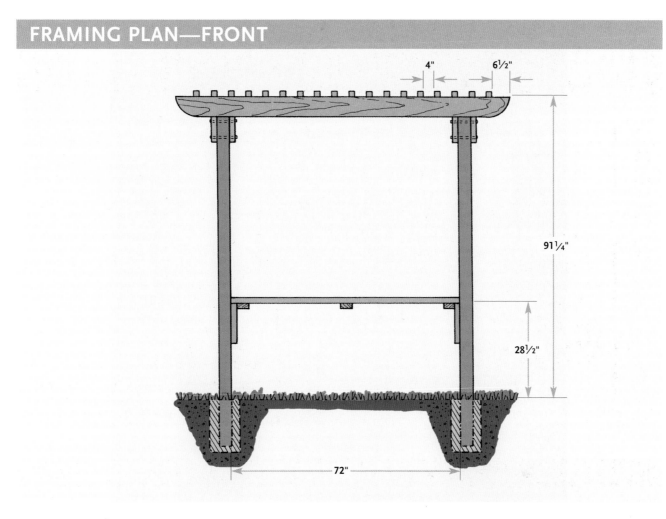

4" 6½"

91¼"

28½"

72"

CONSTRUCT THE ARBOR

1 LOCATE AND INSTALL POSTS. Lay out two postholes 75½ in. on center. Check with your local building department for the right footing depth, and adjust the post length as needed. Set the posts in concrete as directed. Brace the posts with stakes and furring strips on two adjacent sides, and check for plumb. Run a string across the bottoms of the posts to make sure they are in line with each other. Let the concrete set overnight; then measure up one post 91¼ in. and mark it. Using a line level, run a tight string to the other post, and mark it. Trim the posts at the line.

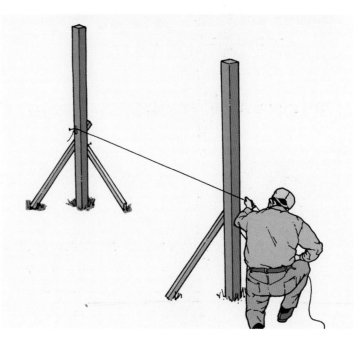

197

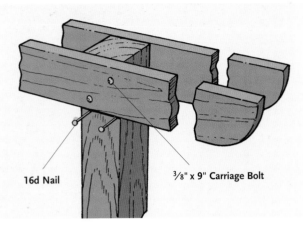

16d Nail   3/8" x 9" Carriage Bolt

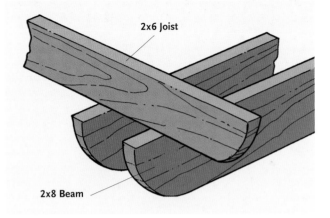

2x6 Joist

2x8 Beam

2 INSTALL BEAMS. Cut the beams to 63 in. long. Choose a curve design (see page 184) and draw it on the end of one beam. Cut the beam using a saber saw; sand it smooth; and use it as a template for the other beam ends. Lift the beams to the tops of the posts, resting them temporarily on 16d nails partially driven 7 1/4 in. from the top. Check that the beams and posts are flush on top. At each post, drill two 3/8-in.-dia. holes through the beams and post, and attach the beams to the post using two 3/8 x 9-in. carriage bolts and nuts.

3 INSTALL ROOF JOISTS. Cut the roof joists 9 ft. long. Draw a curve on the end of one joist; then cut and sand it to use as a template for the other end cuts. Space the joists across the beams, and toenail them into place with 10d nails or attach them with metal ties.

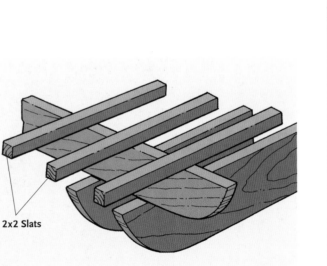

2x2 Slats

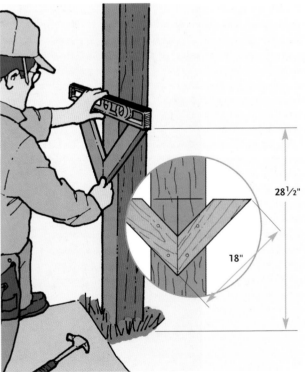

28 1/2"

18"

4 CUT AND NAIL LATTICE SLATS. Cut the slats to 63 in. long. Position the first slat 6 1/2 in. from one end of the joists. Space the remaining slats 4 in. apart on the joists, and fasten them with 10d nails.

5 ASSEMBLE V-BRACES. Cut tabletop V-braces to the dimensions shown, mitering the ends to 45 deg. Measure up one post 28 1/2 in., and mark on the inside. Use a line level to transfer this height to the other post. Draw a pencil line down as shown, centered beneath the 28 1/2-in. mark. Align the top of a V-brace with the 28 1/2-in. mark, and align the bottom along the centerline. Tack each piece in place with one 16d nail. When all four brace pieces are in place, check each assembly with a level, and nail them in place.

CONSTRUCT THE TABLE AND BENCHES

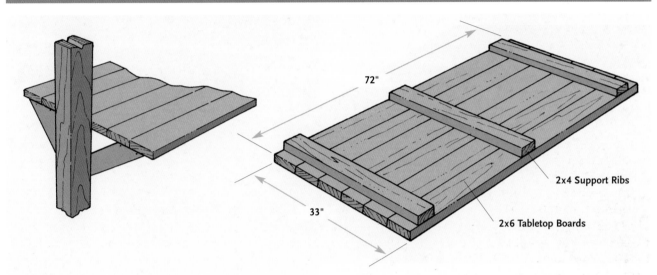

2x4 Support Ribs

2x6 Tabletop Boards

72"

33"

1 MAKE TABLETOP. Measure and cut six 2x6 pieces to fit between the posts. Next, cut three 2x4 table-top support ribs. Align the ends of the tabletop pieces, and screw a support rib across the center with 3-in. galvanized deck screws. Put the table temporarily on the braces, and trace along the braces to mark their locations on the tabletop. Remove the tabletop, and screw the two end ribs along the lines you drew. Put the table-top back on the braces, and secure by screwing through the braces into the end ribs with 3-in. screws.

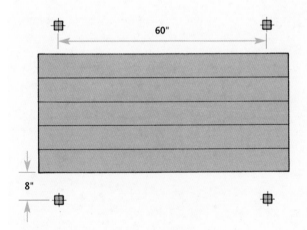

60"

8"

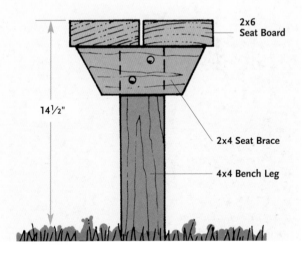

2x6 Seat Board

14½"

2x4 Seat Brace

4x4 Bench Leg

2 INSTALL BENCH LEGS. Center the bench legs on points that are 8 in. from the sides of the table, 60 in. apart, and equidistant from the ends of the table. Dig bench leg holes that are at least 18 in. deep. Place the bench legs in the holes, and fill the holes with concrete. Run a string across the bottoms of the posts to make sure they are in line. Check the posts for plumb, and brace with furring strips if necessary. Allow the concrete to set overnight, then measure up one post 14½ in. and mark it. Transfer this height to the other posts, and cut them to length.

3 MAKE BENCH SEATS. Cut the seat boards to 72 in. Then cut 8 seat braces to 10 in., mitering the ends to 45 deg. as shown. Tack each brace piece to the post with one 10d nail. Check that the braces are level. Drill ⅜-in.-dia. holes through the braces and bench legs. Fasten the braces to the posts with ⅜ x 7-in. carriage bolts. Put a pair of seat boards on each pair of braces, leaving ½ in. of space between the boards. Fasten the boards to the braces with 3-in. galvanized deck screws, driving the screws below the surface. Round off the edges of the tabletop and seat boards with a few passes of a block plane.

This list of manufacturers and associations is meant to be a general guide to additional industry and product-related sources. It is not intended as a listing of products and manufacturers represented by the photographs in this book.

Backyard Products LLC
1000 Ternes Dr.
Monroe, MI 48162
734-242-6900
www.heartlandind.com
Backyard Products sells prefabricated gazebos.

Baldwin Pergolas
440 Middlefield St.
Middletown, CT 06457
www.BaldwinPergolas.com
860-514-4313
Baldwin Pergolas manufactures pergola and arbor kits in western red cedar.

California Redwood Association
888-CALREDWOOD
www.calredwood.org
California Redwood Association is a source of information about building with redwood.

DEWALT Industrial Tool Co.
701 E. Joppa Rd., TW425
Baltimore, MD 21286
800-4-DEWALT
www.dewalt.com
DEWALT Industrial Tool Co. makes power tools and accessories.

Fire Stone Home Products
12400 Portland Ave. S., Suite 195
Burnsville, MN 55337
866-303-4028
www.firestonehp.com
Fire Stone Home Products makes outdoor furniture, grills, lighting, and pergolas.

HomePlace Structures
301 Commerce Dr., Suite 400
New Holland, PA 17557
877-768-0804
www.homeplacestructures.com
HomePlace Structures sells prefabricated gazebos.

Lancaster County Barns/Amish Gazebos
340 Hostetter Rd.
Manheim, PA 17545
717-556-0394
www.amishgazeboshop.com
Lancaster County Barns/Amish Gazebos sells both gazebos and gazebo kits.

Portland Cement Association
5420 Old Orchard Rd.
Skokie, IL 70077
847-966-6200
www.cement.org
Portland Cement Association is a source of information about mixing, pouring, and finishing concrete.

Robert Bosch Tool Corporation
1800 W. Central Rd.
Mt. Prospect, IL 60056-2230
877-BOSCH-99
www.boschtools.com
Robert Bosch Tool Corporation is a maker of power tools and accessories.

Ryobi Technologies, Inc.
1428 Pearman Rd.
Anderson, SC 29625
800-525-2579
www.ryobitools.com
Ryobi Technologies, Inc. is a maker of power tools and accessories.

Simpson Strong Tie
P.O. Box 10789
5956 W. Las Positas Blvd.
Pleasanton, CA 94588
925-560-9000
www.strongtie.com
Simpson Strong Tie makes hanger hardware.

Southern Pine Council
2900 Indiana Ave.
Kenner, LA 70065-4605
504-443-4464
www.southernpine.com
Southern Pine Council is a source of information about pressure-treated wood and southern pine.

The Stanley Works
1000 Stanley Dr.
New Britain, CT 06053
860-827-3833
www.stanleyworks.com
The Stanley Works makes hand tools and measuring devices.

Vintage Woodworks
Hwy. 34 S.–P.O. Box 39
Quinlan, TX 75474-0039
903-356-2158
www.vintagewoodworks.com
Vintage Woodworks is a source of Victorian-style trim.

Western Red Cedar Lumber Association
PMB #1705
914–164th St., SE, #B12
Mill Creek, WA 98012-6339
877-316-8845
www.wrcla.org
Western Red Cedar Lumber Association is a source of information about building with western red cedar.

Waddell Manufacturing Company
1676 Commerce Dr.
Stow, OH 44224
800-433-1737
www.waddellmfg.com
Waddell Manufacturing Company is a source of Victorian-style trim.

glossary

Actual Dimensions The exact measurements of a piece of lumber after it has been cut, surfaced, and left to dry. For example, a 2x4's actual dimensions are $1\frac{1}{2}$ x $3\frac{1}{2}$ inches.

Arbor An openwork structure that usually consists of slats or lattice that support climbing vines.

Baluster A vertical railing member that supports the upper and lower rails.

Beam A framing member used to support joists.

Bird's Mouth A notch in a common rafter that fits over the cap plate. It consists of a level cut, called the seat cut, and a short plumb cut.

Bull Float A flat metal tool equipped with a long handle, used to bring sand and cement to the surface of poured concrete while knocking down the small ridges left by screeding.

Cap Plate Horizontal framing member that goes on top of the top plate, tying walls together.

Ceiling Joist Roof framing member that spans the width of a building.

Chalk Line String or cord that is covered with colored chalk. It is snapped against a surface to make a mark for cutting or aligning.

Chromated Copper Arsenic (CCA) A chemical used to pressure-treat wood to make it resist decay.

Clinching Bending over the exposed tip of a nail, after it has been driven through a board.

Color Value The lightness or darkness of a color.

Color Wheel A chart that identifies associations between colors.

Common Rafter A rafter that meets the cap plate with a bird's-mouth cut and the ridge or key block with a plumb cut.

Complementary Colors Any two colors opposite each other on the color wheel.

Composite Shingles Commonly made of asphalt and fiberglass. They are often made into a three-tab strip, which is one of the most popular roofing materials available.

Crook A deviation in a piece of lumber from a flat plane on the narrow face, end to end. A crook makes wood unsuitable for framing.

Curing The slow chemical action that hardens concrete.

Decay The destruction of wood by fungi or insects.

Deck Height The height above grade of the top of the decking.

Decking Boards or plywood nailed to joists to form the deck surface.

Decking Cleats Small pieces that provide support for the decking boards whenever a board ends at a post.

Dipping A treatment where wood is immersed in a bath of sealant for several minutes, and then allowed to air-dry.

Fascia The horizontal lumber placed at the roofline that covers the ends of the rafters.

Footing The concrete base that supports posts or steps.

Form Lumber set around the edge to define the shape of the concrete slab.

Framing Square A piece of steel or aluminum that forms an "L" shape. Used to figure rise and run of stringers and roofs, to check for square, and to strike square cutting lines.

Frieze An ornamental horizontal band that is positioned near the roofline.

Frost Heave Shifting or upheaval of the ground due to alternate freezing and thawing of water in the soil.

Frost Line The maximum depth to which soil freezes in winter. Your local building department can provide information on the frost line depth in your area.

Gable Roof A roof with two slopes forming triangles on the ends.

Galvanizing Coating a metal with a thin protective layer (e.g., zinc) to prevent rust. Connectors and fasteners should be galvanized for outdoor use.

Gazebo A freestanding structure intended to offer a panoramic view of the surrounding scenery.

Grade The ground level. On-grade means at or on the natural ground level.

Hand Edger A hand tool used to round the edges of a concrete slab.

Hardwood Wood that comes from deciduous trees (those that lose their leaves in fall).

Hip-Jack Rafters Short rafters that run between the cap plate and a hip rafter.

Hip Rafter A rafter that runs diagonally from the ridge to the corners of a building.

Hurricane Ties Connectors used to secure rafters and trusses to the top plates.

Joist One in a series of parallel framing members that supports a floor or ceiling load. Joists are supported by beams or bearing walls.

Joist Hanger Metal connectors used to join a joist and a beam so that the tops of both are in the same plane.

Key Block A piece of wood at the peak of a gazebo roof designed to meet the rafters.

Kickback The action that happens when a saw suddenly jumps backward out of the cut.

Knots The high-density roots of limbs that are very strong, but are not connected to the surrounding wood.

Lag Screw/Lag Bolt A large hex-head screw or bolt used to fasten framing members face-to-face; typically used for joining horizontal framing member to posts.

Lattice A cross-pattern structure that is made of wood, metal, or plastic.

Lignin The binding agent that holds the cells in wood together.

Lumber Grade A label that reflects the lumber's natural growth characteristics (such as knots), defects that result from milling errors, and manufacturing techniques.

Miter Joint A joint in which the ends of two boards are cut at equal angles (typically 45 degrees) to form a corner.

Nail Set A pointed tool with one round or square end, used to drive nails below surface level.

Nominal Dimensions The identifying dimensions of a piece of lumber (e.g., 2x4), which are larger than the actual dimensions ($1\frac{1}{2}$ x $3\frac{1}{2}$ inches).

On-Center (o.c.) A point of reference for measuring. For example, "16 inches on center" means 16 inches from the center of one post to the center of the next post.

Pastel Colors Colors mixed with white.

Pavilion A rectangular structure with a slat, lattice, or gable roof.

Penny (abbreviated "d") Unit of nail measurement; e.g., a 10d nail is 3 inches long.

Permanent Structure Any structure that is anchored to the ground or a house.

Pitch Pocket An accumulation of natural resins in wood.

Plumb Vertically straight, in relation to a horizontally level surface.

Post Vertical framing member (e.g., a 4x4 or 4x6) set on the foundation to support the structure.

Post Anchors Connectors that secure the base of a load-bearing post to a concrete slab or deck.

Posthole Digger A clamshell-type tool used to dig holes for posts.

Premade Lumber Pieces that are factory cut and/or assembled.

Premixed Concrete Bagged, dry concrete that is used for small jobs such as securing individual posts. It is mixed with sand and aggregate.

Pressure-Treated Lumber Wood that has had preservatives forced into it under pressure to make it repel rot and insects.

Primary Colors Three colors (pure red, pure blue, and pure yellow) that cannot be mixed from other colors.

Primer An essential undercoat layer of paint. It provides a good surface onto which to apply layers of paint.

Purlin Clips Connectors used to install purlins (crosspieces) between joists or rafters.

Rafter Tail The part of the rafter that overhangs the wall.

Rafter Ties Connectors used to provide wind and seismic ties for trusses and rafters.

Rail A horizontal member that is placed between posts and used for support or as a barrier.

Ready-Mix Concrete Wet concrete that is transported from a concrete supplier in a cement truck with a revolving drum. The concrete is ready to pour.

Redwood A straight-grained weather-resistant wood used for outdoor building.

Ridge The uppermost horizontal line of the roof.

Rim Joist Joist at the perimeter of a structure.

Rise The vertical distance between the cap plate and the peak of a roof.

Roofer's Hatchet A specialized tool combining a nonskid hammer head with a hatchet. It also has an adjustable pin for gauging shingle exposure and a wrist strap to prevent it from falling off the roof.

Run The measure of the horizontal distance over which a rafter rises.

Screeding Using a straight 2x4, moved from one end of a concrete pour to the other, to strike off excess concrete.

Secondary Colors Three colors (orange, green, and violet) that are mixed from equal amounts of two primary colors.

Skewing Nails driven into wood at opposing angles to hook the boards together.

Slope Number of inches a roof rises per 12 inches of run. For example, a shallow roof would be 4 in 12, while a steeper roof would be 9 in 12.

Softwood Wood that comes from coniferous trees (i.e.., evergreens).

Spaced Slats 1x4s or 1x6s nailed directly to the rafters.

Spading Inserting a shovel vertically into the concrete to remove air pockets that may have occurred in corners or along the sides of the forms.

Span The horizontal distance that's covered by a roof.

Split A crack that passes completely through a piece of lumber.

Square Roofing material is sold by the square; one square is equal to 100 square feet. To determine the number of squares on a roof, measure the area and then divide by 100 (add 10 percent to allow for waste).

Stair Angles Clips that support stair treads, eliminating the need for notching the stringers.

Stringers Diagonal boards that support stair treads.

Tacknail To nail one structural member to another temporarily with a minimum of nails.

Tamping Using a rake in concrete work to jab aggregate down and to work out any air bubbles.

Toenail Joining two boards together by nailing at an angle through the end, or toe, of one board into the face of another.

Tongue-and-Groove Flooring Floor boards that are milled with a tongue on one edge and a groove on the other edge. The tongue of one board fits into the groove of the next to make a tight, strong floor.

Top Plate Horizontal framing member that forms the top of a wall. In a gazebo, top plates are attached to the top of posts.

Treads The horizontal boards on stairs, supported by the stringer.

UV Absorbers and Blockers Particles that absorb, or in the case of blockers, reflect, UV light to minimize its effect on the wood.

UV Inhibitors Compounds that are designed to disrupt the normal chemical action caused by UV light.

V-Braces Two pieces of 2x4 that are cut at 45-degree miters to form a V shape. They attach to the posts and help support a picnic table top.

Wane The presence of bark, or lack of wood at an edge.

Waste Cut The part of the cut that can be used for scrap or thrown away.

index

index

METRIC EQUIVALENTS

Length

1 inch	25.4 mm
1 foot	0.3048 m
1 yard	0.9144 m
1 mile	1.61 km

Area

1 square inch	645 mm²
1 square foot	0.0929 m²
1 square yard	0.8361 m²
1 acre	4046.86 m²
1 square mile	2.59 km²

Volume

1 cubic inch	16.3870 cm³
1 cubic foot	0.03 m³
1 cubic yard	0.77 m³

Common Lumber Equivalents

Metric cross sections are so close to their U.S. sizes, as noted below, that for most purposes they may be considered equivalents.

Dimension lumber	1 x 2	19 x 38 mm
	1 x 4	19 x 89 mm
	2 x 2	38 x 38 mm
	2 x 4	38 x 89 mm
	2 x 6	38 x 140 mm
	2 x 8	38 x 184 mm
	2 x 10	38 x 235 mm
	2 x 12	38 x 286 mm
Sheet sizes	4 x 8 ft.	1200 x 2400 mm
	4 x 10 ft.	1200 x 3000 mm
Sheet thicknesses	¼ in.	6 mm
	⅜ in.	9 mm
	½ in.	12 mm
	¾ in.	19 mm
Stud/joist spacing	16 in. o.c.	400 mm o.c.
	24 in. o.c.	600 mm o.c.

Capacity

1 fluid ounce	29.57 mL
1 pint	473.18 mL
1 quart	0.95 L
1 gallon	3.79 L

Weight

1 ounce	28.35 g
1 pound	0.45 kg

Temperature

Fahrenheit = Celsius x 1.8 + 32
Celsius = 0.55 x (Fahrenheit – 32)

Nail Size and Length

Penny Size	Nail Length
2d	1"
3d	1¼"
4d	1½ "
5d	1¾"
6d	2"
7d	2¼"
8d	2½"
9d	2¾"
10d	3"
12d	3¼"
16d	3½"

photo credits

page 1: Angela Hill **page 4:** courtesy of Lancaster County Barns – Walter Kuhn **page 6:** Verena Matthew **page 7:** *top* Donna H. Chiarelli **page 8:** *top* Harry Thomas; *middle left* Steven Gibson; *bottom left* Dick Dietrich, Phoenix, AZ; *bottom right* Rodale Stock Images – Marilyn Stouffer **page 9:** Richard Goldberg **page 10:** *top* courtesy of California Redwood Association; *bottom* courtesy of Max W. Baldwin, Designer, Craftsman, Pergola specialist **page 11:** *top* Peter Leyden; *bottom* courtesy of Terry Anderson Photography, Edina, MN **page 12:** *top* constantgardener photography; *bottom* Lauri Wiberg **page 13:** *top* udigthis photography; *bottom* Paige Foster **page 14:** *top* courtesy of Backyard Products, LLC; *middle* Jane Norton; *bottom* courtesy of California Redwood Association **page 15:** Doug Brown **page 16:** Classic Pool & Patio, Indianapolis, IN, courtesy of National Spa and Pool Institute, Alexandria, VA **page 17:** Rodale Stock Images – T. L. Gettings **page 18:** Bob Braun Photography, Orlando, FL **page 22:** *top* Verena Matthew; *middle* Nicola Stratford; *bottom* George Mattei Photography, Hackensack, NJ **page 23:** Carrie Nielson **page 24:** *left* Rodale Stock Images – Mitch Mandel; *right* Scott Star Photography, New York, NY **page 25:** *left* Nathan Gutshall-Kresge; *right* Rodale Stock Images – J. Michael Kanouff **page 26:** Rodale Stock Images – J. Michael Kanouff **page 27:** *left* Mark Gibson, Mount Shasta, CA; *top right* Specialized PhotoGraphic Design, Convent Station, NJ; *center right* Rodale Stock Images – Marilyn Stouffer **page 30:** *top* John Schwartz Photography, New York, NY; *bottom* Michael Schimpf Photography, Lansing, MI **page 33:** Olivier le Queinec **page 36:** *top* Debi Gardiner; *middle* YinYang Design; *bottom* The Terry Wild Studios, Williamsport, PA **page 37:** courtesy of HomePlace Structures **page 38:** Don Wilkie **page 39:** Darryl Brooks **page 46:** courtesy of Wolman Wood Care Products **page 47:** Mary Lane **page 50:** *top* Donna H. Chiarelli; *middle* Donna H. Chiarelli; *bottom* Macie J. Noskowski **page 51:** André Weyer **page 54:** *all* Neal Barrett **page 57:** *top center* Todd Taulman; *bottom left* Dave Pilibosian; *bottom right* Donna H. Chiarelli; *all others* Neal Barrett **page 65:** courtesy of California Redwood Association **page 68:** *all* courtesy of California Redwood Association **page 72:** *top* Ann Marie Kurtz; *middle* Gary Woodard; *bottom* Nick Schlax **page 73:** Scott Williams **page 87:** Stacey McRae **page 88:** *top* Miroslava Arnaudova; *middle* Tammy Bryngelson; *bottom* Steven Robertson **page 89:** Angus Plummer **page 96:** *top* Ynona Photography; *middle* Photo/Nats, Auburndale, MA; *bottom* courtesy of Lancaster County Barns – Walter Kuhn **page 97:** Tammy Beans **page 104:** Carrie Nielson **page 109:** courtesy of Cedar Shake & Shingle Bureau **page 110:** *top* Dick Dietrich, Phoenix, AZ; *bottom left* courtesy of Lancaster County Barns – Walter Kuhn; *bottom right* Judy Picciotto **page 111:** courtesy of Owens Corning **page 112:** courtesy of California Redwood Association **page 113:** Specialized PhotoGraphic Design, Convent Station, NJ **page 116:** Photo/Nats, Auburndale, MA **page 124:** *top* Shmuel M. Bowles; *middle* Jeffrey Sheldon; *bottom* Jill Fromer **page 125:** Patrick Moyer **page 126:** courtesy of Wolman Wood Care Products **page 128:** courtesy of Lancaster County Barns – Walter Kuhn **page 201:** Nancy Kennedy **page 207:** Peter Albrektsen

Have a home improvement, decorating, or gardening project? Look for these and other fine Creative Homeowner books wherever books are sold.

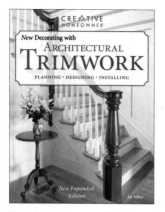

Transform a room with trimwork. Over 550 color photos and illustrations. 240 pp.; 8¹/₂" × 10⁷/₈"
BOOK #: 277500

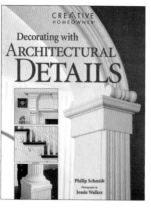

Covers design treatments such as moldings and window seats. 300+ color photos. 224 pp.; 8¹/₂" × 10⁷/₈"
BOOK #: 278225

A complete guide covering all aspects of drywall. Over 450 color photos 160 pp.; 8¹/₂" × 10⁷/₈"
BOOK #: 278320

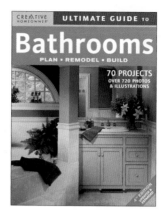

Includes step-by-step projects and over 630 photos.
272 pp.; 8¹/₂" × 10⁷/₈"
BOOK#: 278632

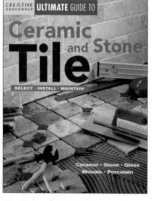

Complete DIY tile instruction. Over 550 color photos and illustrations. 224 pp.; 8¹/₂" × 10⁷/₈"
BOOK #: 27753

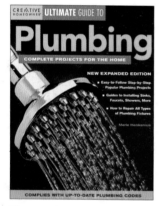

The complete manual for plumbing. Over 750 color photos and illustrations. 288 pp.; 8¹/₂" × 10⁷/₈"
BOOK#: 278200

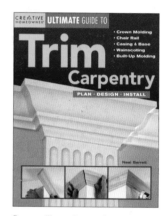

Best-selling trimwork manual. Over 500 color photos and illustrations. 208 pp.; 8¹/₂" × 10⁷/₈"
BOOK#: 277516

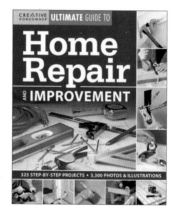

The ultimate home-improvement reference manual. Over 300 step-by-step projects. 608 pp.; 9" × 10⁷/₈"
BOOK#: 267870

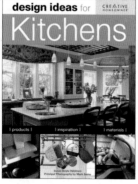

Design inspiration for creating a new kitchen. Over 500 color photographs. 224 pp.; 8¹/₂" ×10⁷/₈"
BOOK #: 279415

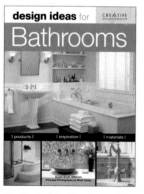

Design inspiration for creating a new bathroom. Over 500 color photos. 224 pp.; 8¹/₂" × 10⁷/₈"
BOOK #: 279268

An impressive guide to garden design and plant selection. 950 color photos and illustrations. 384 pp.; 9" × 10"
BOOK #: 274610

Lavishly illustrated with portraits of over 100 flowering plants; more than 700 photos. 240 pp.; 9" × 10"
BOOK #: 274222

For more information and to order direct, visit our Web site at www.creativehomeowner.com